Japanese

🔊 Phrasebook & CD

Acknowledgments
Product Editor Shona Gray
Language Writers Yoshi Abe, Keiko Hagiwara
Book Designer Virginia Moreno
Cover Researcher Naomi Parker

Thanks
James Hardy, Elizabeth Jones, Catherine Naghten, Angela Tinson,
Juan Winata

Published by Lonely Planet Global Limited
CRN 554153

4th Edition – June 2020
ISBN 978 1 78657 174 8
Text © Lonely Planet 2020
Cover Image Shinsekai district, Osaka, Sean Pavone/Alamy ©

Printed in China   10 9 8 7 6 5 4 3 2 1

Contact lonelyplanet.com/contact

Although the authors and Lonely Planet try to make the information
as accurate as possible, we accept no responsibility for any loss, injury
or inconvenience sustained by anyone using this book.

Paper in this book is certified against the Forest Stewardship Council™
standards. FSC™ promotes environmentally responsible, socially
beneficial and economically viable management of the world's forests.

Look out for the following icons throughout the book:

 'Shortcut' Phrase
Easy to remember alternative to the full phrase

 Q&A Pair
Question-and-answer pair – we suggest a
response to the question asked

 Look For
Phrases you may see on signs, menus etc

 Listen For
Phrases you may hear from officials, locals etc

 LANGUAGE TIP **Language Tip**
An insight into the foreign language

CULTURE TIP **Culture Tip**
An insight into the local culture

Download your files:
- Download audio files directly onto your device at:
  https://phrasebook.lonelyplanet.com/japanese

How to read the phrases:
- Coloured words and phrases throughout the book are
  phonetic guides to help you pronounce the foreign language.

Abbreviations to help you choose the right words:

a	adjective	n	noun	sg	singular
inf	informal	pl	plural	v	verb
lit	literal	pol	polite		

Contents

PAGE 6

 About Japanese
Learn about Japanese, build your own sentences and pronounce words correctly.

Introduction 6
Top Phrases 8
Pronunciation 10
Grammar 16

PAGE 33

Travel Phrases
Ready-made phrases for every situation – buy a ticket, book a hotel and much more.

 Basics 33
Understanding 34
Numbers & Amounts 36
Time & Dates 40

 Practical 45
Transport 46
Border Crossing 62
Directions 64
Accommodation 68
Shopping 80
Communications 88
Money & Banking 95
Business 98

Sightseeing 102
Senior & Disabled Travellers 107
Travel with Children 109

💬 Social 111

Meeting People 112
Interests 122
Feelings & Opinions 126
Going Out 132
Romance 138
Beliefs & Culture 142
Sports 145
Outdoors 153

➕ Safe Travel 157

Emergencies 158
Police 160
Health 162

🍽️ Food 171

Eating Out 172
Self-Catering 189
Vegetarian & Special Meals 193

PAGE
196

📖 Menu Decoder
Dishes and ingredients explained –
order with confidence and try new foods.

PAGE
219

📖 Two-Way Dictionary
Quick reference vocabulary guide –
3500 words to help you communicate.

English–Japanese Dictionary 219
Japanese–English Dictionary 253

Index 267

INTRO **Japanese**
日本語 ni·hon·go

Who speaks Japanese?

Regional Dialects

Standard Language

TOKYO DIALECT
WHOLE COUNTRY

WESTERN
SHIKOKU; HONSHŪ WEST OF THE JAPAN ALPS

EASTERN
HOKKAIDŌ; HONSHŪ EAST OF THE JAPAN ALPS

RYŪKYŪAN DIALECTS
RYŪKYŪ ISLANDS

KYŪSHŪ DIALECTS
KYŪSHŪ

Why Bother

Japanese people are often too shy or worried about making mistakes to speak to visitors using what English they may know. Even the smallest effort to speak to locals in Japanese will be very warmly received.

Distinctive Sounds

Note the reduced, almost silent u (especially when it appears at the end of a word); and the r, which is pronounced halfway between an 'l' and an 'r'. Japanese has fewer sounds than most other major languages.

126 MILLION
speak Japanese as their first language

1 MILLION
speak Japanese as their second language

Japanese Script

Written Japanese is a combination of three different scripts. Kanji are ideographs (symbols that represent a concept as well as pronunciation), borrowed from Chinese. Hiragana and katakana are both indigenous, syllabic scripts (each character represents a syllable).

Japanese Lexicon

Japanese has many onomatopoeic expressions (describing something by its sound). For example, pouring rain can be described with zā zā ざあざあ, and a rumbling stomach might go go·ro go·ro ごろごろ.

Borrowings from English

Japanese has borrowed many words from English, often shortening and adapting them, eg pa·so·kon パソコン for 'personal computer' and kom·bi·ni コンビニ for 'convenience store'.

Language Family

It bears some resemblance to Altaic languages such as Mongolian and Turkish, and shows strong grammatical similarities to Korean, but linguists have not been able to prove the origins of Japanese.

Must-Know Grammar

Japanese has various levels of formality, shown with particular words or verb forms. The standard polite ending ·mas ます (given in this book) is the safe middle ground and will be suitable for most situations you'll encounter.

Donations to English

There are several – you may recognise *futon, karaoke, tsunami, bento box* and *manga,* to name a few.

5 Phrases to Learn Before You Go

1 **Is there a Western-/Japanese-style room?**

洋室/和室はありますか?

yō·shi·tsu/wa·shi·tsu wa a·ri·mas ka

Some lodgings have only Japanese-style rooms, or a mix of Western and Japanese – ask if you have a preference.

2 **Please bring a (spoon/knife/fork).**

(スプーン/ナイフ/フォーク)をください。

(spūn/nai·fu/fō·ku) o ku·da·sai

If you haven't quite mastered the art of eating with chopsticks don't be afraid to ask for cutlery at a restaurant.

3 **How do I get to ...?**

…へはどう行けばいいですか?

... e wa dō i·ke·ba ī des ka

Finding a place from its address can be difficult in Japan. Addresses usually give an area (not a street) and numbers aren't always consecutive. Practise asking for directions.

4 **I'd like a nonsmoking seat, please.**

禁煙席をお願いします。

kin·en·se·ki o o·ne·gai shi·mas

There are smoking seats in many restaurants and on bullet trains so be sure to specify if you want to be smoke-free.

5 **What's the local speciality?**

地元料理は何がありますか?

ji·mo·to·ryō·ri wa na·ni ga a·ri·mas ka

Throughout Japan most areas have a speciality dish and local usually love to talk food.

10 Phrases to Sound Like a Local

Great!	すごい!	su·goy
Sure.	もちろん。	mo·chi·ron
Hey!	ちょっと、ちょっと!	chot·to chot·to
Just a minute.	ちょっと待って。	chot·to mat·te
It's OK.	いいよ。	ī·yo
No problem.	大丈夫。	dai·jō·bu
Good luck.	頑張って。	gam·bat·te
No kidding?	マジ?	ma·ji
Really?	ほんと?	hon·to
Fat chance!	ありえない!	a·ri·e·nai

ABOUT JAPANESE

Pronunciation

Japanese pronunciation is not considered difficult for English speakers. Unlike some other Asian languages, it has no tones and most of its sounds are also found in English.

Vowel Sounds

Vowels in Japanese can be either short or long. The long ones should be held twice as long as the short ones and are represented in our pronunciation guides with a horizontal line on top of them.

~ SYMBOL ~	~ ENGLISH ~	~ JAPANESE EXAMPLE ~
a	run	na·ka
ā	father	sak·kā
e	red	sa·ke
ē	reign	pē·ji
i	bit	ni·ji
ī	bee	shī·tsu
o	pot	mot·to
ō	paw	pas·pō·to
u	put	mu·ra
ū	moon	kū·ki

It's important to make the distinction between short and long vowels as vowel length can change the meaning of a word, as in these examples:

彼	ka·re	**he**
カレー	ka·rē	**curry**
おじさん	o·ji·san	**uncle**
おじいさん	o·jī·san	**grandfather**

All vowels in the table on the previous page are 'pure', meaning they're pronounced individually – they do not tend to run together to form vowel sound combinations (diphthongs). Pronounce them clearly and slowly to make yourself understood, eg i·e (家) for 'house' and ī·e (いいえ) for 'no'.

There are a few vowel sound combinations, however, that roughly correspond to diphthongs in English:

~ SYMBOL ~	~ ENGLISH ~	~ JAPANESE EXAMPLE ~
ai	aisle	d**ai**·ga·ku
air	pair	**air**·kon
ow	cow	t**ow**·ru
oy	toy	k**oy**

The vowel u is sometimes not pronounced in Japanese. This so-called 'reduced' vowel most often occurs between k and s and in verb endings like des (です) and mas (ます). Where it's a silent vowel, we haven't included it in the coloured pronunciation guides.

Consonant Sounds

As the next table shows, most consonant sounds are pretty close to their English counterparts.

To make yourself understood clearly, it's important to make the distinction between single and double consonants as this can produce a difference in meaning, eg:

坂	sa·ka	**slope**
作家	sak·ka	**writer**
過去	ka·ko	**past**
かっこ	kak·ko	**brackets**

Pronounce the double consonants with a slight pause between them.

~ SYMBOL ~	~ ENGLISH ~	~ JAPANESE EXAMPLE ~
b	big	**ba**·sho
ch	chili	**chi**·zu
d	din	**d**ai·ga·ku
f	fun (almost like 'fw' with the lips in a rounded position, especially before 'u')	**fu**·ro
g	go (always a hard sound as in 'go')	**g**ai·jin
h	hit	hi·to
j	jam	**jū**·su
k	kick	**k**an·ji
m	man	**mu**·su·me
n	no	**no**·ri
p	pig	**p**an·tsu
r	run (halfway between 'l' and 'r')	**r**en·ji
s	so	**s**a·ba·ku
sh	show	**shi**·ma
t	tin	**t**a·bi
ts	hits	**tsu**·na·mi
w	win	**w**a·sa·bi
y	yes	**yu**·ki
z	is/zoo	**z**a·ru

Word Stress

Syllables are pronounced fairly evenly in Japanese, so there's no need to indicate stressed syllables.

Reading & Writing Japanese

Written Japanese is actually a combination of three different scripts. The first, kanji, consists of ideographic characters. The other two, hiragana and katakana, are syllabic scripts – each character represents a syllable.

Kanji

Kanji are ideographs (symbols that each represent a concept, idea or thing as well as pronunciation, rather than a word or set of words) borrowed from Chinese, eg 本 (hon) for 'book', 娘 (mu·su·me) for 'daughter' and 日本語 (ni·hon·go) for 'Japanese language'. Each kanji may be made up of anything from one to over 20 strokes written in a particular order. Some kanji characters have two or more ways of being pronounced depending on the context. For example, the kanji 水 is pronounced mi·zu when it means 'water', but su·i when it's part of another word like 水筒 (pronounced su·i·tō) for 'water bottle'.

There are over 2000 kanji in use in modern Japanese, of which 1945 are considered essential for everyday use. Of these, the Ministry of Education has designated 1006 characters as basic – these are taught at primary school level.

Hiragana

Hiragana is used to represent particles and grammatical endings particular to Japanese and are placed alongside the ideographic characters – one single Japanese word can contain both scripts. There are 46 basic hiragana characters, each representing a particular syllable. They can be combined to represent over 100 different syllables (see the table, p15).

| **Where's the market?** | 市場はどこですか? |
| | i·chi·ba wa do·ko des ka |

Note that in the phrase above the word for 'market' (i·chi·ba) is written in kanji (市場), but the rest – the particle wa (は), the question word do·ko (どこ), the verb des (です) and the interrogative particle ka (か) – in hiragana.

Katakana

Each hiragana character also has a katakana equivalent. Katakana are used to represent recent borrowings from other languages, especially English. They're also used to write foreign names – you might want to figure out how to write your own name in Japanese.

credit card	クレジットカード ku·re·jit·to·kā·do
My name is Anthony.	私の名前はアンソニーです。 wa·ta·shi no na·ma·e wa an·so·ī des
I'm from Australia.	オーストラリアから来ました。 ō·sto·ra·rya ka·ra ki·mash·ta

Note that the Japanese words for 'credit card', 'Anthony' and 'Australia' are all written in katakana.

The table (p15) shows the basic as well as some of the combined hiragana and katakana characters. For each syllable you'll find the pronunciation (in blue) with its hiragana symbol above and katakana symbol below it.

Hiragana & Katakana Script Table

あ a ア	い i イ	う u ウ	え e エ	お o オ
か ka カ	き ki キ	く ku ク	け ke ケ	こ ko コ
さ sa サ	し shi シ	す su ス	せ se セ	そ so ソ
た ta タ	ち chi チ	つ tsu ツ	て te テ	と to ト
な na ナ	に ni ニ	ぬ nu ヌ	ね ne ネ	の no ノ
は ha ハ	ひ hi ヒ	ふ fu フ	へ he ヘ	ほ ho ホ
ま ma マ	み mi ミ	む mu ム	め me メ	も mo モ
や ya ヤ		ゆ yu ユ		よ yo ヨ
ら ra ラ	り ri リ	る ru ル	れ re レ	ろ ro ロ
わ wa ワ				を o ヲ
ん n ン				

きゃ kya キャ	きゅ kyu キュ	きょ kyo キョ
しゃ sha シャ	しゅ shu シュ	しょ sho ショ
ちゃ cha チャ	ちゅ chu チュ	ちょ cho チョ
にゃ nya ニャ	にゅ nyu ニュ	にょ nyo ニョ
ひゃ hya ヒャ	ひゅ hyu ヒュ	ひょ hyo ヒョ
みゃ mya ミャ	みゅ myu ミュ	みょ myo ミョ
りゃ rya リャ	りゅ ryu リュ	りょ ryo リョ

が ga ガ	ぎ gi ギ	ぐ gu グ	げ ge ゲ	ご go ゴ
ざ za ザ	じ ji ジ	ず zu ズ	ぜ ze ゼ	ぞ zo ゾ
だ da ダ	ぢ ji ヂ	づ zu ヅ	で de デ	ど do ド
ば ba バ	び bi ビ	ぶ bu ブ	べ be ベ	ぼ bo ボ
ぱ pa パ	ぴ pi ピ	ぷ pu プ	ぺ pe ペ	ぽ po ポ

ぎゃ gya ギャ	ぎゅ gyu ギュ	ぎょ gyo ギョ	びゃ bya ビャ	びゅ byu ビュ	びょ byo ビョ
じゃ ja ジャ	じゅ ju ジュ	じょ jo ジョ	ぴゃ pya ピャ	ぴゅ pyu ピュ	ぴょ pyo ピョ

ABOUT JAPANESE

Grammar

This chapter will help you make your own sentences. It's arranged alphabetically for ease of navigation. If you can't find the exact phrase in this book, remember that with just a little grammar, a few gestures, and a couple of well-chosen words, you'll generally get the message across.

Note that we have added literal translations to every phrase to clarify Japanese sentence structures. The use of particles in Japanese – shown in blue in the literal translations – has been explained in **particles** and **prepositions**.

Adjectives & Adverbs

Describing People/Things • Doing Things

As in English, adjectives come before the noun they describe. There are two types of adjectives: 'i adjectives' that end in a vowel or ·i (い) and 'na adjectives' that end in na (な).

We had a nice meal.	おいしい食事をしました。 (lit: nice meal o did) oy·shī sho·ku·ji o shi·mash·ta
That is a beautiful building.	あれはきれいな建物です。 (lit: that-over-there wa beautiful building is) a·re wa ki·rē na ta·te·mo·no des

Adverbs, which describe a verb or an adjective, can be formed by replacing the ·i (い) ending of 'i adjectives' with the ending

·ku (く). The adjective ha·yai (速い), for example, becomes the adverb ha·ya·ku (速く).

Many adverbs in Japanese, however, exist as a word in their own right. For example, to·te·mo (とても) 'very', yuk·ku·ri (ゆっくり) 'slowly', and kyō (今日) 'today', to name a few.

Articles

Naming People/Things

Japanese does not have words equivalent to the English indefinite and definite articles 'a/an' and 'the':

| **It's a/the hotel.** | ホテルです。 (lit: hotel is) |
| | ho·te·ru des |

Words are used without articles and context will tell you whether 'a' or 'the' is meant. If you do want to point out a specific item (indicated by 'the' in English), you can use a demonstrative (see **demonstratives**).

Be

Describing People/Things • Making Statements • Pointing Things Out

The word des (です) roughly corresponds to the English verb 'be' and, like any verb in Japanese, it doesn't change according to who or what it refers to; des can mean 'I am' or 'she is' or 'we are' etc depending on the situation – there's one form only for all subjects. Japanese verbs do change their form when they're expressing the past tense and/or negative. The following table shows how des changes in these cases:

~ PRESENT POSITIVE ~		~ PRESENT NEGATIVE ~	
です	des	じゃありません	ja a·ri·ma·sen
~ PAST POSITIVE ~		~ PAST NEGATIVE ~	
でした	desh·ta	じゃありません でした	ja a·ri·ma·sen desh·ta

I'm Australian.	私はオーストラリア人です。 (lit: I wa Australian is) wa·ta·shi wa ō·sto·ra·rya·jin des
I'm not a medical doctor.	私は医者じゃありません。 (lit: I wa doctor is-not) wa·ta·shi wa i·sha ja a·ri·ma·sen
It was rainy yesterday.	きのうは雨でした。 (lit: yesterday wa rain was) ki·nō wa a·me desh·ta
The person I met last night was not Mr Takagi.	ゆうべ会った人は高木さんじゃ ありませんでした。 (lit: yesterday met person wa Tagaki-Mister not-was) yū·be at·ta hi·to wa ta·ka·gi·san ja a·ri·ma·sen desh·ta

Note that you drop the particle of the word that immediately precedes a form of the verb des (see **particles**).

There is/There are

There are two ways of expressing that something exists in Japanese. For animate objects (people and animals) the verb i·mas (います) is used. For inanimate objects (things) a·ri·mas (あります) is used.

| There are many good restaurants in Tokyo. | 東京にはいいレストランが
たくさんあります。(lit: Tokyo
in wa good restaurant ga many
there-are-*inanimate*)
tō·kyō ni wa ī res·to·ran ga
ta·ku·san a·ri·mas |
| There are four dogs in the garden. | 庭に犬が4匹います。(lit: garden
in dog ga four there-are-*animate*)
ni·wa ni i·nu ga yon·hi·ki i·mas |

Counters/Classifiers

Counting People/Things

For information on numbers and counters, see **numbers & amounts** (p36).

Demonstratives

Pointing Things Out • Indicating Location • Making Statements

To refer to or point out a person or object, use one of the words in the table below. Note that the element ko· (こ) refers to someone or something close to the speaker, so· (そ) to someone or something close to the listener and a· (あ) to something far from both the speaker and listener.

~ NEAR SPEAKER ~		~ NEAR LISTENER ~		~ FAR FROM BOTH ~	
this	これ ko·re	**that**	それ so·re	**that over there**	あれ a·re
this (book)	この(本) ko·no (hon)	**that (book)**	その(本) so·no (hon)	**that (book) over there**	あの(本) a·no (hon)
here	ここ ko·ko	**there**	そこ so·ko	**over there**	あそこ a·so·ko
this way	こちら ko·chi·ra	**that way**	そちら so·chi·ra	**that way over there**	あちら a·chi·ra

How much does this cost?

これはいくらですか? (lit: this wa how-much is question)
ko·re wa i·ku·ra des ka

That train is full.

その電車は満員です。 (lit: that train wa full is)
so·no den·sha wa man·in des

Have

Possessing

Possession can be shown in various ways in Japanese. The easiest way is to use the possessive particle no (の) after the noun, pronoun or proper noun that indicates who or what possesses something:

my friend	私の友達 (lit: I no friend) wa·ta·shi no to·mo·da·chi
It's hers.	これは彼女のです。 (lit: this wa she no is) ko·re wa ka·no·jo no des
Takashi's hotel	たかしのホテル (lit: Takashi no hotel) ta·ka·shi no ho·te·ru

An alternative way of expressing possession is to use the verb mot·te i·mas (持っています), 'have', or the expression ga a·ri·mas (があります), 'there is something to me':

I have money.	(私は)お金を 持っています。 (lit: (I wa) honourable-money o have) (wa·ta·shi wa) o·ka·ne o mot·te i·mas
I have a car	(私は)自動車 があります。 (lit: (I wa) car there-is) (wa·ta·shi wa) ji·dō·sha ga a·ri·mas

Negatives

Negating

To make a verb in the present tense negative, replace the ending ·mas (ます) with ·ma·sen (ません):

I smoke.	タバコを吸います。 (lit: cigarette o inhale) ta·ba·ko o su·i·mas

I don't smoke.	タバコを吸いません。
	(lit: cigarette o inhale-not)
	ta·ba·ko o su·i·ma·sen

To make a verb in the past tense negative, replace ·mash·ta (ました) with ·ma·sen desh·ta (ませんでした):

I came by train.	電車で来ました。
	(lit: train by did-come)
	den·sha de ki·mash·ta
I did not come by train.	電車で来ませんでした。
	(lit: train by come did-not)
	den·sha de ki·ma·sen desh·ta

In Japanese, adjectives also have a negative form. For 'i adjectives' replace the ending ·i (い) with ·ku (く) and negate them by adding a·ri·ma·sen (ありません) or nai des (ないです):

| 新しい | a·ta·ra·shī | **new** | 新しく ありません | a·ta·ra·shi·ku a·ri·ma·sen | **negative form of 'new'** |
| 古い | fu·ru·i | **old** | 古く ありません | fu·ru·ku a·ri·ma·sen | **negative form of 'old'** |

For 'na adjectives', keep the stems of the word (ie drop the ending na (な)), then negate them by adding ja a·ri·ma·sen (じゃ ありません) or de wa a·ri·ma·sen (ではありません), or the more informal ja nai des (じゃないです):

| 簡単な | kan·tan na | **easy** | 簡単じゃ ありません | kan·tan ja a·ri·ma·sen | **negative form of 'easy'** |

Nouns

Naming People/Things • Making Statements

Japanese nouns have no gender (masculine or feminine) or plural forms: you always use the same form of the noun whether you're referring to a masculine or feminine person, object, place or concept, and whether it's singular or plural.

box/boxes	箱	ha·ko
person/people	人	hi·to
ticket/tickets	切符	kip·pu

Make sure you always use a particle after the nouns when using them in a phrase (see **particles**).

Particles

Making Statements • Doing Things • Indicating Location • Possessing • Asking Questions

A Japanese noun or pronoun is almost always followed by a particle. Particles are short elements that display the function of the preceding word in the sentence. They show, for example, whether the preceding word is the subject (who or what is doing something) or the object (the person or thing that's affected by the action expressed by the verb) of the sentence. Sometimes particles act as prepositions, eg like the English 'to' or 'in'. You'll often come across the following particles in Japanese:

ga (が) **subject particle**
The particle ga (が) indicates the subject of the sentence when this is not omitted from the sentence (as often happens in Japanese):

| **This is my address.** | これが私の住所です。
(lit: this ga I no address is)
ko·re ga wa·ta·shi no jū·sho des |

wa (は) **topic particle**
The particle wa (は) marks the topic or the focal point of the sentence. It's often used when clarifying or stressing a particular point.

I'm a teacher.

私は教師です。
(lit: I wa teacher is)
wa·ta·shi wa kyō·shi des

When the subject of the sentence is stressed or contrasted, it's also the topic of the sentence, in which case the form ga will appear.

o (を) object particle
The particle o (を) marks the object of the sentence.

I ate sushi.

すしを食べました。
(lit: sushi o eat-did)
su·shi o ta·be·mash·ta

no (の) possessive particle
The particle no (の) shows that something belongs to some-one/something (also see **have**):

Miyuki's house

みゆきさんの家
(lit: Miyuki-Miss no house)
mi·yu·ki·san no i·e

ni (に) particle
The particle ni (に) can be used in four different ways.

day/month/year	on Monday	月曜日に	ge·tsu·yō·bi ni
time	at five o'clock	5時に	go·ji ni
location	in the shop	店に	mi·se ni
destination	to the station	駅に	e·ki ni

e (へ) particle (direction)
The particle e (へ) indicates direction and is very similar to the destination function of ni.

I'm going to Ginza.

銀座へ行きます。
(lit: Ginza e go)
gin·za e i·ki·mas

de（で）**particle**

The de（で）particle indicates location – it has a similar function to the location function of ni. It can also express the means of doing something:

at the entrance	入口で (lit: entrance de)
	i·ri·gu·chi de
I'm going by train.	電車で行きます。
	(lit: train de go)
	den·sha de i·ki·mas

ka（か）**interrogative particle**

The particle ka（か）is added to the end of a statement to turn it into a question. Also see **questions**.

I speak English.	英語が話せます。
	(lit: English ga speak)
	ê·go ga ha·na·se·mas
Do you speak English?	英語が話せますか?
	(lit: English ga speak ka)
	ê·go ga ha·na·se·mas ka

Plurals

Naming People/Things

Japanese nouns are the same whether they refer to one or more persons, objects, places or concepts. If you want to count or express a particular number of items you'll have to add a classifier (also called counter) to the noun.

For more details, see **nouns** and **counters** (p37).

Polite Forms

Naming People/Things • Being Polite

Japanese shows different forms of formality with particular words and often changing the forms of the verbs. This phrasebook uses standard polite ·mas（ます）forms, which will be suitable for most situations you encounter. To keep this safe middle ground, also avoid the use of second person pronouns, as they might sound too direct (see **pronouns**). You'll also notice that the Japanese often add the prefixes o- (お) and go- (ご) to certain nouns to indicate politeness or reverence:

sake	お酒	o·sa·ke
rice/meal	ごはん	go·han
I'll introduce you.	ご紹介します。 (lit: honourable-introduction do)	go·shō·kai shi·mas

Sometimes these prefixes mean 'your honourable ...'. Only use these when talking about or to others, never when talking about yourself or your situation.

your husband	ご主人 (lit: your-honourable-husband) go·shu·jin
my husband	主人 (lit: husband) shu·jin
How are you?	お元気ですか? (lit: your-honourable-healthy is ka) o·gen·ki des ka
I'm fine.	元気です。(lit: healthy is) gen·ki des

Possessives

Possessing

To indicate possession, use a pronoun (see **pronouns**), noun or proper noun followed by the particle no (の):

This is my book	これは私の本です。 (lit: this wa I no book is) ko·re wa wa·ta·shi no hon des

Mr Kamimura's suitcase	上村さんのスーツケース (lit: Kamimura-Mister no suitcase) ka·mi·mu·ra·san no sūts·kēs
school teacher	学校の先生 (lit: school no teacher) gak·kō no sen·sē

Also see **have** and **particles**.

Prepositions

Giving Instructions • Indicating Location • Pointing Things Out

The equivalent of English prepositions are often rendered by particles such as ni (に), e (へ) and de (で) in Japanese. Also see **particles**.

above	上に	u·e ni	in (time)	なか	na·ka
across	横切って	yo·ko·git·te	in front of	前	ma·e
after	あと	a·to	near	近く	chi·ka·ku
at (time)	に	ni	on	上に	u·e ni
at (place)	で	de	over	むこうに	mu·kō ni
before (time)	前	ma·e	through	通って	tōt·te
during	あいだ	ai·da	to	へ	e
for	ため	ta·me	under	下に	shi·ta ni
from	から	ka·ra	with	いっしょに	is·sho ni
in (place)	に	ni	without	なしで	na·shi de

Pronouns

Making Statements • Naming People/Things

Subject pronouns are often omitted in Japanese when the person being spoken about is obvious from context. Japanese pronouns vary based on the level of formality – in this phrasebook we have used an appropriate pronoun for each phrase.

I/me	(polite)	私	wa·ta·shi
	(formal)	わたくし	wa·tak·shi
	(used by men only)	僕/おれ	bo·ku/o·re
you sg	(polite)	あなた	a·na·ta
	(used by men to sub-ordinates)	きみ	ki·mi
she/her		彼女	ka·no·jo
he/him		彼	ka·re
we/us		私たち	wa·ta·shi ta·chi
you pl		あなたたち	a·na·ta ta·chi
they/them	m	彼ら	ka·re ra
	f	彼女たち	ka·no·jo ta·chi

Note that there are no different pronouns for subjects (eg I, she), objects (eg me, her) and possessives (eg my, her). The difference between these is indicated by the particle that follows the pronouns in the sentence: wa (は) for the topic, ga (が) for the subject, o (を) for the object and no (の) for the possessive (for more details see **particles**). See the following examples:

I saw her.	私が彼女を見ました。 (lit: I ga she o see-did) wa·ta·shi ga ka·no·jo o mi·mash·ta
She saw me.	彼女が私を見ました。 (lit: she ga I o see-did) ka·no·jo ga wa·ta·shi o mi·mash·ta
It's hers.	それは彼女のです。 (lit: that wa she no is) so·re wa ka·no·jo no des

Note that often it's better to avoid using second person pronouns altogether, as this might seem too direct.

Questions

Asking Questions • Answering Questions

To ask a yes/no question, just add ka (か) to the end of a statement and raise your intonation towards the end of the sentence as you would in English.

| This is the tourist office. | これは観光案内所です。
(lit: this wa tourist-office is)
ko·re wa kan·kō·an·nai·jo des |
| Is this the tourist office? | これは観光案内所ですか?
(lit: this wa tourist-office is ka)
ko·re wa kan·kō·an·nai·jo des ka |

To ask more specific questions, you can use the Japanese equivalents of 'who', 'where', 'what', 'how', 'why' etc. Note that these words often tend to come towards the end of the sentence, after the subject.

~ QUESTION WORDS ~

who	だれ/どなた	da·re/do·na·ta pol
Who is it?	だれですか?	da·re des ka
what	何/なに	nan/na·ni
What is this? **What are you doing?**	これは何ですか? なにをしますか?	ko·re wa nan des ka na·ni o shi·mas ka
which	どちら	do·chi·ra
Which train goes to Ginza?	どちらの電車 が銀座に行きますか?	do·chi·ra no den·sha ga gin·za ni i·ki·mas ka
when	いつ	i·tsu
When's the next bus?	次のバスはいつ ですか?	tsu·gi no bas wa i·tsu des ni
at what time	何時に	nan·ji ni
At what time does the boat leave?	船は何時に出ますか?	fu·ne wa nan·ji ni de·mas ka
where	どこ	do·ko
Where are the toilets?	トイレはどこですか?	toy·re wa do·ko des ka
how	どのように	do·no yō ni
How does this work?	どのようにしますか?	do·no yō ni shi·mas ka
how much/ how many	どのくらい/いくつ	do·no·ku·rai/i·ku·tsu
How much do you want? **How many are there?**	どのくらいほしい ですか? いくつありますか?	do·no·ku·rai ho·shī des ka i·ku·tsu a·ri·mas ka
how much (money)	いくら	i·ku·ra
How much does it cost?	いくらですか?	i·ku·ra des ka
why	なぜ	na·ze
Why (is that so)?	なぜですか?	na·ze des ka

When answering yes/no questions, the complete verb is often repeated after the 'yes' or 'no'.

yes	はい	hai
no	いいえ	ī·e

Do you understand?	わかりましたか？ (lit: understand-did ka) wa·ka·ri·mash·ta ka
Yes, I do (understand).	はい、わかりました。 (lit: yes understand did) hai wa·ka·ri·mash·ta
No, I don't (understand).	いいえ、わかりません。 (lit: no understand-did-not) ī·e wa·ka·ri·ma·sen

Verbs

Doing Things

Verbs are pretty straightforward in Japanese. First of all, they don't change according to the person. The form shi·mas (します) can mean 'I do', 'you do', 'they do' etc. Secondly, Japanese only has two basic tenses, present and past.

In Japanese dictionaries, verbs will usually be listed in their 'plain form'. This form is not appropriate for most conversations, though. In this phrasebook, we have chosen the polite ·mas (ます) form for most phrases, and for ease of use we have also listed the verbs in the dictionary in that form.

~ VERB ~	~ ·MAS FORM ~		~ PLAIN FORM ~	
eat	食べます	ta·be·mas	食べる	ta·be·ru
drink	飲みます	no·mi·mas	飲む	no·mu
do	します	shi·mas	する	su·ru
buy	買います	kai·mas	買う	kau
come	来ます	ki·mas	来る	ku·ru
go	行きます	i·ki·mas	行く	i·ku

There are some contexts in which the verb forms change. This is the case, for example, in negative phrases (for more details on this, see **negatives**), when making a request, or when using the verbs with other verbs such as 'can' and 'must'. These more complex cases have not been included in this chapter, however, as you can make yourself easily understood without knowing the ins and outs of these constructions.

Remember that the verb goes at the end of the sentence.

Future

Future tense is expressed by using the same forms as for the present tense – in Japanese it's most often understood from context that the future is concerned. If you'd like to make it crystal clear that you're talking about the future, you can also use a word or expression of time such as a·shi·ta (明日) for 'tomorrow', rai·ge·tsu (来月) for 'next month' or su·gi ni (すぐに) for 'soon' in your sentence.

Past

To form the past tense, simply replace the ending ·mas (ます) (ie the polite verb ending used in this phrasebook) with the ending ·mash·ta (ました).

I study at university.	大学で勉強します。 (lit: university de study do) dai·ga·ku de ben·kyō shi·mas
I've studied marketing.	マーケティングを勉強 しました。 (lit: marketing o study did) mā·ke·tin·gu o ben·kyō shi·mash·ta

As with the present tense, Japanese verbs in the past tense don't change according to the subject (ie whether the subject is I, you, he/she/it, we, you (pl) or they).

Word Order

Making Statements

Unlike English, in which word order is typically subject–verb–object, the order of a Japanese sentence is typically subject–object–verb. The subject is often omitted from the sentence if it's clear from context.

I bought a ticket to Hiroshima.

(私は)広島までの
チケットを買いました。
(lit: (I wa) Hiroshima to no ticket o bought)
(wa·ta·shi wa) hi·ro·shi·ma ma·de no chi·ket·to o kai·mash·ta

When building Japanese phrases it's important to keep each particle (see **particles**) straight after the word it belongs to – no other element should come between a word and its particle. These 'building blocks' – ie words and their particles – can be moved around in a sentence, as long as the basic subject–object–verb order is respected and the verb goes at the end of the sentence. Compare the following phrases, in which the building blocks are ordered in two possible ways.

I write a postcard in Japanese.

(私は)日本語ではがきを書きます。
(lit: (I wa) Japanese de postcard o write)
(wa·ta·shi wa) ni·hon·go de ha·ga·ki o ka·ki·mas
(私は)はがきを日本語で書きます。
(lit: (I wa) postcard o Japanese de write)
(wa·ta·shi wa) ha·ga·ki o ni·hon·go de ka·ki·mas

Basics

UNDERSTANDING 34

NUMBERS & AMOUNTS 36

TIME & DATES 40

Understanding

KEY PHRASES

Do you speak English?	英語が 話せますか?	ē·go ga ha·na·se·mas ka
I don't understand.	わかりません。	wa·ka·ri·ma·sen
What does ... mean?	…はどういう意味 ですか?	...wa dō yū i·mi des ka

1a Q **Do you speak (English)?**	英語が話せますか? (ē·go) ga ha·na·se·mas ka
A **I speak (English).**	(英語)が話せます。 (ē·go) ga ha·na·se·mas
A **I don't speak (Japanese).**	(日本語)が 話せません。 (ni·hon·go) ga ha·na·se·ma·sen
Does anyone speak English?	どなたか英語が 話せますか? do·na·ta ka ē·go ga ha·na·se·mas ka
1b Q **Do you understand?**	わかりますか? wa·ka·ri·mas ka
1c A **(Yes,) I understand.**	(はい、)わかります。 (hai) wa·ka·ri·mas
1d **I don't understand.**	わかりません。 wa·ka·ri·ma·sen
A **No, I don't understand.**	いいえ、わかりません。 ī·e wa·ka·ri·ma·sen

BASICS UNDERSTANDING

I understand.	わかります。 wa·ka·ri·mas
I speak a little.	少し話せます。 su·ko·shi ha·na·se·mas
2a What does (this) mean?	この意味は何ですか？ ko·no i·mi wa nan des ka
What does 'deguchi' mean?	「出口」はどういう意味ですか？ de·gu·chi wa dō yū i·mi des ka
2b How do you pronounce this?	これはどう発音 しますか。 ko·re wa dō ha·tsu·on shi·mas ka
2c Could you please repeat that?	繰り返して頂けますか？ ku·ri·ka·e·shi·te i·ta·da·ke·mas ka
2d Could you please speak more slowly?	もっとゆっくり話して 頂けますかか？ mot·to yuk·ku·ri ha·na·shi·te i·ta·da·ke·mas ka

✂	**Slowly, please!**	ゆっくり話して！	yuk·ku·ri ha·na·shi·te

2e Could you please write it down?	書いて頂けますか？ kai·te i·ta·da·ke·mas ka
How do you write 'shiatsu'?	「指圧」はどう書きますか？ shi·a·tsu wa dō ka·ki·mas ka
I'd like to learn some of your local dialects.	方言を習いたいのですが。 hō·gen o na·rai·tai no des ga
Would you like to learn some English?	英語を習いたいですか？ ē·go o na·rai·tai des ka

Numbers & Amounts

KEY PHRASES

How many?	どのくらい？	do·no ku·rai
How much?	いくつ？	i·ku·tsu
a little	ちょっと	chot·to
a lot/many	たくさん	ta·ku·san

Cardinal Numbers

The numbers 4, 7 and 9 – and all other numbers containing these numbers – have alternative pronunciations.

3a	0	0	ze·ro
3b	1	一	i·chi
3c	2	二	ni
3d	3	三	san
3e	4	四	yon/shi
3f	5	五	go
3g	6	六	ro·ku
3h	7	七	na·na/shi·chi
3i	8	八	ha·chi
3j	9	九	kyū/ku
3k	10	十	jū
3l	11	十一	jū·i·chi
3m	12	十二	jū·ni

4a 20	二十	ni·jū
21	二十一	ni·jū·i·chi
22	二十二	ni·jū·ni
4b 30	三十	san·jū
4c 40	四十	yon·jū
4d 50	五十	go·jū
4e 60	六十	ro·ku·jū
4f 70	七十	na·na·jū
4g 80	八十	ha·chi·jū
4h 90	九十	kyū·jū
4i 100	百	hya·ku
200	二百	ni·hya·ku
300	三百	sam·bya·ku
4j 1,000	千	sen
4k 10,000	一万	i·chi·man
4l 1,000,000	百万	hya·ku·man

Note that Japanese has no unit for 'a million'. Millions are expressed in units of 10 thousand, so one million is 100 ten-thousand units.

Ordinal Numbers

To use an ordinal number in Japanese, just add ·ban (番) to the end of the corresponding cardinal number.

1st	一番	i·chi·ban
2nd	二番	ni·ban
3rd	三番	sam·ban

Counters

In Japanese, when expressing a certain number of objects, people or animals, the cardinal number is followed by a counter. Counters, also commonly known as 'classifiers', indicate the size, shape and function of things and distinguish between objects, people and animals.

The following generic counters can be used to count most objects, but not to count people or animals:

1	一つ	hi·to·tsu
2	二つ	fu·ta·tsu
3	三つ	mit·tsu
4	四つ	yot·tsu
5	五つ	i·tsu·tsu
6	六つ	mut·tsu
7	七つ	na·na·tsu
8	八つ	yat·tsu
9	九つ	ko·ko·no·tsu
10	十	tō
numbers higher than 10	…個	…ko

Note that apart from the last generic counter mentioned in the list above, there's no need to add the cardinal number before as this already makes part of the counter, eg the phrase 'Give me an apple, please.' is rin·go o hi·to·tsu ku·da·sai (りんごを一つください), literally 'apple-o one please', not rin·go o i·chi hi·to·tsu ku·da·sai (りんごを一一つください), literally 'apple-o one one please'.

Here are also some basic specific counters frequently used in everyday speech, including the ones for people and animals:

age	…歳	…·sai
animals*	…匹	…·hi·ki/pi·ki/bi·ki
books	…冊	…·sa·tsu
bottles, pens (long objects)*	…本	…·hon/pon/bon
floors (of buildings)	…階	…·kai
objects (small)	…個	…·ko
people	…人	…·nin
scoops, glasses, cups*	…杯	…·hai/pai/bai

sheets (paper, sliced objects)	…枚	…mai
time	…時	…ji
vehicles	…台	…dai

*Note that the pronunciation of these three counters changes according to the preceding number. For these, generally use the first option (·hi·ki, ·hon, ·hai) but change to ·pi·ki, ·pon, ·pai after the numbers 1, 6 and 10, and to ·bi·ki, ·bon and ·bai after the number 3. Don't forget to add the cardinal number before each of the specific counters listed above!

Useful Amounts

How much?	どのくらい? do·no ku·rai
How many?	いくつ? i·ku·tsu
(100) grams	(100) グラム (hya·ku)·gu·ra·mu
a kilo	1キロ i·chi·ki·ro
a quarter	4分の1 yom·bun no i·chi
a third	3分の1 sam·bun no i·chi
a half	半分 ham·bun
all	全部 zem·bu
none	なし na·shi

For other useful amounts, see **self-catering** (p189).

Time & Dates

KEY PHRASES

What time is it?	何時ですか？	nan·ji des ka
At what time ...?	何時に…	nan·ji ni ...
What date?	何月 何日ですか？	nan·ga·tsu nan·ni·chi des ka

Telling the Time

To specify the hour, add the number of the hour before the word ·ji (時) 'o'clock'. Note that four o'clock is an exception: yo·ji (4時), not shi·ji. The minutes come after the hour and are expressed by adding ·fun/·pun (分) after the number – see **numbers & amounts** for how to form numbers in Japanese. To say 'half past' use ·ji han (時半). For times leading up to the hour (in English 'to') use ma·e des (前です), meaning literally 'before it is' instead of des (です), 'it is'.

5a Q	What time is it?	何時ですか？ nan·ji des ka
5b A	It's (one) o'clock.	(1)時です。 (i·chi)·ji des
	Five past (ten).	(10)時5分です。 (jū)·ji go·fun des
5c	Quarter past (one).	(1)時15分です。 (i·chi)·ji jū·go·fun des
5d	Half past (one).	(1)時半です。 (i·chi)·ji han des
5e	Quarter to (one).	(1)時15分前です。 (i·chi)·ji jū·go·fun ma·e des

Twenty to (ten).	(10)時20分前です。
	(jū)·ji ni·jup·pun ma·e des
Q At what time ...?	何時に…
	nan·ji ni ...
A At (ten).	(10時)に。
	(jū·ji) ni

Combining numbers with minutes produces some special forms:

one minute	1分	ip·pun
two minutes	2分	ni·fun
three minutes	3分	sam·pun
four minutes	4分	yom·pun
five minutes	5分	go·fun
six minutes	6分	rop·pun
seven minutes	7分	na·na·fun
eight minutes	8分	hap·pun
nine minutes	9分	kyū·fun
10 minutes	10分	jup·pun
15 minutes	15分	jū·go·fun
20 minutes	20分	ni·jup·pun
am	午前	go·zen
pm	午後	go·go
6a morning	朝	a·sa
day	日中	nit·chū
midday	正午	shō·go
6b afternoon	午後	go·go
6c evening	夕方	yū·ga·ta
midnight	真夜中	ma·yo·na·ka
night	夜	yo·ru

BASICS TIME & DATES

The Calendar

7a	Monday	月曜日	ge·tsu·yō·bi
7b	Tuesday	火曜日	ka·yō·bi
7c	Wednesday	水曜日	su·i·yō·bi
7d	Thursday	木曜日	mo·ku·yō·bi
7e	Friday	金曜日	kin·yō·bi
7f	Saturday	土曜日	do·yō·bi
7g	Sunday	日曜日	ni·chi·yō·bi
8a	January	1月	i·chi·ga·tsu
8b	February	2月	ni·ga·tsu
8c	March	3月	san·ga·tsu
8d	April	4月	shi·ga·tsu
8e	May	5月	go·ga·tsu
8f	June	6月	ro·ku·ga·tsu
8g	July	7月	shi·chi·ga·tsu
8h	August	8月	ha·chi·ga·tsu
8i	September	9月	ku·ga·tsu
8j	October	10月	jū·ga·tsu
8k	November	11月	jū·i·chi·ga·tsu
8l	December	12月	jū·ni·ga·tsu
9a	summer	夏	na·tsu
9b	autumn	秋	a·ki
9c	winter	冬	fu·yu
9d	spring	春	ha·ru

To express the date, use the cardinal number plus ·ni·chi (日).

What date is it?	何月何日ですか？（lit: what month and day） nan·ga·tsu nan·ni·chi des ka
10a 🇶 **What date is it today?**	今日は何日ですか？ kyō wa nan·ni·chi des ka
🇦 **It's (18 October).**	（10月18日）です。 （jū·ga·tsu jū·ha·chi·ni·chi) des

There are irregular forms for the 1st to the 10th, the 14th, 20th and 24th when referring to dates:

1st	1日	tsu·i·ta·chi
2nd	2日	fu·tsu·ka
3rd	3日	mik·ka
4th	4日	yok·ka
5th	5日	i·tsu·ka
6th	6日	mu·i·ka
7th	7日	na·no·ka
8th	8日	yō·ka
9th	9日	ko·ko·no·ka
10th	10日	tō·ka
14th	14日	jū·yok·ka
20th	20日	ha·tsu·ka
24th	24日	ni·jū·yok·ka

Present

now	今	i·ma
this afternoon	今日の午後	kyō no go·go
this morning	今朝	ke·sa
this month	今月	kon·ge·tsu
this week	今週	kon·shū
this year	今年	ko·to·shi

| 10b today | 今日 | kyō |
| 10c tonight | 今夜 | kon·ya |

Past

(three days) ago	(3日)前	(mik·ka) ma·e
day before yesterday	おととい	o·to·toy
11a last month	先月	sen·ge·tsu
11b last night	ゆうべ	yū·be
11c last week	先週	sen·shū
11d last year	去年	kyo·nen
since (May)	(5月)から	(go·ga·tsu) ka·ra
12a yesterday	きのう	ki·nō
12b yesterday afternoon	きのうの午後	ki·nō no go·go
12c yesterday evening	きのうの晩	ki·nō no ban
12d yesterday morning	きのうの朝	ki·nō no a·sa

Future

day after tomorrow	あさって	a·sat·te
in (six days)	(6日)後	(mu·i·ka) go
next ...	来…	rai...
13a next month	来月	rai·ge·tsu
13b next week	来週	rai·shū
13c next year	来年	rai·nen
14a tomorrow	明日	a·shi·ta
14b tomorrow afternoon	明日の午後	a·shi·ta no go·go
14c tomorrow evening	明日の晩	a·shi·ta no ban
14d tomorrow morning	明日の朝	a·shi·ta no a·sa
until (June)	(6月)まで	(ro·ku·ga·tsu) ma·de

Practical

TRANSPORT	46
BORDER CROSSING	62
DIRECTIONS	64
ACCOMMODATION	68
SHOPPING	80
COMMUNICATIONS	88
MONEY & BANKING	95
BUSINESS	98
SIGHTSEEING	102
SENIOR & DISABLED TRAVELLERS	107
TRAVEL WITH CHILDREN	109

Transport

KEY PHRASES

What time's the next bus?	次のバスは何時ですか?	tsu·gi no bas wa nan·ji des ka
A ticket to ..., please.	…行きの切符をください。	... yu·ki no kip·pu o ku·da·sai
Please tell me when we get to ...	…に着いたら教えてください。	... ni tsu·i·ta·ra o·shi·e·te ku·da·sai
Please take me to this address.	この住所までお願いします。	ko·no jū·sho ma·de o·ne·gai shi·mas
I'd like to hire a car.	自動車を借りたいのですが。	ji·dō·sha o ka·ri·tai no des ga

Getting Around

Which ... goes to (Nagasaki)?	(長崎)行きの…はどれですか?	(na·ga·sa·ki)·yu·ki no ... wa do·re des ka
boat	船	fu·ne
bullet train	新幹線	shin·kan·sen
bus	バス	bas
plane	飛行機	hi·kō·ki
train	電車	den·sha

15a	Is this the boat to (Tokyo)?	（東京）行きの船は これですか？ (tō·kyō)·yu·ki no fu·ne wa ko·re des ka
15b	Is this the bus to (Tokyo)?	（東京）行きのバスは これですか？ (tō·kyō)·yu·ki no bas wa ko·re des ka
15c	Is this the train to (Tokyo)?	（東京）行きの電車は これですか？ (tō·kyō)·yu·ki no den·sha wa ko·re des ka
16a	What time's the first bus?	始発のバスは何時 ですか？ shi·ha·tsu no bas wa nan·ji des ka
16b	What time's the last bus?	最終のバスは何時 ですか？ sai·shū no bas wa nan·ji des ka
16c	What time's the next bus?	次のバスは何時 ですか？ tsu·gi no bas wa nan·ji des ka
17a	At what time does it leave?	何時に出ますか？ nan·ji ni de·mas ka
17b	At what time does it arrive?	何時に着きますか？ nan·ji ni tsu·ki·mas ka
	What time does it get to (Nagoya)?	（名古屋）に何時に 着きますか？ (na·go·ya) ni nan·ji ni tsu·ki·mas ka
17c	How long will it be delayed?	どのくらい遅れますか？ do·no ku·rai o·ku·re·mas ka
18a	That's my seat.	そこは私の席です。 so·ko wa wa·ta·shi no se·ki des

18b Is this seat available? この席は空いていますか?
ko·no se·ki wa ai·te i·mas ka

✂ **Is it free?** 空いてますか? ai·te·i·mas ka

18c Please tell me when we get to (Tokyo).
(東京)に着いたら
教えてください。
(tō·kyō) ni tsu·i·ta·ra
o·shi·e·te ku·da·sai

Please stop here. ここで停めてください。
ko·ko de to·me·te ku·da·sai

Can we get there by public transport?
そこに公共交通機関で
行けますか?
so·ko ni kō·kyō·kō·tsū·ki·kan de
i·ke·mas ka

I'd prefer to walk there. 歩いて行きたいです。
a·ru·i·te i·ki·tai des

Buying Tickets

19a Where can I buy a ticket?
切符はどこで買えますか?
kip·pu wa do·ko de ka·e·mas ka

19b Do I need to book a seat?
席の予約が必要ですか?
se·ki no yo·ya·ku ga hi·tsu·yō
des ka

A ticket (to Tokyo), please.
(東京行きの)切符をください。
(tō·kyō·yu·ki no) kip·pu o
ku·da·sai

19c A one-way ticket, please.
片道切符一枚を
ください。
ka·ta·mi·chi kip·pu i·chi mai o
ku·da·sai

19d One return ticket, please.
往復切符一枚を
ください。
ō·fu·ku kip·pu i·chi mai o
ku·da·sai

Buying a Ticket

What time's the next ...?
次の…は何時ですか?
tsu·gi no ... wa nan·ji des ka

 boat
船
fu·ne

 bus
バス
bas

 train
電車
den·sha

A ... ticket, please.
…切符一枚をください。
... kip·pu i·chi mai o ku·da·sai

 one-way
片道
ka·ta·mi·chi

 return
往復
ō·fu·ku

I'd like a/an ... seat.

…席をお願いします。
... se·ki o o·ne·gai shi·mas

aisle
通路側
tsū·ro·ga·wa

window
窓側
ma·do·ga·wa

Which platform does it depart from?

何番のプラットホームから出ますか?
nam·ban no pu·rat·to·fō·mu ka·ra de·mas ka

I'd like an aisle seat, please.	通路側席をお願いします。 tsū·ro·ga·wa·se·ki o o·ne·gai shi·mas	
I'd like a window seat, please.	窓側席をお願いします。 ma·do·ga·wa·se·ki o o·ne·gai shi·mas	
19e I'd like a nonsmoking seat, please.	禁煙席を お願いします。 kin·en·se·ki o o·ne·gai shi·mas	
19f I'd like a smoking seat, please.	喫煙席を お願いします。 kit·su·en·se·ki o o·ne·gai shi·mas	
20a Is there (a toilet)?	（トイレ）はありますか？ (toy·re) wa a·ri·mas ka	
20b How much is it?	いくらですか？ i·ku·ra des ka	
20c How long does the trip take?	時間はどのくらい かかりますか？ ji·kan wa do·no·ku·rai ka·ka·ri·mas ka	
20d Is it a direct route?	直行便ですか？ chok·kō·bin des ka	
21a I'd like to cancel my ticket, please.	切符のキャンセルを お願いします。 kip·pu no kyan·se·ru o o·ne·gai shi·mas	
21b I'd like to change my ticket, please.	切符の変更を お願いします。 kip·pu no hen·kō o o·ne·gai shi·mas	
21c I'd like to confirm my ticket, please.	切符の確認を お願いします。 kip·pu no ka·ku·nin o o·ne·gai shi·mas	

Can I get a stand-by ticket?	スタンドバイチケットは ありますか？ stan·do·bai·chi·ket·to wa a·ri·mas ka

Luggage

Where can I find the left-luggage office?	手荷物預かり所は どこですか？ te·ni·mo·tsu·a·zu·ka·ri·sho wa do·ko des ka
22a Where can I find a luggage locker?	ロッカーはどこですか？ rok·kā wa do·ko des ka
Where can I find a trolley?	トロリーはどこですか？ to·ro·rī wa do·ko des ka
22b My luggage has been damaged.	私の手荷物が壊れました。 wa·ta·shi no te·ni·mo·tsu ga ko·wa·re·mash·ta
22c My luggage has been lost.	私の手荷物が なくなりました。 wa·ta·shi no te·ni·mo·tsu ga na·ku·na·ri·mash·ta
22d My luggage has been stolen.	私の手荷物が ぬすまれました。 wa·ta·shi no te·ni·mo·tsu ga nu·su·ma·re·mash·ta

🔊 LISTEN FOR

時刻表	ji·ko·ku·hyō	timetable
キャンセル	kyan·se·ru	cancelled
窓口	ma·do·gu·chi	ticket window
満席	man·se·ki	full
遅れ	o·ku·re	delayed
プラットフォーム	pu·rat·to·fō·mu	platform

Plane

Where's ...?　…はどこですか?
... wa do·ko des ka

the shuttle bus	シャトルバス	sha·to·ru·bas
arrivals	到着便	tō·cha·ku·bin
departures	出発便	shup·pa·tsu·bin
duty-free	免税店	men·zē·ten
gate number (5)	(5)番ゲート	(go)·ban gē·to

Bus & Coach

How often do buses come?	バスはどのくらいひんぱんに来ますか? bas wa do·no·ku·rai him·pan ni ki·mas ka
Does it stop at (Yokohama)?	(横浜)に停まりますか? (yo·ko·ha·ma) ni to·ma·ri·mas ka
23a What's the next stop?	次の停車はどこですか? tsu·gi no tē·sha wa do·ko des ka
I'd like to get off at (Kurashiki).	(倉敷)で下車します。 (ku·ra·shi·ki) de ge·sha shi·mas

Train

23b What station is this?	ここは何駅ですか? ko·ko wa na·ni·e·ki des ka
23c What's the next station?	次は何駅ですか? tsu·gi wa na·ni·e·ki des ka

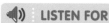

🔊 LISTEN FOR

重量オーバー の手荷物	jū·ryō·ō·bā no te·ni·mo·tsu	excess baggage
機内持込 の手荷物	ki·nai·mo·chi·ko·mi no te·ni·mo·tsu	carry-on baggage

23d **Does it stop at (Tokyo)?**	（東京）に停まりますか？ (tō·kyō) ni to·ma·ri·mas ka
Do I need to change?	乗り換えなければ いけませんか？ no·ri·ka·e·na·ke·re·ba i·ke·ma·sen ka
Which line goes to (Roppongi) station?	（六本木）駅はどの線ですか？ (rop·pon·gi)·e·ki wa do·no sen des ka
Can I use this ticket on the (Toei) line?	この切符で（都営）線に 乗れますか？ ko·no kip·pu de (to·ē)·sen ni no·re·mas ka
I need to pay the excess fare.	清算したいのですが。 sē·san shi·tai no des ga
I'd like to go on a bullet train.	新幹線で行きたいのですが。 shin·kan·sen de i·ki·tai no des ga
Where's exit number (2)?	（２）番出口はどこですか？ (ni)·ban de·gu·chi wa do·ko des ka
Where's the (east) exit?	（東）口はどこですか？ (hi·ga·shi)·gu·chi wa do·ko des ka
Don't push!	押さないで！ o·sa·nai·de

Is it (a/an) ...?*	…ですか? ... des ka

direct (nonstop)	直行便	chok·kō·bin
limited express train (few stops)	特急	tok·kyū
express	急行	kyū·kō
rapid train	快速	kai·so·ku
local	各駅停車	ka·ku·e·ki·tē·sha

* The trains are listed according to how often they stop, starting with the one that stops the least.

Which carriage is for (Hiroshima)?	(広島)行きは 何号車ですか? (hi·ro·shi·ma)·yu·ki wa nan·gō·sha des ka
Which is the dining carriage?	食堂車は 何号車 ですか? sho·ku·dō·sha wa nan·gō·sha des ka
Which is the green-class (1st-class) carriage?	グリーン車は 何号車ですか? gu·rīn·sha wa nan·gō·sha des ka

Boat

What's the sea like today?	今日の海の様子は どうですか? kyō no u·mi no yō·su wa dō des ka
Are there life jackets?	救命胴衣はありますか? kyū·mē·dō·i wa a·ri·mas ka
I feel seasick.	船酔いしました。 fu·na·yoy shi·mash·ta

🔍 LOOK FOR

新幹線	shin·kan·sen	bullet train
モノレール	mo·no·rē·ru	monorail
地下鉄	chi·ka·te·tsu	subway
電車	den·sha	train
市電	shi·den	tram

Taxi

24a I'd like a taxi at (9 o'clock).	(9時)にタクシーを お願いします。	(ku·ji) ni tak·shī o o·ne·gai shi·mas
24b I'd like a taxi now.	今タクシーを お願いします。	i·ma tak·shī o o·ne·gai shi·mas
Where's the taxi rank?	タクシー乗り場はどこ ですか?	tak·shī·no·ri·ba wa do·ko des ka
24c Is this taxi available?	このタクシーは空車ですか?	ko·no tak·shī wa kū·sha des ka
24d How much is it to (Tokyo)?	(東京)までいくらですか?	(tō·kyō) ma·de i·ku·ra des ka
24e Please take me to (this address).	(この住所)まで お願いします。	(ko·no jū·sho) ma·de o·ne·gai shi·mas

✂ **To ...** ……まで。 … ma·de

25a Please slow down.
スピードを落としてください。
spī·do o o·to·shi·te ku·da·sai

25b Please stop here.
ここで停まってください。
ko·ko de to·mat·te ku·da·sai

25c Please wait here.
ここで待っていてください。
ko·ko de mat·te·i·te ku·da·sai

For other useful phrases, see **directions** (p64) and **money** (p95).

Car & Motorbike

26a I'd like to hire a car.
車を借りたいのですが。
ku·ru·ma o ka·ri·tai no des ga

26b I'd like to hire a motorbike.
オートバイを借りたいのですが。
ō·to·bai o ka·ri·tai no des ga

I'd like to hire a/an ...
…を借りたいのですが。
... o ka·ri·tai no des ga

4WD	四駆	yon·ku
automatic	オートマチック	ō·to·ma·chik·ku
manual	マニュアル	ma·nyu·a·ru
scooter	スクーター	skū·tā

26c How much for daily hire?
1日借りるといくらですか?
i·chi·ni·chi ka·ri·ru to i·ku·ra des ka

26d How much for weekly hire?
1週間借りるといくらですか?
is·shū·kan ka·ri·ru to i·ku·ra des ka

Does that include insurance/mileage?
保険料/マイレージが含まれていますか?
ho·ken·ryō/mai·rē·ji ga fu·ku·ma·re·te i·mas ka

Do you have a guide to the road rules in English?	道路交通法の英語の ガイドブックがありますか? dō·ro·kō·tsū·hō no ē·go no gai·do·buk·ku ga a·ri·mas ka
What's the speed limit?	制限速度は何キロ ですか? sē·gen·so·ku·do wa nan·ki·ro des ka
How much is the toll for this road?	この道の通行料は いくらですか? ko·no mi·chi no tsū·kō·ryō wa i·ku·ra des ka
26e Is this the road to (Tokyo)?	これは(東京)へ行く道 ですか? ko·re wa (tō·kyō) e i·ku mi·chi des ka
Where's a petrol station?	ガソリンスタンドはどこ ですか? ga·so·rin·stan·do wa do·ko des ka

PRACTICAL TRANSPORT

windscreen
フロントガラス
fu·ron·to·ga·ra·su

battery
バッテリー
bat·te·ri

engine
エンジン
en·jin

headlight
ヘッドライト
hed·do·rai·to

27a
petrol
ガソリン
ga·so·rin

27b
tyre
タイヤ
tai·ya

🔍 LOOK FOR

一時停止	i·chi·ji·tē·shi	Stop Here
一方通行	ip·pō·tsū·kō	One-way
27c 入口	i·ri·gu·chi	Entrance
工事中	kō·ji·chū	Under Construction
立入り禁止	ta·chi·i·ri·kin·shi	No Entry
駐車	chū·sha	Parking
駐車禁止	chū·sha·kin·shi	No Parking
27d 出口	de·gu·chi	Exit (freeway etc)
止まれ	to·ma·re	Stop
料金所	ryō·kin·jo	Toll

Please fill it up.	満タンにしてください。 man·tan ni shi·te ku·da·sai
I'd like ... litres.	…リットルお願いします。 ... rit·to·ru o·ne·gai shi·mas
Can you check the oil?	オイルのチェックをお願いします。 oy·ru no chek·ku o o·ne·gai shi·mas
Can you check the water?	水のチェックをお願いします。 mi·zu no chek·ku o o·ne·gai shi·mas
Can you check the tyre pressure?	空気圧のチェックをお願いします。 kū·ki·a·tsu no chek·ku o o·ne·gai shi·mas
(How long) Can I park here?	（どのくらい）ここに駐車できますか? (do·no·ku·rai) ko·ko ni chū·sha de·ki·mas ka

Do I have to pay?	料金を払わなければ なりませんか? ryō·kin o ha·ra·wa·na·ke·re·ba na·ri·ma·sen ka
28a I need a mechanic.	整備士が必要です。 sē·bi·shi ga hi·tsu·yō des
I've had an accident.	事故に遭いました。 ji·ko ni ai·mash·ta
The car has broken down (at Minato-ku).	車が(港区で)壊れました。 ku·ru·ma ga (mi·na·to·ku de) ko·wa·re·mash·ta
28b I have a flat tyre.	パンクしました。 pan·ku shi·mash·ta
28c I've run out of petrol.	ガス欠です。 gas·ke·tsu des

ここで停まってください。
ko·ko de to·mat·te ku·da·sai

Please stop here.

PRACTICAL TRANSPORT

Bicycle

29a Can I get there by bicycle?	そこへは自転車で行けますか？ so·ko e wa ji·ten·sha de i·ke·mas ka
I'd like to buy a bicycle.	自転車を買いたいのですが。 ji·ten·sha o kai·tai no des ga
29b I'd like to hire a bicycle.	自転車を借りたいのですが。 ji·ten·sha o ka·ri·tai no des ga
I'd like a mountain bike.	マウンテンバイクが欲しいのですが。 ma·un·ten·bai·ku ga ho·shī no des ga
I'd like a racing bike.	レース用自転車が欲しいのですが。 rē·su·yō ji·ten·sha ga ho·shī no des ga
I'd like a secondhand bike.	中古の自転車が欲しいのですが。 chū·ko no ji·ten·sha ga ho·shī no des ga
How much is it per day?	1日いくらですか？ i·chi·ni·chi i·ku·ra des ka
How much is it per hour?	1時間いくらですか？ i·chi·ji·kan i·ku·ra des ka
Do I need a helmet?	ヘルメットは必要ですか？ he·ru·met·to wa hi·tsu·yō des ka
Is there a bicycle-path map?	自転車道の地図がありますか？ ji·ten·sha·dō no chi·zu ga a·ri·mas ka

| I have a puncture. | パンクしました。
pan·ku shi·mash·ta |
| I'd like my bicycle repaired. | 私の自転車を
直してもらいたいの
ですが。
wa·ta·shi no ji·ten·sha o
now·shi·te mo·rai·tai no
des ga |

CULTURE TIP **Keirin**

An originally Japanese cycling discipline, *keirin* kē·rin (競輪) has made it onto the international stage over the last 20 years. In this 2000m track cycling event, each rider cycles behind a motorised derny (a type of motorcycle specifically designed and built for motor-paced track cycling events) that sets the pace for 1400m, then pulls off the track and leaves the riders to sprint to the finish – fast, furious and spectacular!

Border Crossing

KEY PHRASES

I'm here for ... days.	私は …日滞在 します。	wa·ta·shi wa ... ni·chi tai·zai shi·mas
I'm staying at ...	…に泊まります。	... ni to·ma·ri·mas
I have nothing to declare.	何も申請 するものは ありません。	na·ni mo shin·sē su·ru mo·no wa a·ri·ma·sen

Passport Control

I'm in transit.	トランジットです。 to·ran·jit·to des
30a I'm here on business.	ビジネスで来ました。 bi·ji·nes de ki·ma·shi·ta
30b I'm here on holiday.	休暇で来ました。 kyū·ka de ki·ma·shi·ta
30c I'm here for (10) days.	私は(十)日間滞在します。 wa·ta·shi wa (tō)·ka kan tai·zai shi·mas
30d I'm here for (two) months.	私は(二)ヶ月間滞在します。 wa·ta·shi wa (ni)·ka·ge·tsu kan tai·zai shi·mas
30e I'm here for (three) weeks.	私は(三)週間滞在します。 wa·ta·shi wa (san)·shū kan tai·zai shi·mas
30f I'm going to (Tokyo).	(東京)へ行きます。 (tō·kyō) e i·ki·mas
I'm staying at (Hotel Nikko).	(日航ホテル)に泊まります。 (nik·kō·ho·te·ru) ni to·ma·ri·mas

LOOK FOR

移民	i·min	Immigration
検疫	ken·e·ki	Quarantine
出入国管理	shu·tsu·nyū·ko·ku·kan·ri	Passport Control
税関	zē·kan	Customs
免税	men·zē	Duty-free

At Customs

31a I have nothing to declare.	何も申請するもの はありません。 na·ni mo shin·sē su·ru mo·no wa a·ri·ma·sen
31b I have something to declare.	申請するものがあります。 shin·sē su·ru mo·no ga a·ri·mas
Do I have to declare this?	これを申請しなければ なりませんか? ko·re o shin·sē shi·na·ke·re·ba na·ri·ma·sen ka
31c That's mine.	それは私のです。 so·re wa wa·ta·shi no des
31d That's not mine.	それは私のでは ありません。 so·re wa wa·ta·shi no de wa a·ri·ma·sen
31e I didn't know I had to declare it.	これを申請しなければ ならないのを知りません でした。 ko·re o shin·sē shi·na·ke·re·ba na·ra·nai no o shi·ri·ma·sen desh·ta

For duty-free shopping, see **shopping** (p80), for some handy phrases.

Directions

KEY PHRASES

Where's ...?	…はどこですか?	...wa do·ko des ka
What's the address?	住所は何ですか?	jū·sho wa nan des ka
How far away is it?	どのくらいの距離ですか?	do·no ku·rai no kyo·ri des ka

32a Where's (the tourist office)?

(観光案内所)はどこ
ですか?
(kan·kō·an·nai·jo) wa do·ko
des ka

32b How do I get there?

そこへはどう行けばいい
ですか?
so·ko e wa dō i·ke·ba ī
des ka

32c How far away is it?

どのくらいの距離ですか?
do·no ku·rai no kyo·ri des ka

32d Can you show me (on the map)?

(地図で)教えて
くれますか?
(chi·zu de) o·shi·e·te
ku·re·mas ka

What (street) is this?

この(道路)の名前は
何ですか?
ko·no (dō·ro) no na·ma·e wa
nan des ka

32e What's the address?

住所は何ですか?
jū·sho wa nan des ka

33a Turn left.

左へまがってください。
hi·da·ri e ma·gat·te ku·da·sai

33b Turn right.	右へまがってください。 mi·gi e ma·gat·te ku·da·sai	
33c straight ahead	まっすぐ mas·su·gu	
33d It's far.	遠いです。 tōy des	
33e It's near.	近くです。 chi·ka·ku des	
It's behind ...	…の後ろです。 ... no u·shi·ro des	
It's in front of ...	…の前です。 ... no ma·e des	
33f It's next to ...	…のとなりです。 ... no to·na·ri des	
34a here	ここ ko·ko	
34b there	あそこ a·so·ko	
34c on the corner	角です。 ka·do des	
34d opposite	向かい側 mu·kai·ga·wa	
34e Turn at the corner.	角をまがってください。 ka·do o ma·gat·te ku·da·sai	
34f Turn at the traffic lights.	信号をまがってください。 shin·gō o ma·gat·te ku·da·sai	
35a by bus	バスで bas de	
35b on foot	徒きで a·ru·ki de	
35c by taxi	タクシーで tak·shī de	
35d by train	電車で den·sha de	

PRACTICAL

DIRECTIONS

traffic lights
信号
shin·gō

shop
店
mi·se

pedestrian crossing
横断歩道
ō·dan·ho·dō

bus
バス
bas

intersection
交差点
kō·sa·ten

corner
角
ka·do

taxi
タクシー
tak·shī

36a	**north**	北 ki·ta
36b	**south**	南 mi·na·mi
36c	**east**	東 hi·ga·shi
36d	**west**	西 ni·shi
	kilometres	キロ ki·ro
	metres	メートル mē·to·ru
	minutes	分 fun/pun

LANGUAGE TIP

Japanese Addresses
Some useful language for understanding
Japanese addresses:

avenue	大通り	ō·dō·ri
lane	路地	ro·ji
street (big, surfaced)	道路	dō·ro
street (smaller than dō·ro)	道	mi·chi
city area (a few blocks)	丁目	chō·me
city area (between chō·me and ku)	町	ma·chi
ward (administrative unit)	区	ku
town	町	ma·chi
city	市	shi
Prefecture	県	ken

Note that Tokyo Prefecture is indicated by adding to (都)
to Tokyo – it's often referred to as 'Tokyo Metropolis' – and
Osaka and Kyoto Prefectures by adding fu (府) instead of
ken (県) to the name of the city. Cities like these with a
large population are administratively subdivided in wards,
ku (区).

PRACTICAL DIRECTIONS

Accommodation

KEY PHRASES

Where's a hotel?	ホテルは どこですか?	ho·te·ru wa do·ko des ka
Do you have a double room?	ダブルルームは ありますか?	da·bu·ru·rū·mu wa a·ri·mas ka
How much is it per night?	1泊いくら ですか?	ip·pa·ku i·ku·ra des ka
Is breakfast included?	朝食は 含まれて いますか?	chō·sho·ku wa fu·ku·ma·re·te i·mas ka
What time is checkout?	チェックアウトは 何時ですか?	chek·ku·ow·to wa nan·ji des ka

Finding Accommodation

37a Where's a camping ground?	キャンプ場はどこですか? kyam·pu·jō wa do·ko des ka	
37b Where's a guesthouse?	宿泊施設は どこですか? shu·ku·ha·ku shi·se·tsu wa do·ko des ka	
37c Where's a hotel?	ホテルはどこですか? ho·te·ru wa do·ko des ka	
Where's a Japanese-style inn?	旅館はどこですか? ryo·kan wa do·ko des k	
37d Where's a youth hostel?	ユースホステルはどこ ですか? yū·su·ho·su·te·ru wa do·ko des ka	

37e Can you recommend somewhere cheap?	おすすめの安い ところはありますか? o·su·su·me no ya·su·i to·ko·ro wa a·ri·mas ka
37f Can you recommend somewhere nearby?	近くにおすすめの ところはありますか? chi·ka·ku ni o·su·su·me no to·ko·ro wa a·ri·mas ka

For responses, see **directions** (p64).

ホテルはどこですか?
ho·te·ru wa do·ko des ka

Where's a hotel?

Booking Ahead & Checking In

38a I'd like to book a room, please.	部屋の予約を お願いします。 he·ya no yo·ya·ku o o·ne·gai shi·mas
Are there rooms?	空き部屋は ありますか?	a·ki he·ya wa a·ri·mas ka
38b I have a reservation.	予約をしています。 yo·ya·ku o shi·te·i·mas
38c I'd like to stay for (two) nights.	(2)泊お願いします。 (ni)·ha·ku o·ne·gai shi·mas
For (three) nights/weeks.	(3)泊/週間。 (san)·pa·ku/·shū·kan
From (July 2) to (July 6).	(7月2日)から(7月6日)まで。 (shi·chi·ga·tsu fu·tsu·ka) ka·ra (shi·chi·ga·tsu mu·i·ka) ma·de

PRACTICAL ACCOMMODATION

🔍 LOOK FOR

38f 空室	kū·shi·tsu	rooms available
38g 満室	man·shi·tsu	no vacancy

38d How much is it per night?	1泊いくらですか？ ip·pa·ku i·ku·ra des ka
38e How much is it per person?	1人いくらですか？ hi·to·ri i·ku·ra des ka
How much is it per week?	1週間いくらですか？ is·shū·kan i·ku·ra des ka
Is breakfast included?	朝食は含まれていますか？ chō·sho·ku wa fu·ku·ma·re·te i·mas ka
39a Do you accept credit cards?	クレジットカードで支払えますか？ ku·re·jit·to·kā·do de shi·ha·ra·e·mas ka
39b Do you have a double room?	ダブルルームはありますか？ da·bu·ru·rū·mu wa a·ri·mas ka
39c Do you have a single room?	シングルルームはありますか？ shin·gu·ru·rū·mu wa a·ri·mas ka
39d Do you have a twin room?	ツインルームはありますか？ tsu·in·rū·mu wa a·ri·mas ka
Can I see the room?	部屋を見てもいいですか？ he·ya o mi·te mo ī des ka

Finding a Room

Do you have a ... room?
…ルームはありますか?
…rū·mu wa a·ri·mas ka

double
ダブル
da·bu·ru

single
シングル
shin·gu·ru

How much is it per ...?
…いくらですか?
…i·ku·ra des ka

night
1泊
ip·pa·ku

person
1人
hi·to·ri

Is breakfast included?
朝食は含まれていますか?
chō·sho·ku wa fu·ku·ma·re·te i·mas ka

Can I see the room?
部屋を見てもいいですか?
he·ya o mi·te mo ī des ka

I'll take it.
この部屋にします。
ko·no he·ya ni shi·mas

I won't take it.
ちょっと考えます。
chot·to kan·ga·e·mas

air-conditioning
エアコン
air·kon

key
鍵
ka·gi

door
(Japanese style)
ふすま
fu·su·ma

toilet
トイレ
toy·re

bath
お風呂
o·fu·ro

futon
布団
fu·ton

reed mat
たたみ
ta·ta·mi

bed
ベッド
bed·do

table (low)
ちゃぶ台
cha·bu·dai

chair (legless)
座椅子
za·i·su

cushion
座布団
za·bu·ton

| **I'll take it.** | この部屋にします。
ko·no he·ya ni shi·mas |
| **I won't take it.** | ちょっと考えます。(lit: I'll think about it)
chot·to kan·ga·e·mas |

1泊いくらですか？
ip·pa·ku i·ku·ra des ka
How much is it per night?

Requests & Queries

39e Is there an elevator?	エレベーターはありますか？	e·re·bē·tā wa a·ri·mas ka
Do you have a laundry service?	洗濯サービスがありますか？	sen·ta·ku·sā·bis ga a·ri·mas ka
39f Is there a safe?	金庫はありますか？	kin·ko wa a·ri·mas ka
Do you change money here?	ここで換金できますか？	ko·ko de kan·kin de·ki·mas ka
Can I use the ...?	…を使ってもいいですか？	... o tsu·kat·te mo ī des ka

kitchen (Japanese)	台所	dai·do·ko·ro
kitchen (Western)	キッチン	kit·chin
laundry	洗濯室	sen·ta·ku·shi·tsu
telephone	電話	den·wa

Could I have an extra blanket, please?	スペアの毛布をお願いします。	spair no mō·fu o o·ne·gai shi·mas
40a Could I have my key, please?	鍵をお願いします。	ka·gi o o·ne·gai shi·mas
40b When's breakfast served?	朝食はいつですか？	chō·sho·ku wa i·tsu des ka
40c Where's breakfast served?	朝食はどこですか？	chō·sho·ku wa do·ko des ka
40d Please wake me at (seven o'clock).	(7時)に起こしてください。	(shi·chi·ji) ni o·ko·shi·te ku·da·sai

There's no need to change my sheets.	シーツを替える必要はありません。 shī·tsu o ka·e·ru hi·tsu·yō wa a·ri·ma·sen
Is there a message for me?	伝言はありますか? den·gon wa a·ri·mas ka
Can I leave a message for someone?	伝言を残したいのですが。 den·gon o no·ko·shi·tai no des ga
Do you arrange tours here?	ここでツアーに申し込めますか? ko·ko de tsu·ā ni mō·shi·ko·me·mas ka
I'm locked out of my room.	部屋に鍵を残したまま鍵をかけてしまいました。 he·ya ni ka·gi o no·ko·shi·ta ma·ma ka·gi o ka·ke te shi·mai·mash·ta

Complaints

The room is too bright.	部屋が明るすぎます。 he·ya ga a·ka·ru su·gi·mas
The room is too cold.	部屋が寒すぎます。 he·ya ga sa·mu su·gi·mas
The room is too dark.	部屋が暗すぎます。 he·ya ga ku·ra su·gi·mas
41a The room is too noisy.	部屋がうるさすぎます。 he·ya ga u·ru·sa su·gi·mas
41b The room is too small.	部屋が小さすぎます。 he·ya ga chī·sa su·gi·mas

41c The (fan) doesn't work.	(扇風機)が 壊れています。 (sem·pū·ki) ga ko·wa·re·te i·mas
Can I get another (blanket)?	(毛布)をもう一つ お願いできますか? (mō·fu) o mō hi·to·tsu o·ne·gai de·ki·mas ka
41d This (pillow) isn't clean.	この(枕)はきれい ではありません。 ko·no (ma·ku·ra) wa ki·rē de wa a·ri·ma·sen

Checking Out

42a What time is checkout?	チェックアウトは何時 ですか? chek·ku·ow·to wa nan·ji des ka
Can I have a late checkout?	チェックアウトを遅らせたい のですが。 chek·ku·ow·to o o·ku·ra·se·tai no des ga
Can you call a taxi for me?	タクシーを呼んで もらえますか? tak·shī o yon·de mo·ra·e·mas ka
I'd like a taxi at (11) o'clock.	(11)時にタクシーを呼んで ください (jū·i·chi)·ji ni tak·shī o yon·de ku·da·sai
I'm leaving now.	今、出発します。 i·ma shup·pa·tsu shi·mas
42b Can I leave my luggage here?	ここで荷物を預かって もらえますか? ko·ko de ni·mo·tsu o a·zu·kat·te mo·ra·e·mas ka

42c Could I have my deposit, please?	保証金の返却を お願いします。	ho·shō·kin no hen·kya·ku o o·ne·gai shi·mas
42d Could I have my valuables, please?	貴重品の返却を お願いします。	ki·chō·hin no hen·kya·ku o o·ne·gai shi·mas
Could I have a receipt, please?	レシートをお願いします。	re·shī·to o o·ne·gai shi·mas
I'll be back on (Tuesday).	(火曜日)にもどります。	(ka·yō·bi) ni mo·do·ri·mas
I had a great stay, thank you.	たいへんくつろげました。	tai·hen ku·tsu·ro·ge·mash·ta
I'll recommend it to my friends.	友達に薦めます。	to·mo·da·chi ni su·su·me·mas

Camping

Do you have ...?	…がありますか?	... ga a·ri·mas ka

electricity	電気	den·ki
a laundry	コインランドリー	ko·in·ran·do·rī
shower facilities	シャワー	sha·wā
a site	キャンプサイト	kyam·pu·sai·to
tents for hire	貸しテント	ka·shi·ten·to

How much is it per ...?	…いくらですか?	... i·ku·ra des ka

caravan	キャラバン	kya·ra·ban
	1台	i·chi·dai
person	1人	hi·to·ri
tent	テント1つ	ten·to hi·to·tsu
vehicle	車1台	ku·ru·ma i·chi·dai

42e Am I allowed to camp here?

ここでキャンプしても
いいですか?
ko·ko de kyam·pu shi·te mo ī
des ka

Can I park next to my tent?

テントのとなりに駐車
してもいいですか?
ten·to no to·na·ri ni chū·sha
shi·te mo ī des ka

Is the water drinkable?

水は飲めますか?
mi·zu wa no·me·mas ka

Could I borrow ...?

…を貸してもらえませんか?
... o ka·shi·te mo·ra·e·ma·sen ka

Renting

If you're planning to stick around for a while in Japan, you might
consider staying in a gai·jin hows (外人ハウス), literally meaning
'foreigner house', which offers cheap accommodation for long-term
visitors.

Do you have a/an (monthly/weekly) apartment for rent?

賃貸のための
(マンスリー/ウィークリー)
マンションがありますか?
chin·tai no ta·me no
(man·su·rī/wī·ku·rī)
man·shon ga a·ri·mas ka

Do you have a house for rent?

賃貸のための家が
ありますか?
chin·tai no ta·me no i·e ga
a·ri·mas ka

🔊 LISTEN FOR

一部家具付き	(i·chi·bu) ka·gu·tsu·ki	(partly) furnished
家具なし	ka·gu·na·shi	unfurnished

Do you have a room for rent?	賃貸のための部屋が ありますか? chin·tai no ta·me no he·ya ga a·ri·mas ka

Staying with Locals

Can I stay at your place?	お宅に泊めて いただけませんか? o·ta·ku ni to·me·te i·ta·da·ke·ma·sen ka
I have my own mattress/ sleeping bag.	私はマットレス/ 寝袋を持っています。 wa·ta·shi wa mat·to·res/ ne·bu·ku·ro o mot·te i·mas
Is there anything I can do to help?	何か手伝うことは ありませんか? na·ni ka te·tsu·dow ko·to wa a·ri·ma·sen ka
Can I bring anything for the meal?	食事を運びましょうか? sho·ku·ji o ha·ko·bi·ma·shō ka
Can I clear the table?	テーブルの片付けを しましょうか? tē·bu·ru no ka·ta·zu·ke o shi·ma·shō ka
Can I do the dishes?	食器を洗いましょうか? shok·ki o a·rai·ma·shō ka

CULTURE TIP

Visiting Etiquette

It's customary in Japan to bring a small gift when visiting someone's home. Cakes, chocolates, fruit and flowers are common and relatively safe gifts. Something for the kids or from your country will go down a treat and it doesn't need to be big.

Take your shoes off in the entrance hall (gen·kan 玄関), the foyer that specifically serves this purpose. Slippers are usually provided to guests but it's strictly socks only on the ta·ta·mi (たたみ), the straw-mat flooring you'll see in Japanese houses.

For women it's best to sit with the legs to one side rather than cross-legged. The sē·za (正座) position, in which you tuck your knees directly underneath you, is required in very formal situations only. If unsure, simply follow your hosts' example.

If you stay over, remember that body-washing takes place before entering the bath – not inside it.

Thanks for your hospitality.	たいへんお世話に なりました。 tai·hen o·se·wa ni na·ri·mash·ta

To compliment your hosts' cooking, see **eating out** (p172).

Shopping

KEY PHRASES

I'd like ...	…をください。	... o ku·da·sai
Can I look at it?	見せて もらえますか?	mi·se·te mo ra·e·mas ka
Can I try it on?	試着 できますか?	shi·cha·ku de·ki·mas ka
How much is it?	いくらですか?	i·ku·ra des ka
That's too expensive.	高すぎます。	ta·ka·su·gi·mas

Looking for ...

43a Where's (a supermarket)?	(スーパー)はどこですか? (sū·pā) wa do·ko des ka
43b Where can I buy (a padlock)?	(鍵)はどこで 買えますか? (ka·gi) wa do·ko de ka·e·mas ka
43c I'm looking for...	…を探しています。 ... o sa·ga·shi·te·i·mas
Where can I buy locally produced goods/souvenirs?	地元産の製品/ お土産は、どこで 買えますか? ji·mo·to·san no sē·hin/ o·mi·ya·ge wa do·ko de ka·e·mas ka

To find your way to the shops, see **directions** (p64).

🔍	**LOOK FOR**		
43d 営業中	ē·gyō·chū	Open
43e 閉店	hē·ten	Closed
押す	o·su	Push
引く	hi·ku	Pull

Making a Purchase

I'm just looking.	見ているだけです。 mi·te i·ru da·ke des	
44a I'd like (a pen).	(ペン)をください。 (pen) o ku·da·sai	
44b How much is it?	いくらですか? i·ku·ra des ka	
✂ How much?	おいくら?	o·i·ku·ra
44c Can you write down the price?	値段を書いてもらえますか? ne·dan o kai·te mo·ra·e·mas ka	
44d Do you have any others?	ほかに何かありますか? ho·ka ni na·ni ka a·ri·mas ka	
44e Can I look at it?	見せてもらえますか? mi·se·te mo ra·e·mas ka	
Could I have it wrapped?	包んでもらえますか? tsu·tsun·de mo·ra·e·mas ka	
45a Does it have a guarantee?	保証(書)はありますか? ho·shō·(sho) wa a·ri·mas ka	
45b Can I have it sent abroad?	海外に送れますか? kai·gai ni o·ku·re·mas ka	
Can I pick it up later?	受け取りは後でできますか? u·ke·to·ri wa a·to de de·ki·mas ka	

45c	It's faulty.	不良品です。 fu·ryō·hin des
45d	Do you accept credit cards?	クレジットカードで 支払えますか? ku·re·jit·to· kā·do de shi·ha·ra·e·mas ka
45e	Do you accept travellers cheques?	トラベラーズチェックで 支払えますか? to·ra·be·rāz· chek·ku de shi·ha·ra·e·mas ka
46a	I'd like a receipt, please.	レシートをください。 re·shī·to o ku·da·sai
46b	I'd like a bag, please.	袋をください。 fu·ku·ro o ku·da·sai
46c	I'd like my change, please.	お釣りをお願いします。 o·tsu·ri o o·ne·gai shi·mas
46d	I'd like a refund, please.	払い戻しを お願いします。 ha·rai·mo·do·shi o o·ne·gai shi·mas
46e	I'd like to return this, please.	返品をしたいのですが。 hem·pin o shi·ta·i no des·ga

Bargaining

47a	That's too expensive.	高すぎます。 ta·ka·su·gi·mas
	Do you have something cheaper?	もっと安いものが ありますか? mot·to ya·su·i mo·no ga a·ri·mas ka
47b	Can you lower the price?	安くしてもらえませんか? ya·su·ku shi·te mo·ra·e·ma·sen ka
	I'll give you (5000 yen).	(5千円)払います。 (go·sen·en) ha·rai·mas

Making a Purchase

I'd like ...
…をください。
... o ku·da·sai

How much is it?
いくらですか？
i·ku·ra des ka

----- OR -----

Can you write down the price?
値段を書いてもらえますか？
ne·dan o kai·te mo·ra·e·mas ka

Do you accept credit cards?
クレジットカードで支払えますか？
ku·re·jit·to·kā·do de shi·ha·ra·e·mas ka

I'd like a ...., please.
…をください。
... o ku·da·sai

receipt
レシート
re·shī·to

bag
袋
fu·ku·ro

CULTURE TIP

Japanese Souvenirs

Common Japanese souvenirs (o·mi·ya·ge おみやげ) and gifts include folding fans (sen·su 扇子), ceramics (tō·gē 陶芸), tea sets (cha·ki 茶器), lacquerware (shik·ki 漆器), handmade paper (wa·shi 和紙) and Japanese dolls (ni·hon nin·gyō 日本人形). Art lovers will find beautiful scrolls (ka·ke·ji·ku 掛け軸) and woodblock prints (u·ki·yo·e 浮世絵), samurai enthusiasts can look for Japanese swords (ka·ta·na 刀), and the cotton kimono (yu·ka·ta 浴衣) is an ever-popular lightweight souvenir.

Clothes

48a My size is (32).	私のサイズは(32)号です。 wa·ta·shi no sai·zu wa (san·jū ni)·gō des
My size is (L/M/S).	私のサイズは(L/M/S)です。 wa·ta·shi no sai·zu wa (e·ru/ e·mu/e·su) des
48b Can I try it on?	試着できますか? shi·cha·ku de·ki·mas ka
48c It doesn't fit.	サイズが合いません。 sai·zu ga ai·ma·sen

For clothing items, see the **dictionary**. For sizes, see **numbers & amounts** (p36).

Books & Reading

Do you have a book by (Yukio Mishima)?	(三島由紀夫)の本はありますか? (mi·shi·ma yu·ki·o) no hon wa a·ri·mas ka
Is there an English-language section?	英語のセクションは ありますか? ē·go no sek·shon wa a·ri·mas ka

I'd like a dictionary.	辞書をください。 ji·sho o ku·da·sai
I'd like a newspaper (in English).	(英字)新聞をください。 (ē·ji) shim·bun o ku·da·sai

Music & DVD

I'd like a CD/DVD.	CD/DVDをください。 shī·dī/dī·bī·dī o ku·da·sai
I'm looking for something by (Dreams Come True).	(ドリームズ・カム・トゥルー)の曲を探しています。 (do·rī·mu·zu ka·mu tu·rū) no kyo·ku o sa·ga·shi·te i·mas
What's their best recording?	どの曲がいちばんですか？ do·no kyo·ku ga i·chi·ban des ka
Can I listen to this?	これを聴いてもいいですか？ ko·re o kī·te mo ī des ka
What region is this DVD for?	このDVDのリージョンは何ですか？ ko·no dī·bī·dī no rī·jon wa nan des ka
Will this work on any DVD player?	これはどんなDVDプレーヤーでも大丈夫ですか？ ko·re wa don·na dī·bī·dī·pu·rē·yā de·mo dai·jō·bu des ka

いくらですか？
i·ku·ra des ka
How much is it?

Photography

49a I need a B&W film for this camera.	このカメラに合う 白黒フィルムを ください。 ko·no ka·me·ra ni a·u shi·ro·ku·ro fi·ru·mu o ku·da·sai
49b I need a colour film for this camera.	このカメラに合うカラー フィルムをください。 ko·no ka·me·ra ni a·u ka·rā fi·ru·mu o ku·da·sai
I need ... speed film for this camera.	このカメラに合う ISO/ASA…のフィルムを ください。 ko·no ka·me·ra ni a·u ai·es·ō/ ā·sā ... no fi·ru·mu o ku·da·sai
Can you print digital photos?	デジタル写真の 印刷はできますか? de·ji·ta·ru·sha·shin no in·sa·tsu wa de·ki·mas ka
49c Can you transfer photos from my camera to CD?	カメラからCDに 写真をコピーできますか? ka·me·ra ka·ra shī·dī ni sha·shin o ko·pī de·ki·mas ka
49d Could you develop this film?	このフィルムを現像は できますか? ko·no fi·ru·mu o gen·zō wa de·ki·mas ka
Do you have batteries for this camera?	このカメラの電池は ありますか? ko·no ka·me·ra no den·chi wa a·ri·mas ka

Do you have memory cards for this camera?	このカメラの メモリーカードは ありますか? ko·no ka·me·ra no me·mo·ri·kā·do wa a·ri·mas ka
49e When will it be ready?	いつ出来上がりますか? i·tsu de·ki·a·ga·ri·mas ka
I need a passport photo taken.	パスポート用の写真が 必要です。 pas·pō·to·yō no sha·shin ga hi·tsu·yō des

Repairs

Can I have my (backpack) repaired here?	(バックパック)を直して もらえますか? (bak·ku·pak·ku) o na·o·shi·te mo·ra·e·mas ka
When will my (camera) be ready?	(カメラ)はいつできますか? (ka·me·ra) wa i·tsu de·ki·mas ka

Communications

KEY PHRASES

Where's an internet cafe?	インターネット カフェはどこ ですか?	in·tā·net·to· ka·fe wa do·ko des ka
I'd like to check my email.	Eメールをチェック したいのですが。	ī·mē·ru o chek·ku shi·tai no des ga
I want to send a parcel.	小包を 送りたいの ですが。	ko·zu·tsu·mi o o·ku·ri·tai no des ga
I'd like a SIM card.	SIMカードを お願いします。	shi·mu·kā·do o o·ne·gai shi·mas

Post Office

50a	**I want to send a letter.**	手紙を出したいの ですが。 te·ga·mi o da·shi·tai no des ga
50b	**I want to send a postcard.**	はがきを送りたいのですが。 ha·ga·ki o o·ku·ri·tai no des ga
50c	**I want to send a parcel.**	小包を送りたいの ですが。 ko·zu·tsu·mi o o·ku·ri·tai no des ga
50d	**I want to buy an envelope.**	封筒をください。 fū·tō o ku·da·sai
50e	**I want to buy stamps.**	切手をください。 kit·te o ku·da·sai

🔍 LOOK FOR

関税申告	kan·zē·shin·ko·ku	customs declaration
国内	ko·ku·nai	domestic
壊れ物	ko·wa·re·mo·no	fragile
国際	ko·ku·sai	international
郵便番号	yū·bin·ban·gō	postcode
郵便局	yū·bin·kyo·ku	post office

PRACTICAL COMMUNICATIONS

Please send it to (Australia).	（オーストラリア）まで お願いします。 (ō·sto·ra·rya) ma·de o·ne·gai shi·mas
51a Please send it to (Australia) by airmail.	（オーストラリア）まで航空便 でお願いします。 (ō·sto·ra·rya) ma·de kō·kū·bin de o·ne·gai shi·mas
51b Please send it to (Australia) by express mail.	（オーストラリア）まで 速達でお願いします。 (ō·sto·ra·rya) ma·de so·ku·ta·tsu de o·ne·gai shi·mas
Please send it ...	… お願いします。 ... o·ne·gai shi·mas

by surface mail	普通便で	fu·tsū·bin de
registered	書留で	ka·ki·to·me de
by sea mail	船便で	fu·na·bin de

It contains (souvenirs).	（お土産）が入っています。 (o·mi·ya·ge) ga hait·te i·mas
Is there any mail for me?	私宛の郵便物 はありますか？ wa·ta·shi·a·te no yū·bin·bu·tsu wa a·ri·mas ka

Phone

52a Q **What's your phone number?**	あなたの電話番号は 何番ですか?	a·na·ta no den·wa·ban·gō wa nam·ban des ka
A **The number is ...**	電話番号は…です。	den·wa·ban·gō wa ... des
52b **Where's the nearest public phone?**	いちばん近くの 公衆電話はどこですか?	i·chi·ban chi·ka·ku no kō·shū·den·wa wa do·ko des ka
52c **I'd like to buy a phonecard.**	テレフォンカードを買いたい のですが。	te·re·fon·kā·do o kai·tai no des ga
52d **I want to call (Singapore).**	(シンガポール)に電話 したいのですが。	(shin·ga·pō·ru) ni den·wa shi·tai no des ga
52e **I want to reverse the charges.**	コレクトコールで電話 したいのですが。	ko·re·ku·to·kō·ru de den·wa shi·tai no des ga
How much does a (three)-minute call cost?	(3)分間の通話 料金はいくらですか?	(san)·pun·kan no tsū·wa ryō·kin wa i·ku·ra des ka
What's the area code for (Osaka)?	(大阪)の市内局番 は何番ですか?	(ō·sa·ka) no shi·nai·kyo·ku·ban wa nam·ban des ka
What's the country code for (New Zealand)?	(ニュージーランド)の国番号 は何番ですか?	(nyū·jī·ran·do) no ku·ni·ban·gō wa nam·ban des ka

PRACTICAL COMMUNICATIONS

🔊 **LISTEN FOR**

ちょっと待って ください。	chot·to mat·te ku·da·sai	One moment.
どなたですか?	do·na·ta des ka	Who's calling?
どなたに代わりま しょうか?	do·na·ta ni ka·wa·ri·ma·shō ka	Who do you want to speak to?
…はいません。	... wa i·ma·sen	... is not here.
間違い電話 です。	ma·chi·gai·den·wa des	Wrong number.

It's engaged.	お話中です。 o·ha·na·shi·chū des
I've been cut off.	電話が切れました。 den·wa ga ki·re·mash·ta
The connection's bad.	電話のかかりが 悪いです。 den·wa no ka·ka·ri ga wa·ru·i des
Hello. It's ...	もしもし。…です。 mo·shi·mo·shi ... des
Is ... there?	…はいらっしゃいますか? ... wa i·ras·shai·mas ka
Please tell him/her I called.	私が電話したと お伝えください。 wa·ta·shi ga den·wa shi·ta to o·tsu·ta·e ku·da·sai
Can I leave a message?	伝言をお願いできますか? den·gon o o·ne·gai de·ki·mas ka
My number is ...	私の電話番号は…です。 wa·ta·shi no den·wa·ban·gō wa ... des
I'll call back later.	また後で電話します。 ma·ta a·to de den·wa shi·mas

Mobile/Cell Phone

I'd like a ...　　　　　　　　…をお願いします。
　　　　　　　　　　　　　… o o·ne·gai shi·mas

charger for my phone	携帯電話の充電器	kē·tai·den·wa no jū·den·ki
mobile/cell phone for hire	携帯電話のレンタル	kē·tai·den·wa no ren·ta·ru
prepaid mobile/cell phone	プリペイドの携帯電話	pu·ri·pē·do no kē·tai·den·wa
SIM card	SIMカード	shi·mu·kā·do

What are the rates?	通話料金はいくらですか？ tsū·wa·ryō·kin wa i·ku·ra des ka
(10) yen per (1) minute.	(1)分間(10)円。 (ip)·pun·kan (jū)·en

Internet

53a Where's the local internet cafe?	インターネットカフェはどこですか？ in·tā·net·to·ka·fe wa do·ko des ka
Do you have internet access here?	ここでインターネットは使えますか？ ko·ko de in·tā·net·to wa tsu·ka·e·mas ka
Is there wireless internet access here?	ここはインターネットを無線で使えますか？ ko·ko de in·tā·net·to o mu·sen de tsu·ka·e·mas ka

Can I connect my laptop here?	私のノートパソコンに 接続してもいいですか? wa·ta·shi no nō·to·pa·so·kon ni se·tsu·zo·ku shi·te mo ī des ka
Do you have PCs?	PCがありますか? pī·shī ga a·ri·mas ka
Do you have Macs?	マッキントッシュが ありますか? mak·kin·tos·shu ga a·ri·mas ka
Do you have headphones (with a microphone)?	(マイク付きの) ヘッドフォン がありますか? (mai·ku tsu·ki no) hed·do·fōn ga a·ri·mas ka
53b **I'd like to check my email.**	Eメールをチェックしたいの ですが。 ī·mē·ru o chek·ku shi·tai no des ga
I'd like to download photos.	写真をダウンロードしたいの ですが。 sha·shin o down·rōd shi·tai no des ga

インターネットカフェはどこ ですか?

in·tā·net·to·ka·fe wa do·ko des ka

Where is an internet cafe?

53c I'd like to use a printer.	プリントしたいのですが。 prin·to shi·tai no des ga
I'd like to use a scanner.	スキャンしたいのですが。 skyan shi·tai no des ga
I'd like to use Skype.	スカイプを使いたいのですが。 skaip o tsu·kai·tai no des ga
53d How much is it per hour?	1時間いくらですか? i·chi·ji·kan i·ku·ra des ka
How much per (five) minutes?	(5)分間いくらですか? (go)·fun·kan i·ku·ra des ka
How much per page?	1ページいくらですか? i·chi·pē·ji i·ku·ra des ka
How do I log on?	どうすればログオンできますか? dō·su·re ba ro·gu·on de·ki·mas ka
Please change it to the English-language setting.	英語のセッティングにしてください。 ē·go no set·tin·gu ni shi·te ku·da·sai
It's crashed.	クラッシュしています。 ku·ras·shu shi·te i·mas
I've finished.	終わりました。 o·wa·ri·mash·ta

Money & Banking

KEY PHRASES

How much is it?	いくらですか？	i·ku·ra des ka
What's the exchange rate?	為替レートは いくらですか？	ka·wa·se·rē·to wa i·ku·ra des ka
Where's an ATM?	ATMはどこ ですか？	ē·tī·e·mu wa do·ko des ka

Japan is still a cash-based country, although credit cards are becoming more common – carry some yen with you and don't assume you can use credit cards at restaurants, hotels and shops. For more info on the availability of various methods of payment, see Lonely Planet's guidebook to Japan.

Paying the Bill

54a Q **How much is it?**	いくらですか？	i·ku·ra des ka
A **It's free.**	ただです。	ta·da des
A **It's (4000) yen.**	(4000)円です。	(yon·sen)·en des
54b Do you accept credit cards?	クレジットカードで 支払えますか？	ku·re·jit·to·kā·do de shi·ha·ra·e·mas ka
54c Do you accept debit cards?	デビットカードで 支払えますか？	de·bit·to·kā·do de shi·ha·ra·e·mas ka

54d	Do you accept travellers cheques?	トラベラーズチェックで支払えますか？ to·ra·be·rāz·chek·ku de shi·ha·ra·e·mas ka
54e	I'd like a receipt, please.	レシートをください。 re·shī·to o ku·da·sai
54f	I'd like my change, please.	お釣りをお願いします。 o·tsu·ri o o·ne·gai shi·mas
54g	There's a mistake in the bill.	請求書に間違いがあります。 sē·kyū·sho ni ma·chi·gai ga a·ri·mas

Banking

55a	Where's an ATM?	ATMはどこですか？ ē·tī·e·mu wa do·ko des ka
55b	Where's a foreign exchange office?	両替所はどこですか？ ryō ga·e·jo wa do·ko des·ka
55c	What time does the bank open?	銀行は何時に開きますか？ gin·kō wa nan·ji ni hi a·ki·mas ka
56a	I'd like to cash a cheque.	小切手の換金をお願いします。 ko·git·te no kan·kin o o·ne·gai shi·mas
56b	I'd like to change travellers cheques.	トラベラーズチェックの換金をお願いします。 to·ra·be·rāz chek·ku no kan·kin o o·ne·gai shi·mas
56c	I'd like to change money.	両替をお願いします。 ryō·ga·e o o·ne·gai shi·mas
	I'd like to get a cash advance.	キャッシュアドバンスをお願いします。 kyas·shu·a·do·ban·su o o·ne·gai shi·mas

🔊 LISTEN FOR

身分証明書	mi·bun·shō·mē·sho	identification
ここにサインを お願いします。	ko·ko ni sain o o·ne·gai shi·mas	Sign here.
残高がありません。	zan·da·ka ga a·ri·ma·sen	You have no funds left.

Do you change money here?	ここで換金できますか? ko·ko de kan·kin de·ki·mas ka
What's the charge?	料金はいくらですか? ryō·kin wa i·ku·ra des ka
56d What's the exchange rate?	為替レートはいくら ですか? ka·wa·se·rē·to wa i·ku·ra des ka
The automated teller machine took my card.	ATMにカードを取られて しまいました。 ē·tī·e·mu ni kā·do o to·ra·re·te shi·mai·mash·ta
I've forgotten my PIN.	暗証番号を 忘れました。 an·shō·ban·gō o wa·su·re·mash·ta
Can I use my credit card to withdraw money?	クレジットカードで現金を 引き出せますか? ku·re·jit·to·kā·do de gen·kin o hi·ki·da·se·mas ka
Has my money arrived yet?	お金は届いていますか? o·ka·ne wa to·doy·te i·mas ka

Business

KEY PHRASES

I'm attending a conference.	会議に出席します。	kai·gi ni shus·se·ki shi·mas
I have an appointment with ...	…とアポがあります。	... to a·po ga a·ri·mas
Can I please have your business card?	名刺をいただけませんか?	mē·shi o i·ta·da·ke·ma·sen ka

Doing Business

I'm attending a conference.	会議に出席します。 kai·gi ni shus·se·ki shi·mas
I'm attending a meeting.	ミーティングに出席します。 mī·tin·gu ni shus·se·ki shi·mas
I'm attending a trade fair.	展示会に出席します。 ten·ji·kai ni shus·se·ki shi·mas
I'm attending a course.	コースに出席します。 kōs ni shus·se·ki shi·mas
I'm with (Mr Suzuki).	(鈴木さん)といっしょです。 (su·zu·ki·san) to is·sho des
I'm with (two) others.	ほかの（2人）といっしょです。 ho·ka no (fu·ta·ri) to is·sho des
I'm with my colleagues.	同僚といっしょです。 dō·ryō to is·sho des

PRACTICAL BUSINESS

CULTURE TIP	**Business Cards**

Business cards (mē·shi 名刺) are exchanged at the start of the meeting. Hand over your card with the writing facing the receiver so he or she can read it, and preferably hold the card with both hands.

Always read the card you're given on the spot, and treat it with care. Never write on the card, fold it or leave it behind as this is interpreted as a sign of disrespect.

During a meeting, it's best to keep the card in front of you on the table – file it away appropriately at the end of the meeting.

Q	**Can I please have your business card?**	名刺をいただけませんか？ mē·shi o i·ta·da·ke·ma·sen ka
A	**Here's my business card.**	これが私の 名刺です。 ko·re ga wa·ta·shi no mē·shi des
Q	**What's your (mobile number)?**	あなたの(携帯番号)は 何ですか？ a·na·ta no (kē·tai·ban·gō) wa nan des ka
A	**Here's my (mobile number).**	これが私の (携帯番号)です。 ko·re ga wa·ta·shi no (kē·tai·ban·gō) des
57a	**What's your fax number?**	あなたのファックス番号は 何ですか？ a·na·ta no fak·kus·ban·gō wa nan des ka
57b	**Here's my email address.**	これが私のEメール アドレスです。 ko·re ga wa·ta·shi no ī·mē·ru a·do·res des

CULTURE TIP

Business Etiquette
Always give ample notice of your visit and start a meeting by exchanging business cards. A small present representing your country or company always goes down well.

The seating is linked to status, so wait to be directed to your seat and don't sit (or stand) before the person highest in the pecking order does. Never initiate the use of first names – let your Japanese contacts decide. It's more likely that titles will be used instead.

Don't try to rush or push decisions. Entertainment makes up part of the process so try not to skip these occasions. Be aware, though, that talking business during a meal is a no-no and that controversial topics are better avoided.

I have an appointment with …	…とアポがあります。	… to a·po ga a·ri·mas
I need …	…が必要です。	… ga hi·tsu·yō des

a computer	コンピュータ	kom·pyū·ta
an internet connection	インターネットの接続	in·tā·net·to no se·tsu·zo·ku
an interpreter	通訳	tsū·ya·ku
more business cards	もっと名刺	mot·to mē·shi
some space to set up	セットアップするスペース	set·to·ap·pu su·ru spēs
to send a fax	ファックス送信	fak·kus·sō·shin

Where's the business centre?	ビジネスセンターはどこですか？ bi·ji·nes·sen·tā wa do·ko des ka

Where's the conference?	会議はどこですか? kai·gi wa do·ko des ka
Where's the meeting?	ミーティングはどこですか? mī·tin·gu wa do·ko des ka
Thank you for your time.	お時間をどうもありがとう ございました。 o·ji·kan o dō·mo a·ri·ga·tō go·zai·mash·ta
Shall we go for a drink?	飲みに行きましょうか? no·mi ni i·ki·ma·shō ka
Shall we go for a meal?	食事に行きましょうか? sho·ku·ji ni i·ki·ma·shō ka
It's on me.	私のおごりです。 wa·ta·shi no o·go·ri des

See **eating out** (p172) for more food and drink phrases. See **going out** (p132) for arranging social get-togethers.

Sightseeing

KEY PHRASES

I'd like a guide.	ガイドをお願い します。	gai·do o o·ne·gai shi·mas
Can I take a photo?	写真を撮っても いいですか?	sha·shin o tot·temo ī des ka
What time does it open?	何時に 開きますか?	nan·ji ni a·ki·mas ka
I'm interested in ...	…に興味が あります。	... ni kyō·mi ga a·ri·mas

58a I'd like a guide.
ガイドをお願いします。
gai·do o o·ne·gai shi·mas

I'd like a catalogue.
パンフレットを
お願いします。
pan·fu·ret·to o
o·ne·gai shi·mas

58b I'd like a (local) map.
(市街) 地図を
お願いします。
(shi·gai) chi·zu o
o·ne·gai shi·mas

Do you have information on cultural sights?
文化的見どころに
ついての案内は
ありますか?
bun·ka·te·ki mi·do·ko·ro ni
tsu·i·te no an·nai wa
a·ri·mas ka

Do you have information on historical sights?
史跡についての案内は
ありますか?
shi·se·ki ni tsu·i·te no an·nai wa
a·ri·mas ka

LANGUAGE TIP

Say Cheeeeeese!
When taking a picture of your Japanese friends
and acquaintances, ensure their attention – and
best smiles – with hai, chī·zu (ハイ、チーズ), 'Say cheese!'

Do you have information on religious sights?	宗教的見どころについての案内はありますか? shū·kyō·te·ki mi·do·ko·ro ni tsu·i·te no an·nai wa a·ri·mas ka
58c I'd like to see ...	…が見たいです。 ... ga mi·tai des
59a What's that?	あれは何ですか? a·re wa nan des ka
How old is it?	どのくらい古いですか? do·no ku·rai fu·ru·i des ka
Could you take a photo of me?	私の写真を撮ってもらえませんか? wa·ta·shi no sha·shin o tot·te mo·ra·e·ma·sen ka
Can I take a photograph (of you)?	(あなたの)写真を撮ってもいいですか? (a·na·ta no) sha·shin o tot·te mo ī des ka

Getting In

59b What time does it open?	何時に開きますか? nan·ji ni a·ki·mas ka
59c What time does it close?	何時に閉まりますか? nan·ji ni shi·ma·ri·mas ka
59d Can I take a photo?	写真を撮ってもいいですか? sha·shin o tot·temo ī des ka

60a	What's the admission charge?	入場料はいくらですか？ nyū·jō·ryō wa i·ku·ra des ka
60b	Is there a discount for children?	子供割引がありますか？ ko·do·mo·wa·ri·bi·ki ga a·ri·mas ka
60c	Is there a discount for students?	学生割引がありますか？ gak·sē·wa·ri·bi·ki ga a·ri·mas ka
	Is there a discount for older people?	高齢者割引がありますか？ kō·rē·sha·wa·ri·bi·ki ga a·ri·mas ka

何時に開きますか？
nan·ji ni a·ki·mas ka
What time does it open?

Galleries & Museums

Q	What's in the collection?	所蔵品には何が ありますか？ sho·zō·hin ni wa na·ni ga a·ri·mas ka
A	It's a/an ... exhibition.	…の展覧会です。 ... no ten·ran·kai des
	I like the works of ...	…の作品が好きです。 ... no sa·ku·hin ga su·ki des
	I'm interested in ...	…に興味があります。 ... ni kyō·mi ga a·ri·mas

(Edo) art	(江戸)アート	(e·do) ā·to
calligraphy	書道	sho·dō
ceramics	陶芸	tō·gē
ink painting	水墨画	su·i·bo·ku·ga
ukiyo-e prints	浮世絵	u·ki·yo·e
yamato-e (Japanese painting)	大和絵	ya·ma·to·e

Tours

Can you recommend a tour?	おすすめのツアーは ありますか?	o·su·su·me no (tsu·ā) wa a·ri·mas ka
61a When's the next tour?	次のツアーはいつですか?	tsu·gi no tsu·ā wa i·tsu des ka
61b When's the next day trip?	次の1日観光は いつですか?	tsu·gi no i·chi·ni·chi kan·kō wa i·tsu des ka
61c Is accommodation included?	宿泊料は 含まれていますか?	shu·ku·ha·ku·ryō wa fu·ku·ma·re·te i·mas ka
61d Is food included?	食事代は 含まれていますか?	sho·ku·ji·dai wa fu·ku·ma·re·te i·mas ka
61e Is transport included?	交通費は 含まれていますか?	kō·tsū·hi wa fu·ku·ma·re·te i·mas ka

61f How long is the tour?	ツアーにかかる時間は どのくらいですか？ tsu·ā ni ka·ka·ru ji·kan wa do·no ku·rai des ka
I've lost my group.	グループから はぐれました。 gu·rū·pu ka·ra ha·gu·re·mash·ta

> **CULTURE TIP**
>
> ### Japanese Theatre
> For a night of culture in Japan, choose from the many forms of contemporary or classical theatre. Well-known traditional forms include bun·ra·ku (文楽), puppet theatre involving large puppets manipulated by up to three puppeteers; ka·bu·ki (歌舞伎), a combination of dancing and speaking in conventional intonation patterns and performed exclusively by men; and nō (能), a Zen-influenced classical dance-drama including a chorus, drummers and a flautist. Comedy performances include man·zai (漫才), a dialogue in which witticisms are exchanged on current themes; ra·ku·go (落語) – literally meaning 'dropped word' – a traditional monologue ending in a punch line; and kyō·gen (狂言), comic vignettes in everyday language performed in between *no* performances.

Accessible Travel

KEY PHRASES

I need assistance.	手を貸して ください。	te o ka·shi·te ku·da·sai
Is there wheelchair access?	車椅子で 入れますか?	ku·ru·ma·i·su de hai·re·mas ka
Are there disabled toilets?	障害者用トイレ はありますか?	shō·gai·sha·yō·toy·re wa a·ri·mas ka

I have a disability.	私は障害者です。 wa·ta·shi wa shō·gai·sha des
I need assistance.	手を貸してください。 te o ka·shi·te ku·da·sai
Are there disabled toilets?	障害者用トイレは ありますか? shō·gai·sha·yō·toy·re wa a·ri·mas ka
Are there disabled parking spaces?	障害者優先の 駐車場はありますか? shō·gai·sha yū·sen no chū·sha·jō wa a·ri·mas ka
Is there wheelchair access?	車椅子で入れますか? ku·ru·ma·i·su de hai·re·mas ka
I have a hearing aid.	補聴器をしています。 ho·chō·ki o shi·te i·mas
Are guide dogs permitted?	盲導犬は入れますか? mō·dō·ken wa hai·re·mas ka

How many steps are there?	段差は何段ありますか？ dan·sa wa nan·dan a·ri·mas ka
Is there an elevator?	エレベータはありますか？ e·re·bē·ta wa a·ri·mas ka
Are there rails in the bathroom?	バスルームに手すりは ありますか？ bas·rū·mu ni te·su·ri wa a·ri·mas ka
Could you call me a taxi for the disabled?	障害者用タクシーを 呼んでもらえますか？ shō·gai·sha·yō·tak·shī o yon·de mo·ra·e·mas ka
Are there train carriages for people with a disability?	障害者のための 車両はありますか？ shō·gai·sha no ta·me no sha·ryō wa a·ri·mas ka
Could you help me cross the street safely?	道を渡るのを 手伝ってもらえますか？ mi·chi o wa·ta·ru no o te·tsu·dat·te mo·ra·e·mas ka
Is there somewhere I can sit down?	座れるところは ありますか？ su·wa·re·ru to·ko·ro wa a·ri·mas ka
guide dog	盲導犬 mō·dō·ken
ramp	傾斜路 kē·sha·ro
walking frame	歩行車 ho·kō·sha
walking stick	杖 tsu·e
wheelchair	車椅子 ku·ru·ma·i·su

Travel with Children

KEY PHRASES

Are children allowed?	子供は入れますか?	ko·do·mo wa hai·re·mas ka
Is there a child discount?	子供割引はありますか?	ko·do·mo·wa·ri·bi·ki wa a·ri·mas ka
Is there a baby change room?	授乳室はありますか?	ju·nyū·shi·tsu wa a·ri·mas ka

Are children allowed?	子供は入れますか?
	ko·do·mo wa hai·re·mas ka

Is there a ...?	…はありますか?
	... wa a·ri·mas ka

baby change room	授乳室	ju·nyū·shi·tsu
child discount	子供割引	ko·do·mo·wa·ri·bi·ki
child-minding service	託児サービス	ta·ku·ji·sā·bis
children's menu	子供のメニュー	ko·do·mo no me·nyū
crèche	託児所	ta·ku·ji·sho

Do you sell baby wipes?	おしり拭きはありますか?
	o·shi·ri·fu·ki wa a·ri·mas ka

Do you sell disposable nappies?	紙おむつはありますか?
	ka·mi·o·mu·tsu wa a·ri·mas ka

I need a ...		…が必要です。 ... ga hi·tsu·yō des
baby seat	ベビーシート	be·bī·shī·to
cot	ベビーベッド	be·bī·bed·do
highchair	ベビーチェア	be·bī·chair
potty	おまる	o·ma·ru
stroller	ベビーカー	be·bī·kā

Where's the nearest toy shop?	この近くの おもちゃ屋はどこですか? ko·no chi·ka·ku no o·mo·cha·ya wa do·ko des ka
Where's the nearest playground?	この近くの遊び場 はどこですか? ko·no chi·ka·ku no a·so·bi·ba wa do·ko des ka
Do you hire out strollers?	ベビーカーのレンタルは ありますか? be·bī·kā no ren·ta·ru wa a·ri·mas ka
Where can I change a nappy?	おむつはどこで 換えられますか? o·mu·tsu wa do·ko de ka·e·ra·re·mas ka
Do you mind if I breast-feed here?	ここで母乳をあげても いいですか? ko·ko de bo·nyū o a·ge·te mo ī des ka
Is this suitable for ... year old children?	これは…歳の子供向き ですか? ko·re wa ...sai no ko·do·mo·mu·ki des ka

To talk about health issues, see **health** (p162).

Social

MEETING PEOPLE	112
INTERESTS	122
FEELINGS & OPINIONS	126
GOING OUT	132
ROMANCE	138
BELIEFS & CULTURE	142
SPORTS	145
OUTDOORS	153

Meeting People

KEY PHRASES

My name is ...	私の名前は…です。	wa·ta·shi no na·ma·e wa ... des
I'm from ...	…から来ました。	... ka·ra ki·mash·ta
I work in ...	私は…の仕事をしています。	wa·ta·shi wa ... no shi·go·to o shi·te i·mas
I'm ... years old.	私は…歳です。	wa·ta·shi wa ...·sai des
And you?	あなたは?	a·na·ta wa

Basics

62a Yes.
はい。
hai

62b No.
いいえ。
ī·e

63a Please. (asking)
ください
ku·da·sai

63b Please. (offering)
どうぞ。
dō·zo

63c Thank you.
ありがとう。
a·ri·ga·tō

Thank you very much.
どうもありがとうございます。
dō·mo a·ri·ga·tō go·zai·mas

63d You're welcome.	どういたしまして。 dō·i·ta·shi·mash·te
63e Excuse me. (to get attention)	すみません。 su·mi·ma·sen
63f Sorry.	ごめんなさい。 go·men·na·sai

Greetings & Goodbyes

The most common gesture used when greeting is the bow – introducing yourself, greeting, thanking and saying goodbye are all done bowing. Timing, posture and movement of the bow are meant to be a reflection of sincerity, respect and maturity. As a visitor to Japan you're not expected to emulate this ritual faithfully; a gentle nod will do. Kissing and hugging in Japan are still rare, except with close friends or family. For handshakes, it's best to let the locals take the lead so wait and let them instigate this process if they feel comfortable doing so.

64a Hello.	こんにちは。 kon·ni·chi·wa
64b Hi.	こんにちは。 kon·ni·chi·wa
Good afternoon.	こんにちは。 kon·ni·chi·wa
64c Good evening.	こんばんは。 kom·ban·wa
Good morning.	おはよう（ございます）。 o·ha·yō (go·zai·mas)
65a Q How are you?	お元気ですか？ o·gen·ki des ka
65b A Good, thanks.	はい、元気です。 hai, gen·ki des
And you?	あなたは？ a·na·ta wa

66a Q	What's your name?	お名前は何ですか？ o·na·ma·e wa nan des ka
66b A	My name is (Sato).	私の名前は (佐藤）です。 wa·ta·shi no na·ma·e wa (sa·tō) des
	I'd like to introduce you to ...	…を紹介します。 ... o shō·kai shi·mas

✂	**This is...**	こちらは...です。	ko·chi·ra wa ... des

	This is my child.	こちらは私の子供です。 ko·chi·ra wa wa·ta·shi no ko·do·mo des
	This is my colleague.	こちらは私の同僚です。 ko·chi·ra wa wa·ta·shi no dō·ryō des
66c	This is my friend.	こちらは私の友達です。 ko·chi·ra wa wa·ta·shi no to·mo·da·chi des
66d	This is my husband.	こちらは私の主人です。 ko·chi·ra wa wa·ta·shi no shu·jin des
66e	This is my wife.	こちらは私の妻です。 ko·chi·ra wa wa·ta·shi no tsu·ma des

For family members, see **family** (p119).

66f	I'm pleased to meet you.	お会いできてうれしいです。 o·ai de·ki·te u·re·shī des
67a	See you later.	また会いましょう。 ma·ta ai·ma·shō
67b	Goodbye.	さようなら。 sa·yō·na·ra

67c Bye.	じゃ、また。 ja ma·ta
67d Good night.	おやすみ（なさい）。 o·ya·su·mi (na·sai)
Bon voyage!	よい旅を！ yoy·ta·bi o

Addressing People

Avoid using all forms of the second person pronoun 'you' in Japanese speech as it can sound too direct – it will be understood from context who you're referring to when speaking (for more information regarding pronouns, see **grammar**, p27).

| **Mr/Ms/Mrs/Miss** | …さん
…·san |
| **Sir/Madam** | …さま
…·sama |

Making Conversation

The Japanese love a chat – just avoid criticising aspects of the Japanese culture too vigorously as your comments might be taken quite personally. Never get visibly angry or shout as this leaves a bad impression. For more conversation topics, see **interests** (p122) and **feelings & opinions** (p126).

Isn't it (hot) today?	今日は（暑い）ですね。 kyō wa (a·tsu·i) des ne
What a beautiful day.	素晴らしい日ですね。 su·ba·ra·shī hi des ne
(Nice/Awful/Strange) weather, isn't it?	（いい/ひどい/変な）天気 ですね。 (ī/hi·doy/hen·na) ten·ki des ne
Do you live here?	ここに住んでいますか? ko·ko ni sun·de i·mas ka

LANGUAGE TIP

The Suffix '-san'

In Japan people normally call each other by their surname and add the suffix ·san (さん), eg su·zu·ki·san (鈴木さん) – avoid using first names unless invited to do so. It's also common to call people by their title instead of their name, like sha·chō (社長) for a company president and sen·sē (先生) for a doctor or teacher (literally meaning 'master'). You may also notice older people addressing children or young women with the suffix ·chan (ちゃん) as a term of endearment.

Where are you going?	どこに行きますか? do·ko ni i·ki·mas ka
What are you doing?	何をしていますか? na·ni o shi·te i·mas ka
Q Do you like it here?	ここが好きですか? ko·ko ga su·ki des ka
A I love it here.	ここが大好きです。 ko·ko ga dai·su·ki des
That's (beautiful), isn't it?	(きれい)ですね。 (ki·rē) des ne
Q Are you here on holidays?	休暇でここに 来ましたか? kyū·ka de ko·ko ni ki·mash·ta ka
A I'm here for a holiday.	休暇でここに来ました。 kyū·ka de ko·ko ni ki·mash·ta
A I'm here on business.	仕事でここに 来ました。 shi·go·to de ko·ko ni ki·mash·ta
A I'm here to study.	勉強のためにここに 来ました。 ben·kyō no ta·me ni ko·ko ni ki·mash·ta

Q How long are you here for?	いつまでここにいますか? i·tsu ma·de ko·ko ni i·mas ka
A I'm here for (two) weeks.	ここに(2)週間います。 ko·ko ni (ni)·shū·kan i·mas
A I'm here for (four) days.	ここに(4)日間います。 ko·ko ni (yok)·ka·kan i·mas

Nationalities

68a Q Where are you from?	どちらから来ましたか? do·chi·ra ka·ra ki·mash·ta ka
68b A I'm from (Singapore).	(シンガポール)から 来ました。 (shin·ga·pō·ru) ka·ra ki·mash·ta

For more countries, see the **dictionary**.

Age

Talking about age did not use to be a big issue, but more recently the topic is best avoided when speaking to women.

69a Q How old are you?	おいくつですか? oy·ku·tsu des ka
69b A I'm (25) years old.	私は(25)歳です。 wa·ta·shi wa (ni·jū go)·sai des
Q How old is your (son/daughter)?	(息子/娘)さんは おいくつですか? (mu·su·ko/mu·su·me)·san wa oy·ku·tsu des ka
A He's ... years old.	彼は…歳です。 ka·re wa ...sai des
A She's ... years old.	彼女は…歳です。 ka·no·jo wa ...sai des

| Too old! | もう歳です。
mō to·shi des |
| I'm younger than I look. | 私は見た目より
若いです。
wa·ta·shi wa mi·ta·me yo·ri
wa·kai des |

For your age, see **numbers & amounts** (p36).

Occupations & Studies

70a Q What's your occupation?	お仕事は何ですか? o·shi·go·to wa nan des ka
70b A I'm a (scientist).	私は(科学者)です。 wa·ta·shi wa (ka·ga·ku·sha) des
I work in (sales).	私は(営業)の 仕事をしています。 wa·ta·shi wa (ē·gyō) no shi·go·to o shi·te i·mas
I'm retired.	私は退職者です。 wa·ta·shi wa tai·sho·ku·sha des
I'm self-employed.	私は自営業者です。 wa·ta·shi wa ji·ē·gyō·sha des
I'm unemployed.	私は失業者 です。 wa·ta·shi wa shi·tsu·gyō·sha des
I've been made redundant.	リストラされました。 ri·su·to·ra sa·re·mash·ta
Q What are you studying?	何を勉強していますか? na·ni o ben·kyō shi·te i·mas ka
A I'm studying (science).	私は(自然科学) を勉強しています。 wa·ta·shi wa (shi·zen·ka·ga·ku) o ben·kyō shi·te i·mas

Family

Japanese uses different forms for certain words and verbs depending on social context and the specific relationship between the speaker and the listener. One category of such words are the kinship terms, which take different forms depending on whether you're talking about your own family or the listener's family.

	MY		YOUR	
brother	兄弟	kyō·dai	ご兄弟	go·kyō·dai
daughter	娘	mu·su·me	娘さん	mu·su·me·san
family	家族	ka·zo·ku	ご家族	go·ka·zo·ku
father	父	chi·chi	お父さん	o·tō·san
grand-daughter	孫娘	ma·go·mu·su·me	孫娘さん	ma·go·mu·su·me·san
grand-father	祖父	so·fu	おじいさん	o·jī·san
grand-mother	祖母	so·bo	おばあさん	o·bā·san
grandson	孫	ma·go	お孫さん	o·ma·go·san
husband	夫	ot·to	ご主人	go·shu·jin
mother	母	ha·ha	お母さん	o·kā·san
partner	パートナー	pā·to·nā	パートナー	pā·to·nā
sister	姉妹	shi·mai	ご姉妹	go·shi·mai
son	息子	mu·su·ko	息子さん	mu·su·ko·san
wife	妻	tsu·ma	奥さん	o·ku·san

Q Do you have a (brother)?
(ご兄弟)がいますか?
(go·kyō·dai) ga i·mas ka

A I have a (daughter).
(娘)がいます。
(mu·su·me) ga i·mas

A I don't have a (partner).
(パートナー)がいません。
(pā·to·nā) ga i·ma·sen

71a Q	Are you married?	結婚していますか？ kek·kon shi·te i·mas ka
71b A	I'm married.	私は結婚しています。 wa·ta·shi wa kek·kon shi·te i·mas
A	I'm separated.	私は離婚しました。 wa·ta·shi wa ri·kon shi·mash·ta
71c A	I'm single.	私は独身です。 wa·ta·shi wa do·ku·shin des

Talking with Children

When's your birthday?	お誕生日はいつ？ o·tan·jō·bi wa i·tsu
Do you go to school/ kindergarten?	学校/幼稚園に行っているの？ gak·kō/yō·chi·en ni it·te i·ru no
What grade are you in?	何年生？ nan·nen·sē
Do you learn English?	英語を勉強してる？ ē·go o ben·kyō shi·te·ru
I come from very far away.	私はとても遠くからきたの。 wa·ta·shi wa to·te·mo tō·ku ka·ra ki·ta no

Farewells

| 72a Q | What's your
(address)? | あなたの (住所) は
何ですか？
a·na·ta no (jū·sho) wa
nan des ka |
| 72b A | Here's my
(address). | これが私の (住所)
です。
ko·re ga wa·ta·shi no (jū·sho)
des |

72c What's your phone number?	あなたの電話番号は 何番ですか? a·na·ta no den·wa·ban·gō wa nam·ban des ka
72d What's your email address?	あなたのEメールアドレスは 何ですか? a·na·ta no ī·mē·ru·a·do·res wa nan des ka
Keep in touch.	連絡をとりましょう。 ren·ra·ku o to·ri·ma·shō
It's been great meeting you.	あなたに会えてとても よかったです。 a·na·ta ni a·e·te to·te·mo yo·kat·ta des

Well-Wishing

Note that when you're in a more formal situation, you can add go·zai·mas (ございます), 'very much', after some of these wishes.

Bon voyage!	よい旅を! yoy ta·bi o
Congratulations!	おめでとう(ございます)。 o·me·de·tō (go·zai·mas)
Good luck!	がんばって! gam·bat·te
Happy birthday!	誕生日おめでとう (ございます)。 tan·jō·bi o·me·de·tō (go·zai·mas)
Happy New Year!	明けましておめでとう (ございます)。 a·ke·mash·te o·me·de·tō (go·zai·mas)
Look after yourself. (to a sick person)	お大事に。 o·dai·ji ni

Interests

What do you do in your spare time?	ひまなとき 何をしますか?	hi·ma na to·ki na·ni o shi·mas ka
Do you like ...?	…が好きですか?	... ga su·ki des ka
I like ...	…が好きです。	... ga su·ki des
I don't like ...	…が好きでは ありません。	... ga su·ki de wa a·ri·ma·sen

Common Interests

What do you do in your spare time?	ひまなとき何を しますか? hi·ma na to·ki na·ni o shi·mas ka
73a Q Do you like (movies)?	(映画)が好きですか? (ei·ga) ga su·ki des ka
73b A I like (movies).	(映画)が好きです。 (ei·ga) ga su·ki des
73c A I don't like (movies).	(映画)が好きでは ありません。 (ei·ga) ga su·ki de wa a·ri·ma·sen

For more activities, see **sports** (p145) and the **dictionary**.

Music

What bands do you like?	どんなバンドが好きですか? don·na ban·do ga su·ki des ka

What music do you like?	どんな音楽が好きですか?	don·na on·ga·ku ga su·ki des ka
What singers do you like?	どんな歌手が好きですか?	don·na ka·shu ga su·ki des ka
Do you ...?	…ますか?	...·mas ka

dance	ダンスをし	dan·su o shi
go to concerts	コンサートに行き	kon·sā·to ni i·ki
listen to music	音楽を聴き	on·ga·ku o ki·ki
play an instrument	楽器を演奏し	gak·ki o en·sō shi
sing	歌い	u·tai

I like...	…が 好きです。	ga su·ki des
I don't like...	…が好きではありません。	... ga su·ki de wa a·ri·ma·sen

blues	ブルース	bu·rū·su
classical music	クラシック	ku·ra·shik·ku
enka (genre of popular ballads)	演歌	en·ka
hip hop	ヒップホップ	hip·pu·hop·pu
jazz	ジャズ	ja·zu
(Japanese) pop	(J-)ポップ	(jē·)pop·pu
rock	ロック	rok·ku
world music	ワールドミュージック	wā·ru·do·myū·jik·ku

See also **going out** (p132).

CULTURE TIP

Japanese Pastimes

While you're in Japan why not try your hand at some local pastimes, such as bon·sai (盆栽; miniature trees), i·ke·ba·na (生け花; flower arranging), o·ri·ga·mi (折り紙; paper folding) or reading man·ga (漫画). Local board games include go (碁) and shō·gi (将棋; Japanese chess), and in many cities you'll find noisy parlours where you can play pa·chin·ko (パチンコ; a kind of pinball game).

Cinema & Theatre

I feel like going to a ...	…に行こうと思います。 ... ni i·kō to o·moy·mas
What's showing at the cinema/theatre tonight?	今晩はどんな映画/舞台がありますか? kom·ban wa don·na ē·ga/bu·tai ga a·ri·mas ka
Is it in English?	英語ですか? ē·go des ka
Does it have (English) subtitles?	(英語の)字幕がありますか? (ē·go no) ji·ma·ku ga a·ri·mas ka
Is this seat vacant?	この席は空いていますか? ko·no se·ki wa ai·te i·mas ka
Have you seen ...?	…をもう観ましたか? ... o mō mi·mash·ta ka
🇶 **Who's in it?**	だれが演じていますか? da·re ga en·ji·te i·mas ka
🇦 **It stars ...**	主役は…です。 shu·ya·ku wa ... des
🇶 **Did you like the film?**	映画はよかったですか? ē·ga wa yo·kat·ta des ka

Q Did you like the play?	劇はよかったですか? ge·ki wa yo·kat·ta des ka	
A I thought it was excellent.	素晴らしかったと 思います。 su·ba·ra·shi·kat·ta to o·moy·mas	
A I thought it was long.	長すぎたと思います。 na·ga·su·gi·ta to o·moy·mas	
A I thought it was OK.	まあまあだったと思います。 mā·mā dat·ta to o·moy·mas	
I like ...	…が好きです。 ... ga su·ki des	
I don't like ...	…が好きでは ありません。 ... ga su·ki de wa a·ri·ma·sen	

action movies	アクション ムービー	a·ku·shon· mū·bī
anime films	アニメ	a·ni·me
comedies	コメディ	ko·me·di
drama	ドラマ	do·ra·ma
horror movies	ホラー映画	ho·rā·ē·ga
Japanese cinema	日本映画	ni·hon·ē·ga
sci-fi	SF	e·su·e·fu

Feelings & Opinions

KEY PHRASES

What did you think of it?	どう思いますか?	dō o·moy·mas ka
I thought it was OK.	まあまあだ と思いました。	mā·mā da to o·moy·mash·ta
Did you hear about ...?	…について 聞きましたか?	... ni tsu·i·te ki·ki·mash·ta ka

Feelings

74a Are you happy?	幸せですか?	shi·a·wa·se des ka
74b I'm happy.	うれしいです。	u·re·shī des
74c Are you sad?	悲しいですか?	ka·na·shī des ka
74d I'm sad.	悲しいです。	ka·na·shī des
75a Are you thirsty?	のどが渇きましたか?	no·do ga ka·wa·ki·mash·ta ka
75b I'm thirsty.	のどが渇きました。	no·do ga ka·wa·ki·mash·ta
75c Are you tired?	疲れましたか?	tsu·ka·re·mash·ta ka
75e I'm tired.	疲れました。	tsu·ka·re·mash·ta
I'm disappointed.	がっかりしました。	gak·ka·ri shi·mash·ta

I'm embarrassed.	恥ずかしいです。 ha·zu·ka·shī des
I'm worried.	心配しています。 shim·pai shi·te i·mas
I'm (a little) sad.	(ちょっと)悲しいです。 (chot·to) ka·na·shī des
I'm (extremely) sorry.	(本当に)すみません。 (hon·tō ni) su·mi·ma·sen
I feel (very) lucky.	(とても)運が良かったと 思います。 (to·te·mo) un ga yo·kat·ta to o·moy·mas

If feeling unwell, see **health** (p162).

Opinions

Q	Did you like it?	好きですか? su·ki des ka
A	I thought it was ...	…と思いました。 ... to o·moy·mash·ta
Q	What do you think of it?	どう思いますか? dō o·moy·mas ka
A	It's ...	…です。 ... des

awful	ひどい	hi·doy
beautiful	美しい	u·tsu·ku·shī
boring	つまらない	tsu·ma·ra·nai
great	素晴らしい	su·ba·ra·shī
interesting	面白い	o·mo·shi·roy

I thought it was OK.	まあまあだと思いました。 mā·mā da to o·moy·mash·ta
I thought it was strange.	変だと思いました。 hen da to o·moy·mash·ta

SOCIAL FEELINGS & OPINIONS

CULTURE TIP

Etiquette – Taking a Compliment
You'll be complimented on your language skills when making even the slightest effort to speak Japanese. If you're able to respond to these pats on the back in a typically modest Japanese fashion, you'll be even more sure to impress. When they say 'Your Japanese is so good' (日本語がお上手ですね。ni·hon·go ga o·jō·zu des ne), you could answer with 'It's not really' (それほどでも。so·re·ho·do de·mo).

Politics & Social Issues

The Japanese generally tend not to discuss politics openly and avoid mentioning which party they support. Be aware that bold statements regarding Japan and Japanese culture might be taken quite personally and are better avoided.

Q Who do you vote for?	だれに投票しますか？	da·re ni tō·hyō shi·mas ka
A I support the ... party.	私は…党を支持します。	wa·ta·shi wa ...tō o shi·ji shi·mas

communist	共産	kyō·san
conservative	保守	ho·shu
democratic	民主	min·shu
green	緑の	mi·do·ri no
liberal (progressive)	由	ji·yū
liberal democratic	自民	ji·min
social democratic	社会民主	sha·kai·min·shu
socialist	社会	sha·kai

Did you hear about ...?	…について聞きましたか？ ... ni tsu·i·te ki·ki·mash·ta ka
Q Do you agree with it?	それに賛成しますか？ so·re ni san·sē shi·mas ka
A I agree with ...	…に賛成します。 ... ni san·sē shi·mas
A I don't agree with ...	…に賛成しません。 ... ni san·sē shi·ma·sen
How do people feel about the economy?	みんなは経済について どう思っていますか？ min·na wa kē·zai ni tsu·i·te dō o·mot·te i·mas ka
How do people feel about the environment?	みんなは環境について どう思っていますか？ min·na wa kan·kyō ni tsu·i·te dō o·mot·te i·mas ka
How do people feel about the war in ...?	みんなは…戦争について どう思っていますか？ min·na wa ...sen·sō ni tsu·i·te dō o·mot·te i·mas ka
How do people feel about immigration?	みんなは移民について どう思っていますか？ min·na wa i·min ni tsu·i·te dō o·mot·te i·mas ka

SOCIAL FEELINGS & OPINIONS

美しいです。
u·tsu·ku·shī des
It's beautiful.

Environment

Is there a ... problem here?	ここには…の問題が ありますか? ko·ko ni wa ... no mon·dai ga a·ri·mas ka
What should be done about ...?	…について何を しなければなりませんか? ... ni tsu·i·te na·ni o shi·na·ke·re·ba na·ri·ma·sen ka

climate change	気候変動	ki·kō hen·dō
greenhouse effect	温室効果	on·shi·tsu·kō·ka
nuclear energy	原子力	gen·shi·ryo·ku
pollution	公害	kō·gai
recycling	リサイクル	ri·sai·ku·ru
whaling	捕鯨	ho·gē

Where can I recycle this?	これはどこでリサイクル できますか? ko·re wa do·ko de ri·sai·ku·ru de·ki·mas ka
Is this a protected park?	これは保護されている 公園ですか? ko·re wa ho·go sa·re·te i·ru kō·en des ka
Is this a protected species?	これは保護されている 生物ですか? ko·re wa ho·go sa·re·te i·ru sē·bu·tsu des ka

CULTURE TIP

Etiquette – Giving Gifts

It's good manners to exchange some niceties when giving or receiving presents. In addition to a simple thank you, the recipient of the present could add 'You shouldn't have bothered' (そんなに気を使わなくても よかったのに。 son·na ni ki o tsu·ka·wa·na·ku·te mo yo·kat·ta no ni), to which the giver could reply 'It's my pleasure' (どういたしまして。 dō i·ta·shi mash·te) or 'It's nothing really' (つまらないものですが、 tsu·ma·ra·nai mo·no des ga).

Is this a protected forest?	これは保護されている 森ですか? ko·re wa ho·go sa·re·te i·ru mo·ri des ka

Going Out

KEY PHRASES

What's on tonight?	今夜は何が ありますか?	kon·ya wa na·ni ga a·ri·mas ka
What time shall we meet?	何時に 会いましょうか?	nan·ji ni ai·ma·shō ka
Where shall we meet?	どこで 会いましょうか?	do·ko de ai·ma·shō ka

Where to Go

What's on this weekend?	今週の週末は何がありますか? kon·shū no shū·ma·tsu wa na·ni ga a·ri·mas ka
What's on today?	今日は何がありますか? kyō wa na·ni ga a·ri·mas ka
What's on tonight?	今夜は何がありますか? kon·ya wa na·ni ga a·ri·mas ka
76a Where can I find (a bar)?	どこに行けば(バー)が ありますか? do·ko ni i·ke·ba (bā) ga a·ri·mas ka
76b Where can I find a gay venue?	どこに行けばゲイの場所が ありますか? do·ko ni i·ke·ba gē no ba·sho ga a·ri·mas ka
76c Where can I find a nightclub?	どこに行けばクラブが ありますか? do·ko ni i·ke·ba ku·ra·bu ga a·ri·mas ka

76d Where can I find a pub?	どこに行けばパブが ありますか? do·ko ni i·ke·ba pa·bu ga a·ri·mas ka
Is there a local film/ music guide?	地元の映画/音楽 ガイドはありますか? ji·mo·to no ē·ga/on·ga·ku gai·do wa a·ri·mas ka
I feel like going to a cafe.	カフェに行きたい気分です。 ka·fe ni i·ki·tai ki·bun des
77a I feel like going to a concert.	コンサートに行きたい 気分です。 kon·sā·to ni i·ki·tai ki·bun des
77b I feel like going to the movies.	映画に行きたい気分です。 ē·ga ni i·ki·tai ki·bun des
77c I feel like going to a party.	パーティーに行きたい 気分です。 pā·tī ni i·ki·tai ki·bun des
77d I feel like going to a restaurant.	レストランに行きたい 気分です。 res·to·ran ni i·ki·tai ki·bun des
77e I feel like going to the theatre.	劇場に行きたい気分です。 ge·ki·jō ni i·ki·tai ki·bun des

For more on bars and drinks, see **eating out** (p172).

Invitations

What are you doing now?	これから何をする予定 ですか? ko·re·ka·ra na·ni o su·ru yo·tē des ka
What are you doing this weekend?	今週の週末何を する予定ですか? kon·shū no shū·ma·tsu na·ni o su·ru yo·tē des ka

What are you doing tonight?	今夜何をする予定ですか? kon·ya na·ni o su·ru yo·tē des ka
Would you like to go (for a) ...?	…に 行きませんか? ... ni i·ki·ma·sen ka
Would you like to go for a coffee?	コーヒーに 行きませんか? kō·hī ni i·ki·ma·sen ka
Would you like to go out somewhere?	どこか外に 行きませんか? do·ko ka so·to ni i·ki·ma·sen ka
Do you know a good restaurant?	いいレストランを知っていますか? ī res·to·ran o shit·te i·mas ka
Do you want to come to the concert with me?	いっしょにコンサートに行きませんか? is·shō ni kon·sā·to ni i·ki·ma·sen ka
We're having a party.	パーティーをします。 pā·tī o shi·mas
You should come.	来てください。 ki·te ku·da·sai
My round.	私の番です。 wa·ta·shi no ban des

Responding to Invitations

Sure!	もちろん! mo·chi·ron
Yes, I'd love to.	はい、ぜひとも。 hai, ze·hi to·mo
That's very kind of you.	親切にありがとう。 shin·se·tsu ni a·ri·ga·tō
Where shall we go?	どこに行きましょうか? do·ko ni i·ki·ma·shō ka

No, I'm afraid I can't.	すみませんが、ちょっと 都合が悪いんです。 su·mi·ma·sen ga, chot·to tsu·gō ga wa·ru·in des
What about tomorrow?	明日はどうですか? a·shi·ta wa dō des ka
Sorry, I can't sing.	ごめんなさい、 歌えないんです。 go·men·na·sai, u·ta·e·nain des

> コーヒーに 行きませんか?
> kō·hī ni i·ki·ma·sen ka
> *Would you like to go for a coffee?*

Arranging to Meet

Q What time shall we meet?	何時に会いましょうか? nan·ji ni ai·ma·shō ka
A Let's meet at (eight) o'clock.	(8)時に会いましょう。 (ha·chi)·ji ni ai·ma·shō
Where shall we meet?	どこで会いましょうか? do·ko de ai·ma·shō ka
Let's meet at (the entrance).	(入口)で会いましょう。 (i·ri·gu·chi) de ai·ma·shō
I'll pick you up.	迎えに行きます。 mu·ka·e ni i·ki·mas
Q Are you ready?	準備はいいですか? jum·bi wa ī des ka
A I'm ready.	準備はいいです。 jum·bi wa ī des

CULTURE TIP **Karaoke**
Karaoke boxes (ka·ra·o·ke·bok·kus カラオケ
ボックス) – rooms for karaoke that can be booked
on an hourly basis and where you can also be served food
and drinks – are hugely popular in Japan. A few phrases
that might come in handy while out singing: 'Let's sing together' (いっしょに歌いましょう。is·sho ni u·tai·ma·shō),
'Are there English songs?' (英語の曲がありますか? ē·go no
kyo·ku ga a·ri·mas ka), 'I don't know this song' (この曲は
知りません。ko·no kyo·ku wa shi·ri·ma·sen), and, for when
you'd rather just watch, 'I'm not good at singing' (歌うのが
上手じゃありません。u·ta·u no ga jō·zu ja a·ri·ma·sen).

I'll be coming later.	遅れて行きます。 o·ku·re·te i·ki·mas
Where will you be?	どこにいますか? do·ko ni i·mas ka
If I'm not there by (nine), don't wait for me.	(9)時までに私が 行かなかったら待たないで ください。 (ku)·ji ma·de ni wa·ta·shi ga i·ka·na·kat·ta·ra ma·ta·nai de ku·da·sai
OK!	OK! ō·kē
I'll see you there.	じゃ、そこで会いましょう。 ja, so·ko de ai·ma·shō
See you later.	あとで会いましょう。 a·to de ai·ma·shō
See you tomorrow.	明日会いましょう。 a·shi·ta ai·ma·shō
I'm looking forward to it.	楽しみにしています。 ta·no·shi·mi ni shi·te i·mas

| Sorry I'm late. | 遅れてすみません。
o·ku·re·te su·mi·ma·sen |
| Never mind. | だいじょうぶです。
dai·jō·bu des |

Drugs

I don't take drugs.	麻薬はやりません。 ma·ya·ku wa ya·ri·ma·sen
I take ... occasionally.	ときどき…をやります。 to·ki·do·ki ... o ya·ri·mas
Do you want to have a smoke?	吸いたいですか? su·i·tai des ka
Do you have a light?	火はありますか? hi wa a·ri·mas ka

Romance

KEY PHRASES

Will you go out with me?	付き合いませんか?	tsu·ki·ai·ma·sen ka
I love you.	愛しています。	ai shi·te i·mas
Leave me alone, please.	独りにしておいてください。	hi·to·ri ni shi·te oy·te ku·da·sai

Asking Someone Out

Would you like to do something (tomorrow)?	(明日)何かしませんか? (a·shi·ta) na·ni ka shi·ma·sen ka
Yes, I'd love to.	はい、ぜひとも。 hai, ze·hi to·mo
Sorry, I can't.	すみません、行けません。 su·mi·ma·sen, i·ke·ma·sen
Where would you like to go (tonight)?	(今晩)どこに行きたいですか? (kom·ban) do·ko ni i·ki·tai des ka

Pick-Up Lines

Would you like a drink?	何か飲みませんか? na·ni ka no·mi·ma·sen ka
You look like someone I know.	私の知っている人によく似ています。 wa·ta·shi no shit·te i·ru hi·to ni yo·ku ni·te i·mas

You're a fantastic dancer.	踊りがすごくうまい ですね。 o·do·ri ga su·go·ku u·mai des ne
How about some tea?	お茶しませんか? o·cha shi·ma·sen ka
Do you want to come to my place?	うちに来ない? u·chi ni ko·nai
Can I sit here?	ここに座ってもいいですか? ko·ko ni su·wat·te mo ī des ka
Can I dance with you?	いっしょに踊ってもいい ですか? is·sho ni o·dot·te mo ī des ka
Can I take you home?	お宅まで送ってもいい ですか? o·ta·ku ma·de o·kut·te mo ī des ka

Rejections

I'm here with my boyfriend/girlfriend.	彼氏/彼女と一緒なんです。 ka·re·shi/ka·no·jo to is·sho nan des
I'm with someone.	連れがいますので。 tsu·re ga i·mas no·de
Excuse me, I have to go now.	すみませんが、もう 行かなくてはなりません。 su·mi·ma·sen ga, mō i·ka·na·ku·te wa na·ri·ma·sen
No, thank you.	いいえ、けっこうです。 ī·e, kek·kō des
Leave me alone, please.	独りにしておいて ください。 hi·to·ri ni shi·te oy·te ku·da·sai

| Go away! | あっちへ行け！
at·chi e i·ke |
| Stop it! | やめて！
ya·me·te |

Getting Closer

I like you very much.	あなたがとても好き。 a·na·ta ga to·te·mo su·ki
Can I kiss you?	キスしてもいい？ ki·su shi·te mo ī
Do you want to come inside for a while?	ちょっと、うちに寄って いきませんか？ chot·to u·chi ni yot·te i·ki·ma·sen ka
Can I stay over?	泊まってもいいですか？ to·mat·te mo ī des ka

Sex

Kiss me.	キスして。 ki·su shi·te
I want you.	あなたが欲しい。 a·na·ta ga ho·shī
Let's go to bed.	ベッドに行きましょう。 bed·do ni i·ki·ma·shō
🇶 Do you like this?	これは好き？ ko·re wa su·ki
🇦 I like that.	それは好きです。 ko·re wa su·ki des
🇦 I don't like that.	それは好きじゃありません。 ko·re wa su·ki ja a·ri·ma·sen
I think we should stop now.	これ以上はやめましょう。 ko·re i·jō wa ya·me·ma·shō

Let's use a (condom).	（コンドーム）を 使いましょう。 (kon·dō·mu) o tsu·kai·ma·shō
It helps to have a sense of humour.	肩の力を抜いて やろうよ。 ka·ta no chi·ka·ra o nu·i·te ya·rō yo
That's great!	素晴らしい! su·ba·ra·shī
Easy tiger!	ちょっと待って! chot·to mat·te
That was amazing.	すばらしかったです。 su·ba·ra·shi·kat·ta des

Love

I love you.	愛しています。 ai shi·te i·mas
I think we're good together.	いいカップルだと思います。 ī kap·pu·ru da to o·moy·mas
Will you go out with me?	付き合いませんか? tsu·ki·ai·ma·sen ka
Will you marry me?	結婚しませんか? kek·kon shi·ma·sen ka

LANGUAGE TIP

Terms of Endearment

The Japanese are generally more reserved about expressing emotions than some other cultures, so pet names are a lot less used than elsewhere. However, some couples use nicknames derived from their first name. They might affectionately abbreviate each other's first name and add the suffix ·chan（ちゃん）expressing endearment: eg ta·ke·chan（たけちゃん）for ta·ke·shi（たけし）or ha·na·chan（はなちゃん）for ha·na·ko（はなこ）

Beliefs & Culture

SOCIAL BELIEFS & CULTURE

KEY PHRASES

What's your religion?	あなたの宗教は何ですか?	a·na·ta no shū·kyō wa nan des ka
I'm ...	私は…です。	wa·ta·shi wa ... des
I'm sorry, it's against my beliefs.	すみませんが、それは私の信仰に反します。	su·mi·ma·sen ga so·re wa wa·ta·shi no shin·kō ni han·shi·mas

Religion

Q What's your religion?
あなたの宗教は何ですか?
a·na·ta no shū·kyō wa nan des ka

A I'm not religious.
私はあまり宗教的ではありません。
wa·ta·shi wa a·ma·ri shū·kyō·te·ki de wa a·ri·ma·sen

A I'm ...
私は…です。
wa·ta·shi wa ... des

agnostic	不可知論者	fu·ka·chi·ron·ja
atheist	無神論者	mu·shin·ron·ja
Buddhist	仏教徒	buk·kyō·to
Christian	キリスト教徒	ki·ri·su·to·kyō·to
Hindu	ヒンドゥー教徒	hin·dū·kyō·to
Jewish	ユダヤ教徒	yu·da·ya·kyō·to
Muslim	イスラム教徒	i·su·ra·mu·kyō·to

I believe in (God).	(神)を信じています。 (ka·mi) o shin·ji·te i·mas
I don't believe in (astrology).	(星占い)を信じて いません。 (ho·shi·u·ra·nai) o shin·ji·te i·ma·sen
Where can I attend a service?	どこで礼拝に参加 できますか? do·ko de rē·hai ni san·ka de·ki·mas ka
Where can I attend mass?	どこでミサに参加 できますか? do·ko de mi·sa ni san·ka de·ki·mas ka
Where can I meditate?	どこで瞑想できますか? do·ko de mē·sō de·ki·mas ka
Where can I pray?	どこでお祈りできますか? do·ko de oy·no·ri de·ki·mas ka

Cultural Differences

Is this a local custom?	これは地元の習慣 ですか? ko·re wa ji·mo·to no shū·kan des ka
I don't want to offend you.	不愉快な思いを させたくありません。 fu·yu·kai na o·moy o sa·se·ta·ku a·ri·ma·sen
I didn't mean to do anything wrong.	悪意でやったわけでは ありません。 a·ku·i de yat·ta wa·ke de wa a·ri·ma·sen
I'm not used to this.	これに慣れていません。 ko·re ni na·re·te i·ma·sen

I'd rather not join in.	参加を辞退したいと思います。 san·ka o ji·tai shi·tai to o·moy·mas
I'll try it.	やってみます。 yat·te mi·mas
I'm sorry, it's against my beliefs.	すみませんが、それは私の信仰に反します。 su·mi·ma·sen ga so·re wa wa·ta·shi no shin·kō ni han·shi·mas
I'm sorry, it's against my religion.	すみませんが、それは私の宗教に反します。 su·mi·ma·sen ga so·re wa wa·ta·shi no shū·kyō ni han·shi·mas
This is different.	これは変わっています。 ko·re wa ka·wat·te i·mas
This is fun.	これは楽しいです。 ko·re wa ta·no·shī des
This is interesting.	これはおもしろいです。 ko·re wa o·mo·shi·roy des

For phrases relating to cultural differences and food, see **vegetarian & special meals** (p193).

Sports

KEY PHRASES

What sport do you play?	どんなスポーツをしますか?	don·na spō·tsu o shi·mas ka
Who's your favourite team?	どのチームがいちばん好きですか?	do·no chī·mu ga i·chi·ban su·ki des ka
What's the score?	スコアはどうですか?	sko·a wa dō des ka

Sporting Interests

For phrases about hiking, see **outdoors** (p153). For more sports, see the **dictionary**.

Q **What sport do you play?**
どんなスポーツをしますか?
don·na spō·tsu o shi·mas ka

Q **What sport do you follow?**
どのスポーツのファンですか?
do·no spō·tsu no fan des ka

A **I play/do ...**
…をします。
... o shi·mas

A **I follow ...**
…のファンです。
... no fan des

baseball	野球	ya·kyū
basketball	バスケット	bas·ket·to
football (soccer)	サッカー	sak·kā
martial arts	武道	bu·dō
tennis	テニス	te·nis

SOCIAL SPORTS

🔊 LISTEN FOR

If you're going to a Sumo tournament (場所 ba·sho), here are some of the terms you're likely to hear.

土俵	do·hyō	ring/arena
行司	gyō·ji	referee
引き落とし	hi·ki·o·to·shi	pull down the opponent
まわし	ma·wa·shi	loincloth
押し出し	o·shi·da·shi	push the opponent out of the arena
押し倒し	o·shi·tow·shi	knock or throw down the opponent
力士	ri·ki·shi	wrestler
四股	shi·ko	stomping
つり出し	tsu·ri·da·shi	carry the opponent out of the arena
寄り切り	yo·ri·ki·ri	drive the opponent out of the arena

I cycle.	サイクリングをします。 sai·ku·rin·gu o shi·mas
I run.	ジョギングをします。 jo·gin·gu o shi·mas
I walk.	散歩をします。 sam·po o shi·mas
Q Do you like (sumo)?	(相撲) が好きですか? (su·mō) ga su·ki des ka
A Yes, very much.	はい、とても好きです。 hai, to·te·mo su·ki des
A Not really.	あまり好きじゃありません。 a·ma·ri su·ki ja a·ri·ma·sen
A I like watching it.	観るのが好きです。 mi·ru no ga su·ki des

Who's your favourite sportsperson?	どの選手がいちばん 好きですか? do·no sen·shu ga i·chi·ban su·ki des ka
Who's your favourite team?	どのチームがいちばん 好きですか? do·no chī·mu ga i·chi·ban su·ki des ka

Going to a Game

Would you like to go to a game?	試合に行きたいですか? shi·ai ni i·ki·tai des ka
Who are you supporting?	だれを応援していますか? da·re o ō·en shi·te i·mas ka
What's the score?	スコアはどうですか? sko·a wa dō des ka
Who's playing?	だれがプレーしていますか? da·re ga pu·rē shi·te i·mas ka
Who's winning?	だれが勝っていますか? da·re ga kat·te i·mas ka
That was a great/bad game!	素晴らしい/悪い 試合でしたね! su·ba·ra·shī/wa·ru·i shi·ai desh·ta ne
That was a boring game!	つまらない試合 でしたね! tsu·ma·ra·nai shi·ai desh·ta ne
What a great team!	素晴らしいチームだ! su·ba·ra·shī chī·mu da
What a terrible team!	だめなチームだ! da·me na chī·mu da

Playing Sport

Q Do you want to play?	プレーしたいですか？ pu·rē shi·tai des ka
A That would be great.	それはいいですね。 so·re wa ī des ne
A I can't.	できません。 de·ki·ma·sen
Can I join in?	いっしょにやってもいい ですか？ is·sho ni yat·te mo ī des ka
Your/My point.	あなた/私の点。 a·na·ta/wa·ta·shi no ten
Kick/Pass it to me!	こっちにキック/パス！ kot·chi ni kik·ku/pas
You're a good player.	うまいですね。 u·mai des ne
Thanks for the game.	試合、ありがとう。 shi·ai, a·ri·ga·tō
Where's the nearest golf course?	いちばん近いゴルフ場は どこですか？ i·chi·ban chi·kai go·ru·fu·jō wa do·ko des ka
Where's the nearest gym?	いちばん近いジムはどこ ですか？ i·chi·ban chi·kai ji·mu wa do·ko des ka
Where's the nearest tennis court?	いちばん近いテニスコートは どこですか？ i·chi·ban chi·kai te·nis kō·to wa do·ko des ka
What's the charge per day/hour?	1日/1時間の 料金はいくらですか？ i·chi·ni·chi/i·chi·ji·kan no ryō·kin wa i·ku·ra des ka

What's the charge per game?	1ゲームの料金は いくらですか? i·chi·gē·mu no ryō·kin wa i·ku·ra des ka
What's the charge per visit?	1回の料金はいくら ですか? ik·kai no ryō·kin wa i·ku·ra des ka
Can I hire a ...?	…を貸してもらえませんか? ... o ka·shi·te mo·ra·e·ma·sen ka

ball	ボール	bō·ru
bicycle	自転車	ji·ten·sha
court	コート	kō·to
racquet	ラケット	ra·ket·to

Where are the changing rooms?	更衣室はどこですか? kō·i·shi·tsu wa do·ko des ka
Can I take lessons?	レッスンを受けられますか? res·sun o u·ke·ra·re·mas ka

SOCIAL SPORTS

Baseball

base	塁 ru·i
baseball	野球 ya·kyū
batter	バッター bat·tā
curve ball	カーブ kā·bu
dugout	ベンチ ben·chi

fastball	速球	sok·kyū
home run	ホームラン	hō·mu·ran
infielder	内野手	nai·ya·shu
inning	イニング	i·nin·gu
out a/n	アウト	ow·to
outfielder	外野手	gai·ya·shu
pitcher	ピッチャー	pit·chā
run n	ラン	ran
safe	セーフ	sē·fu
strike n	ストライク	sto·rai·ku

Skiing

I'd like to hire ...	…を借りたいの ですが。	... o ka·ri·tai no des ga

boots	ブーツ	bū·tsu
gloves	手袋	te·bu·ku·ro
goggles	ゴーグル	gō·gu·ru
poles	ストック	stok·ku
skis	スキー	skī
a ski suit	スキースーツ	skī·sū·tsu

Is it possible to go ...?	…に行けますか？ ... ni i·ke·mas ka

alpine skiing	アルペンスキー	a·ru·pen·skī
cross-country skiing	クロスカントリー	ku·ros·kan·to·rī
snowboarding	スノーボード	su·nō·bō·do
tobogganing	そり	so·ri

How much is a pass?	券はいくらですか？ ken wa i·ku·ra des ka
What are the conditions like (at Niseko)?	（ニセコの）コンディションは どうですか？ (ni·se·ko no) kon·di·shon wa dō des ka
What level is that slope?	このゲレンデはどの レベルですか？ ko·no ge·ren·de wa do·no re·be·ru des ka
Which are the advanced slopes?	上級レベルのゲレンデは どこですか？ jō·kyū re·be·ru no ge·ren·de wa do·ko des ka
Which are the beginner slopes?	初級レベルのゲレンデは どこですか？ sho·kyū re·be·ru no ge·ren·de wa do·ko des ka
Which are the intermediate slopes?	中級レベルのゲレンデは どこですか？ chū·kyū re·be·ru no ge·ren·de wa do·ko des ka
cable car	ケーブルカー kē·bu·ru·kā
chairlift/ski-lift	リフト ri·fu·to

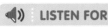
SOCIAL SPORTS

コーナー	kō·nā	corner
ファウル	fow·ru	foul
フリーキック	fu·rī·kik·ku	free kick
ゴール	gō·ru	goal
オフサイド	of·sai·do	offside
ペナルティ	pe·na·ru·tī	penalty
レッドカード	red·do·kā·do	red card
審判	shim·pan	referee
イエローカード	ye·rō·kā·do	yellow card

Soccer

Who plays for (Urawa Reds)?	だれが(浦和レッズ)でプレーしていますか? da·re ga (u·ra·wa rez·zu) de pu·rē shi·te i·mas ka
Which team is at the top of the league?	どのチームがリーグのトップですか? do·no chī·mu ga rī·gu no top·pu des ka
What a goal!	すごいゴール! su·goy gō·ru
What a kick!	すごいキック! su·goy kik·ku

Outdoors

KEY PHRASES

Do we need a guide?	ガイドが必要ですか？	gai·do ga hi·tsu·yō des ka
I'm lost.	迷いました。	ma·yoy·mash·ta
What's the weather like?	天気はどうですか？	ten·ki wa dō des ka

Hiking

Where can I buy supplies?	どこで食料が買えますか？ do·ko·de sho·ku·ryō ga ka·e·mas ka
Where can I get a map?	どこで地図が手に入りますか？ do·ko·de chi·zu ga te ni hai·ri·mas ka
Where can I hire hiking gear?	どこで登山用品が買えますか？ do·ko·de to·zan·yō·hin ga ka·e·mas ka
How high is the climb?	どのくらい高度差がありますか？ do·no·ku·rai kō·do·sa ga a·ri·mas ka
How long is the trail?	どのくらい距離がありますか？ do·no·ku·rai kyo·ri ga a·ri·mas ka

Do we need to take bed linen?	シーツを持っていく必要がありますか？ shī·tsu o mot·te i·ku hi·tsu·yō ga a·ri·mas ka
Do we need to take food/ water?	食料/水を持っていく必要がありますか？ sho·ku·ryō/mi·zu o mot·te i·ku hi·tsu·yō ga a·ri·mas ka
Do we need a guide?	ガイドが必要ですか？ gai·do ga hi·tsu·yō des ka
Are there guided treks?	ガイドが同行してくれるルートがありますか？ gai·do ga dō·kō shi·te ku·re·ru rū·to ga a·ri·mas ka
Is it safe?	安全ですか？ an·zen des ka
Is there a hut?	山小屋がありますか？ ya·ma·go·ya ga a·ri·mas ka
Is the track (well) marked?	山道は標識が（きちんと）ありますか？ ya·ma·mi·chi wa hyō·shi·ki ga (ki·chin·to) a·ri·mas ka
Is the track open?	山道は開通していますか？ ya·ma·mi·chi wa kai·tsū shi·te i·mas ka
Is the track scenic?	山道は眺めがいいですか？ ya·ma·mi·chi wa na·ga·me ga ī des ka
Which is the easiest route?	どのルートがいちばん簡単ですか？ do·no rū·to ga i·chi·ban kan·tan des ka
Which is the shortest route?	どのルートがいちばん短いですか？ do·no rū·to ga i·chi·ban mi·ji·kai des ka

🔊 LISTEN FOR

地震	ji·shin	earthquake
雨季	u·ki	rainy season
津波	tsu·na·mi	tsunami
台風	tai·fū	typhoon
噴火	fun·ka	volcanic eruption
火山	ka·zan	volcano

Where can I find the camping ground?	キャンプ場はどこに ありますか? kyam·pu·jō wa do·ko ni a·ri·mas ka
Where can I find the showers/toilets?	シャワー/トイレはどこに ありますか? sha·wā/toy·re wa do·ko ni a·ri·mas ka
Does this path go to ...?	この道は…に行きますか? ko·no mi·chi wa ... ni i·ki·mas ka
Can I go through here?	ここを通り抜けできますか? ko·ko o tō·ri·nu·ke de·ki·mas ka
Is the water OK to drink?	水を飲んでもだいじょうぶ ですか? mi·zu o non·de mo dai·jō·bu des ka
I'm lost.	迷いました。 ma·yoy·mash·ta

Beach

Where's the nearest beach?	いちばん近いビーチは どこですか? i·chi·ban chi·kai bī·chi wa do·ko des ka

Is it safe to dive here?	ここは安全に 飛び込めますか? ko·ko wa an·zen ni to·bi·ko·me·mas ka
Is it safe to swim here?	ここは安全に 泳げますか? ko·ko wa an·zen ni o·yo·ge·mas ka

Weather

What will the weather be like tomorrow?	明日の天気はどうですか? a·shi·ta no ten·ki wa dō des ka
78a Q What's the weather like?	天気はどうですか? ten·ki wa dō des ka
78b A It's cold.	寒いです。 sa·mu·i des
78c A It's hot.	暑いです。 a·tsu·i des
78d A It's raining.	雨です。 a·me des
78e A It's sunny.	晴れです。 ha·re des
A It's ...	…です。 ... des

cloudy	曇り	ku·mo·ri
humid	蒸し暑い	mu·shi·a·tsu·i
snowing	雪	yu·ki
warm	暖かい	a·ta·ta·kai
windy	風が強い	ka·ze ga tsu·yoy

Safe Travel

EMERGENCIES	158
POLICE	160
HEALTH	162

Emergencies

KEY PHRASES

Help!	たすけて！	tas·ke·te
There's been an accident.	事故です。	ji·ko des
It's an emergency.	緊急です。	kin·kyū des

79a	Help!	たすけて！ tas·ke·te
79b	Stop!	止まれ！ to·ma·re
79c	Go away!	あっちへ行け！ ac·chi e i·ke
79d	Thief!	どろぼう！ do·ro·bō
79e	Fire!	火事だ！ ka·ji da
79f	Watch out!	危ない！ a·bu·nai
	Careful!	気をつけて！ ki o tsu·ke·te
80a	It's an emergency.	緊急です。 kin·kyū des
	There's been an accident.	事故です。 ji·ko des
80b	Call the police.	警察を呼んで。 kē·sa·tsu o yon·de
80c	Call a doctor.	医者を呼んで。 i·sha o yon·de

🔍 LOOK FOR

病院	byō·in	Hospital
警察	kē·sa·tsu	Police
警察署	kē·sa·tsu·sho	Police Station
交番	kō·ban	Police Box
救急	kyū·kyū	Emergency Department

80d Call an ambulance.
救急車を呼んで。
kyū·kyū·sha o yon·de

81a Could you help me, please?
たすけてください。
tas·ke·te ku·da·sai

81b I have to use the telephone.
電話を貸してください。
den·wa o ka·shi·te ku·da·sai

81c I'm lost.
迷いました。
ma·yoy·mash·ta

81d Where's the toilet?
トイレはどこですか?
toy·re wa do·ko des ka

Is it safe at night?
夜は安全ですか?
yo·ru wa an·zen des ka

Is it safe for women?
女性にとって安全ですか?
jo·sē ni tot·te an·zen des ka

Is it safe on your own?
独りで安全ですか?
hi·to·ri de an·zen des ka

Is it safe for travellers?
旅行者にとって安全ですか?
ryo·kō·sha ni tot·te an·zen des ka

Police

KEY PHRASES

Where's the police station?	警察署は どこですか?	kē·sa·tsu·sho wa do·ko des ka
I want to contact my embassy/ consulate.	領事館/大使館 に連絡したい です。	ryō·ji·kan/tai·shi·kan ni ren·ra·ku shi·tai des
My bags were stolen.	私の バッグが 盗まれました。	wa·ta·shi no bag·gu ga nu·su·ma·re·mash·ta

82a Where's the police station?
警察署はどこですか?
kē·sa·tsu·sho wa do·ko des ka

82b I want to report an offence.
犯罪を報告したいの ですが。
han·zai o hō·ko·ku shi·tai no des ga

82c I've been assaulted.
暴行を受けました。
bō·kō o u·ke·mash·ta

82d I've been raped.
レイプされました。
rē·pu sa·re·mash·ta

82e I've been robbed.
強盗に遭いました。
gō·tō ni ai·mash·ta

It was him/her.
やったのは彼/彼女です。
yat·ta no wa ka·re/ka·no·jo des

83a My bags were stolen.
私のバッグが 盗まれました。
wa·ta·shi no bag·gu ga nu·su·ma·re·mash·ta

83b **My passport was stolen.**

私のパスポートが
盗まれました。
wa·ta·shi no pas·pō·to ga
nu·su·ma·re·mash·ta

83c **My wallet was stolen.**

私の財布が盗まれました。
wa·ta·shi no sai·fu ga
nu·su·ma·re·mash·ta

83d **I've lost my bags.**

バッグをなくしました。
bag·gu o na·ku·shi·mash·ta

83e **I've lost my passport.**

パスポートをなくしました。
pas·pō·to o na·ku·shi·mash·ta

83f **I've lost my wallet.**

財布をなくしました。
sai·fu o na·ku·shi·mash·ta

What am I accused of?

どんな理由で告訴
されるのですか?
don·na ri·yū de ko·ku·so
sa·re·ru no des ka

I didn't realise I was doing anything wrong.

違法行為をしているつもり
はありませんでした。
i·hō·kōy o shi·te i·ru tsu·mo·ri
wa a·ri·ma·sen desh·ta

I didn't do it.

私はやっていません。
wa·ta·shi wa yat·te i·ma·sen

Can I make a phone call?

電話をかけてもいいですか?
den·wa o ka·ke·te mo ī des ka

Can I have a lawyer (who speaks English)?

(英語ができる)弁護士を
お願いします。
(ē·go ga de·ki·ru) ben·go·shi o
o·ne·gai shi·mas

84a **I want to contact my consulate.**

領事館に連絡したいです。
ryō·ji·kan ni ren·ra·ku shi·tai des

84b **I want to contact my embassy.**

大使館に連絡
したいです。
tai·shi·kan ni ren·ra·ku
shi·tai des

Health

KEY PHRASES

Where's the nearest hospital?	この近くの病院はどこですか?	ko·no chi·ka·ku no byō·in wa do·ko des ka
I'm sick.	私は病気です。	wa·ta·shi wa byō·ki des
I need a doctor.	お医者さんが必要です。	oy·sha·san ga hi·tsu·yō des
I'm on medication for ...	…の薬を飲んでいます。	... no ku·su·ri o non·de i·mas
I'm allergic to ...	私は…アレルギーです。	wa·ta·shi wa ... a·re·ru·gī des

---

85a Where's the nearest dentist?
この近くの歯医者はどこですか?
ko·no chi·ka·ku no ha·i·sha wa do·ko des ka

85b Where's the nearest doctor?
この近くの医者はどこですか?
ko·no chi·ka·ku no i·sha wa do·ko des ka

85c Where's the nearest hospital?
この近くの病院はどこですか?
ko·no chi·ka·ku no byō·in wa do·ko des ka

85d Where's the nearest (24-hour) pharmacist?
この近くの(24時間営業の)薬局はどこですか?
ko·no chi·ka·ku no (ni·jū·yo·ji·kan ē·gyō no) yak·kyo·ku wa do·ko des ka

86a I need a doctor.

お医者さんが必要です。
oy·sha·san ga hi·tsu·yō des

I need a doctor (who speaks English).

(英語ができる)お医者さん
が必要です。
(ē·go ga de·ki·ru) oy·sha·san ga hi·tsu·yō des

86b Could I see a female doctor?

女性のお医者さんをお願い
できますか?
jo·sē no oy·sha·san o o·ne·gai de·ki·mas ka

Could the doctor come here?

お医者さんはこちらに
来ることができますか?
oy·sha·san wa ko·chi·ra ni ku·ru·ko·to ga de·ki·mas ka

86c I've run out of my medication.

薬がなくなりました。
ku·su·ri ga na·ku·na·ri mash·ta

I don't want a blood transfusion.

輸血はしたくないです。
yu·ke·tsu wa shi·ta·ku·nai des

I've been vaccinated against tetanus.

私は破傷風の
予防注射をしました。
wa·ta·shi wa ha·shō·fū no yo·bō·chū·sha o shi·mash·ta

I've been vaccinated against typhoid.

私はチフスの
予防注射をしました。
wa·ta·shi wa chif·su no yo·bō·chū·sha o shi·mash·ta

I've been vaccinated against hepatitis A/B/C.

私はA/B/C型肝炎の
予防注射をしました。
wa·ta·shi wa ē/bī/shī· ga·ta·kan·en no yo·bō·chū·sha o shi·mash·ta

He/She has been vaccinated against ...

彼/彼女は…の
予防注射をしました。
ka·re/ka·no·jo wa ... no yo·bō·chū·sha o shi·mash·ta

Symptoms & Conditions

86d	I'm sick.	私は病気です。 wa·ta·shi wa byō·ki des
	My friend/child is (very) sick.	友達/子供は (ひどい)病気です。 to·mo·da·chi/ko·do·mo wa (hi·doy) byō·ki des
	He/She is having a/an ...	彼/彼女は…を 起こしています ka·re/ka·no·jo·wa ... o o·ko·shi·te i·mas

allergic reaction	アレルギー反応	a·re·ru·gī·han·nō
asthma attack	喘息発作	zen·so·ku·hos·sa
epileptic fit	てんかん発作	ten·kan·hos·sa
heart attack	心臓発作	shin·zō·hos·sa

I feel ...	私は…	wa·ta·shi wa ...

better	良く なりました	yo·ku na·ri·mash·ta
dizzy	めまいがします	me·mai ga shi·mas
hot and cold	暑くなったり 寒くなったり します	a·tsu·ku nat·ta·ri sa·mu·ku nat·ta·ri shi·mas
weak	ちからが ありません	chi·ka·ra ga a·ri·ma·sen
worse	悪くなって います	wa·ru·ku nat·te i·mas

🔊 LISTEN FOR

どうしましたか？	dō shi·mash·ta ka	
	What's the problem?	
どこが痛いですか？	do·ko ga i·tai des ka	
	Where does it hurt?	
熱がありますか？	ne·tsu ga a·ri·mas ka	
	Do you have a temperature?	
いつからこのような 状態ですか？	i·tsu ka·ra ko·no yō·na jō·tai des ka	
	How long have you been like this?	
前にもなったことが ありますか？	ma·e ni mo nat·ta ko·to ga a·ri·mas ka	
	Have you had this before?	

I've been injured.	けがをしました。 ke·ga o shi·mash·ta	
87a It hurts here.	ここが痛いです。 ko·ko ga i·tai des	
87b I'm nauseous.	吐き気がします ha·ki·ke ga shi·mas	
I've been vomiting.	私はもどしています。 wa·ta·shi wa mo·do·shi·te i·mas	
I can't sleep.	眠れません。 ne·mu·re·ma·sen	
I'm on medication for ...	…の薬を飲んでいます。 ... no ku·su·ri o non·de i·mas	
I have ...	私は…があります。 wa·ta·shi wa ... ga a·ri·mas	
87c I have asthma.	私は喘息が あります wa·ta·shi wa zen·so·ku ga a·ri·mas	
87d I have diarrhoea.	下痢がしています。 ge·ri o shi·te·i·mas	

🔊 LISTEN FOR

お酒を飲みますか?	o·sa·ke o no·mi·mas ka Do you drink?
タバコを吸いますか?	ta·ba·ko o su·i·mas ka Do you smoke?
麻薬を使用して いますか?	ma·ya·ku o shi·yō shi·te i·mas ka Do you take drugs?
アレルギーがありますか?	a·re·ru·gī ga a·ri·mas ka Are you allergic to anything?
薬を使用していますか?	ku·su·ri o shi·yō shi·te i·mas ka Are you on medication?
最近、性交渉が ありましたか?	sai·kin sē·kō·shō ga a·ri·mash·ta ka Are you sexually active?
コンドームなしの性交渉 がありましたか?	kon·dō·mu·na·shi no sē·kō·shō ga a·ri·mash·ta ka Have you had unprotected sex?
入院する必要が あります。	nyū·in su·ru hi·tsu·yō ga a·ri·mas You need to be admitted to hospital.

87e **I have a headache.**	頭痛があります。 zu·tsū ga a·ri·mas	
I've recently had ...	私は最近…が ありました。 wa·ta·shi wa sai·kin ... ga a·ri·mash·ta	
He/She has ...	彼/彼女は…があります。 ka·re/ka·no·jo wa ... ga a·ri·mas	

For more symptoms and conditions, see the **dictionary**.

Allergies

I'm allergic to ...	私は…アレルギーです。 wa·ta·shi wa ... a·re·ru·gī des
He's/She's allergic to ...	…アレルギーです。 ... a·re·ru·gī des
88a I'm allergic to antibiotics.	私は抗生物質 アレルギーです。 wa·ta·shi wa kō·sē·bus·shi·tsu a·re·ru·gī des
88b I'm allergic to anti-inflammatories.	私は抗炎症薬 アレルギーです。 wa·ta·shi wa kō·en·shō·ya·ku a·re·ru·gī des
88c I'm allergic to aspirin.	私はアスピリン アレルギーです。 wa·ta·shi wa as·pi·rin a·re·ru·gī des
88d I'm allergic to penicillin.	私はペニシリン アレルギーです。 wa·ta·shi wa pe·ni·shi·rin a·re·ru·gī des
I have a skin allergy.	皮膚アレルギーです。 hi·fu·a·re·ru·gī des

For food-related allergies, see **vegetarian & special meals** (p193).

Women's Health

(I think) I'm pregnant.	私は妊娠してい （ると思い）ます。 wa·ta·shi wa nin·shin shi·te i(·ru to o·moy)·mas
I'm on the pill.	ピルを飲んでいます。 pi·ru o non·de i·mas

I need a pregnancy test.	妊娠テストをお願い します。 nin·shin·tes·to o o·ne·gai shi·mas
I haven't had my period for (six) weeks.	(6)週間月経が ありません。 (ro·ku)·shū·kan gek·kē ga a·ri·ma·sen
I need contraception.	避妊薬をお願いします。 hi·nin·ya·ku o o·ne·gai shi·mas
I need the morning-after pill.	モーニングアフターピルを お願いします。 mō·nin·gu·af·tā·pi·ru o o·ne·gai shi·mas

89a
eye
目
me

89b
ear
耳
mi·mi

89c
arm
腕
u·de

89d
hand
手
te

bum
お尻
o·shi·ri

89e
foot
足
a·shi

89f
head
頭
a·ta·ma

89g
nose
鼻
ha·na

89h
mouth
口
ku·chi

89i
chest
胸
mu·ne

89j
stomach
お腹
o·na·ka

89k
leg
脚
a·shi

Parts of the Body

My ... hurts.	…が痛いです。 ... ga i·tai des
I can't move my ...	…を動かせません。 ... o u·go·ka·se·ma·sen
I have a cramp in my ...	…がつりました。 ... ga tsu·ri·mash·ta
My ... is swollen.	…が腫れています。 ... ga ha·re·te i·mas

Dentist

I have a broken tooth.	歯が折れました。 ha ga o·re·mash·ta
I have a toothache.	歯が痛いです。 ha ga i·tai des
I've lost a filling.	歯の詰め物が とれました。 ha no tsu·me·mo·no ga to·re·mash·ta
My dentures are broken.	入れ歯がこわれました。 i·re·ba ga ko·wa·re·mash·ta
My gums hurt.	歯茎が痛いです。 ha·gu·ki ga i·tai des
I don't want it extracted.	抜かないでください。 nu·ka·nai·de ku·da·sai

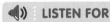

🔊 **LISTEN FOR**

大きく開いて。	ō·ki·ku hi·rai·te	Open wide.
うがいをして ください。	u·gai o shi·te ku·da·sai	Rinse.

🔊 LISTEN FOR

1日2回(食事時)。	i·chi·ni·chi ni·kai (sho·ku·ji·do·ki) Twice a day (with food).
これを使ったことが ありますか?	ko·re o tsu·kat·ta ko·to ga a·ri·mas ka Have you taken this before?

I need a filling.	詰め物をして ください。 tsu·me·mo·no o shi·te ku·da·sai
Ouch!	痛い! i·tai

Chemist

I need something for (a headache).	なにか(頭痛)に 効くものが必要です。 na·ni ka (zu·tsū) ni ki·ku·mo·no ga hi·tsu·yō des
Do I need a prescription for (antihistamines)?	(抗ヒスタミン剤)の 処方箋が必要ですか? (kō·his·ta·min·sai) no sho·hō·sen ga hi·tsu·yō des ka
I have a prescription.	処方箋があります。 sho·hō·sen ga a·ri·mas
How many times a day?	1日何回ですか? i·chi·ni·chi nan·kai des ka
Will it make me drowsy?	眠くなりますか? ne·mu·ku na·ri·mas ka

Food

EATING OUT	172
SELF-CATERING	189
VEGETARIAN & SPECIAL MEALS	193

Eating Out

KEY PHRASES

Can you recommend a restaurant?	どこかいい レストランを 知っていますか?	do·ko ka ī res·to·ran o shit·te i·mas ka
I'd like to reserve a table for two people.	2人の 予約を お願いします。	fu·ta·ri no yo·ya·ku o o·ne·gai shi·mas
I'd like the menu, please.	メニューをお願い します。	me·nyū o o·ne·gai shi·mas
I'd like a beer, please.	ビールをお願い します。	bī·ru o o·ne·gai shi·mas
I'd like the bill, please.	お勘定を お願いします。	o·kan·jō o o·ne·gai shi·mas

Basics

Alternative terms are commonly used for meals, the first options given below being slightly more formal.

90a 90b breakfast	朝食/朝ごはん chō·sho·ku/a·sa·go·han
90c 90d lunch	昼食/昼ごはん chū·sho·ku/hi·ru·go·han
90e 90f dinner	夕食/晩ごはん yū·sho·ku/ban·go·han
90g 90h snack	軽食/おやつ kē·sho·ku/o·ya·tsu
90i eat	食べる ta·be·ru

90j drink	飲む no·mu
I'd like ...	…をください。 ... o·ku·da·sai
91a I'm hungry.	お腹がすきました。 o·na·ka ga su·ki·ma·shi·ta

Finding a Place to Eat

91b Can you recommend a cafe?	どこかいいカフェを知っていますか? do·ko ka ī ka·fe o shit·te i·mas ka
91c Can you recommend a restaurant?	どこかいいレストランを知っていますか? do·ko ka ī res·to·ran o shit·te i·mas ka
Where would you go for a cheap meal?	安い食事をするならどこに行きますか? ya·su·i sho·ku·ji o su·ru na·ra do·ko ni i·ki·mas ka

FOOD EATING OUT

CULTURE TIP

Japanese Meals

Traditional Japanese breakfasts usually consist of rice (go·han ご飯), miso soup (mi·so·shi·ru 味噌汁), raw egg (na·ma·ta·ma·go 生卵), dried fish (hi·mo·no 干物), dried seaweed (no·ri 海苔) and pickles (tsu·ke·mo·no 漬物). Some eat fermented soy beans (nat·tō 納豆) at breakfast. Western-style breakfasts are also common.

Lunch boxes (ben·tō 弁当) often include rice, soup, pickles, a main dish and fruit. Noodles – so·ba (そば), sō·men (そうめん), rā·men (ラーメン) or u·don (うどん) – are also common fare for lunch. Dinner will usually include rice, soup and a side dish (o·ka·zu おかず).

For more Japanese dishes and ingredients, see the **menu decoder** (p196).

Where would you go for local specialities?	名物を食べるなら どこに行きますか? mē·bu·tsu o ta·be·ru na·ra do·ko ni i·ki·mas ka
Where would you go for a celebration?	お祝いをするならどこに 行きいますか? oy·wai o su·ru na·ra do·ko ni i·ki·mas ka
I'd like to reserve a table for one person/two people.	1人/2人の予約を お願いします。 hi·to·ri/fu·ta·ri no yo·ya·ku o o·ne·gai shi·mas
I'd like to reserve a table for (eight) o'clock.	(8)時の予約を お願いします。 (ha·chi)·ji no yo·ya·ku o o·ne·gai shi·mas
Are you still serving food?	まだ食事が できますか? ma·da sho·ku·ji ga de·ki·mas ka
How long is the wait?	どのくらい待ちますか? do·no ku·rai ma·chi·mas ka

At the Restaurant

When you book for more than three, you'll always be seated at a table. When you make a booking for two or less, make sure you request a table if you don't want to end up at the counter. You can say 'at a table, please': tē·bu·ru de o·ne·gai shi·mas.

91d **I'd like a table for (two), please.**
(2)名分のテーブルを
お願いします。
(ni)·mē·bun no tē·bu·ru o
o·ne·gai shi·mas

 For two, please.   2名です。   ni mē des

Eating Out

Can I see the menu, please?

メニューをお願いします。
me·nyū o o·ne·gai shi·mas

What would you recommend for ...?

お勧めの...は何ですか？
o·su·su·me no ... wa nan des ka

 the main meal
メインディッシュ
mēn dish

dessert
デザート
de·zā·to

 drinks
飲み物
no·mi·mo·no

Can you bring me ..., please?

…をください。
... o ku·da·sai

I'd like the bill, please.

お勘定をお願いします。
o·kan·jō o o·ne·gai shi·mas

🔊 LISTEN FOR

閉店です。	hē·ten des	We're closed.
満席です。	man·se·ki des	We're full.
何名様?	nan·mē·sa·ma	How many people?
少々お待ち ください。	shō·shō o·ma·chi ku·da·sai	One moment, please.

91e the nonsmoking section	禁煙席 kin·en·se·ki	
91f the smoking section	喫煙席 ki·tsu·en·se·ki	
91g I'd like the menu, please.	メニューをお願いします。 me·nyū o o·ne·gai shi·mas	
I'd like a children's menu, please.	子供のメニューを お願いします。 ko·do·mo no me·nyū o o·ne·gai shi·mas	
91h I'd like the drink list, please.	ドリンクメニューを お願いします。 do·rin·ku me·nyū o o·ne·gai shi·mas	
I'd like a half portion, please.	半人前を お願いします。 han·nim·ma·e o o·ne·gai shi·mas	
91i What would you recommend?	なにがお勧めですか? na·ni ga o·su·su·me des ka	
What's in that dish?	あの料理に何が入って いますか? a·no ryō·ri ni na·ni ga hait·te i·mas ka	

Can you tell me what traditional foods I should try?	伝統的な食べ物は どんなものがおすすめ ですか？	den·tō·te·ki na ta·be·mo·no wa don·na mo·no ga o·su·su·me des ka
I'll have that.	あれをください。	a·re o ku·da·sai
Please decide for me.	おまかせします。	o·ma·ka·se shi·mas
Does it take long to prepare?	料理に時間がかかりますか？	ryō·ri ni ji·kan ga ka·ka·ri·mas ka
Is service included in the bill?	サービス料込みですか？	sā·bis·ryō ko·mi des ka
Are these complimentary?	これはただですか？	ko·re wa ta·da des ka
I'd like (the chicken).	（鶏肉）をお願いします。	(to·ri·ni·ku) o o·ne·gai shi·mas
I'd like a local speciality.	地元の名物を お願いします。	ji·mo·to no mē·bu·tsu o o·ne·gai shi·mas

Requests

Please bring ...	…をください。	... o ku·da·sai

a knife/fork	ナイフ/フォーク	nai·fu/fō·ku
a glass	グラス	gu·ra·su
a serviette	ナプキン	na·pu·kin
a spoon	スプーン	spūn
a wineglass	ワイングラス	wain·gu·ra·su

FOOD **EATING OUT**

🔊 LISTEN FOR

お決まりでしょうか?	o·ki·ma·ri de·shō ka What can I get for you?
…がお好きですか?	... ga o·su·ki des ka Do you like ...?
…をおすすめします。	... o o·su·su·me shi·mas I suggest the ...
どのように料理 いたしましょうか?	do·no yō ni ryō·ri i·ta·shi·ma·shō ka How would you like that cooked?
どうぞ。	dō·zo Here you go!

I'd like it ...　　　　　　　　…ください。
　　　　　　　　　　　　　　　... ku·da·sai

boiled (in hot water)	ゆでて	yu·de·te
boiled (in stock)	煮て	ni·te
deep fried	揚げて	a·ge·te
fried	炒めて	i·ta·me·te
grilled	グリルして	gu·ri·ru shi·te
medium	ミディアムに して	mi·dya·mu ni shi·te
rare	レアにして	rair ni shi·te
re-heated	温めなお して	a·ta·ta·me·now· shi·te
steamed	蒸して	mu·shi·te
well done	ウェルダンに して	we·ru·dan ni shi·te
with the dressing on the side	ドレッシングを 別にして	do·res·shin·gu o be·tsu ni shi·te

I don't want it deep fried.	揚げないでください。 a·ge·nai·de ku·da·sai
I don't want it fried.	炒めないでください。 i·ta·me·nai·de ku·da·sai
I don't want it re-heated.	温めなおさないで ください。 a·ta·ta·me·now·sa·nai·de ku·da·sai
I'd like it with ...	…を付けてお願いします。 ... o tsu·ke·te o·ne·gai shi·mas
I'd like it without ...	…を抜きでお願いします。 ... o nu·ki de o·ne·gai shi·mas

chilli	唐辛子	tō·ga·ra·shi
garlic	ニンニク	nin·ni·ku
ginger	ショウガ	shō·ga
sauce	ソース	sō·su
seaweed	のり	no·ri
soy sauce	しょう油	shō·yu
horseradish	わさび	wa·sa·bi

See also **vegetarian & special meals** (p193).

Compliments & Complaints

Bon appetit!	いただきます (lit: I receive) i·ta·da·ki·mas
I love this dish.	この料理が大好きです。 ko·no ryō·ri ga dai·su·ki des
I love the local cuisine.	地元料理が大好きです。 ji·mo·to·ryō·ri ga dai·su·ki des
That was delicious!	おいしかった。 oy·shi·kat·ta

table
テーブル
tē·bu·ru

tea cup
湯飲み茶碗
yu·no·mi·ja·wan

side plate
小皿
ko·za·ra

teapot
急須
kyū·su

soup bowl
お椀
o·wan

**soy sauce
bottle**
しょう油注し
shō·yu·sa·shi

spoon
スプーン
spūn

rice bowl
茶碗
cha·wan

hot hand towel
おしぼり
o·shi·bo·ri

chopsticks
はし
ha·shi

chopstick holder
はし置き
ha·shi·o·ki

It was a real feast.	ごちそうさま go·chi·sō·sa·ma
I'm full.	お腹がいっぱいです。 o·na·ka ga ip·pai des
This is cold.	これは冷たいです ko·re wa tsu·me·tai des
This is spicy.	これはスパイシーです ko·re wa spai·shī des
This is superb.	これは素晴らしいです ko·re wa su·ba·ra·shī des

Paying the Bill

| **91j** I'd like the bill, please. | お勘定をお願いします。
o·kan·jō o o·ne·gai shi·mas |
| There's a mistake in the bill. | 請求書に間違いが
あります。
sē·kyū·sho ni ma·chi·gai ga a·ri·mas |

Nonalcoholic Drinks

92a mineral water	ミネラルウォーター mi·ne·ra·ru·wō·tā
sparkling ... /still ...	炭酸…/ 炭酸なしの… tan·san.../ tan·san·na·shi no...
92b boiled water	お湯 o·yu
lemonade	レモネード re·mo·nē·do

🔍 LOOK FOR

前菜	zen·sai	appetisers
スープ	sū·pu	soups
アントレー	an·to·rē	entrees
サラダ	sa·ra·da	salads
メインコース	mēn·kō·su	main courses
デザート	de·zā·to	desserts
一品料理	ip·pin·ryō·ri	à la carte
飲み物	no·mi·mo·no	drinks

For more menu items, see the **menu decoder** (p196).

FOOD EATING OUT

milk	ミルク	mi·ru·ku
92c (orange) juice	(オレンジ)ジュース	(o·ren·ji)·jū·su
92d soft drink	ソフトドリンク	so·fu·to·do·rin·ku
water	水	mi·zu
92e I'd like a cup of tea.	紅茶を1杯お願いします。	kō·cha o ip·pai o·ne·gai shi·mas
92f I'd like a cup of coffee.	コーヒーを1杯お願いします。	kō·hī o ip·pai o·ne·gai shi·mas
92g with milk	ミルク入り	mi·ru·ku·i·ri
92h without milk	ミルクなし	mi·ru·ku·na·shi
92i with sugar	砂糖入り	sa·tō·i·ri
92j without sugar	砂糖なし	sa·tō·na·shi
... coffee	…コーヒー	... kō·hī

black	ブラック	bu·rak·ku
iced	アイス	ai·su
strong	濃い	koy
weak	薄い	u·su·i
white	ホワイト	ho·wai·to

Japanese green tea	お茶	o·cha
barley tea	麦茶	mu·gi·cha

CULTURE TIP

Japanese Eateries

Many eating places specialise in serving up one particular type of dish. Look for the ·ya (屋) after the name of a dish and that's usually where you'll find it. For example, ton·ka·tsu·ya (とんかつ屋) specialise in *tonkatsu* (pork cutlet), sha·bu·sha·bu·ya (しゃぶしゃぶ屋) in *shabu shabu* hot pot, so·ba·ya (そば屋) in *soba* (buckwheat noodles) and su·shi·ya (すし屋) in sushi. Other popular alternatives are ro·ba·ta·ya·ki (ろばた焼き), where food is grilled, ya·ki·to·ri (焼き鳥) restaurants specialising in variations of skewered chicken, and o·den (おでん) shops, whipping up stewed hot pot. For a quick bite and booze, try the i·za·ka·ya (居酒屋), or a kis·sa·ten (喫茶店) cafe-style establishment. Other options are the sho·ku·dō (食堂), cheap restaurants or dining halls dishing up filling and inexpensive food, or kai·ten·zu·shi (回転ずし), where sushi comes on a rotating conveyer belt.

green leaf tea	煎茶	sen·cha
oolong tea	ウーロン茶	ū·ron·cha
powdered green tea	抹茶	mat·cha
roasted rice tea	玄米茶	gem·mai·chai
cappucino	カプチーノ	ka·pu·chī·no
decaffeinated	デカフェ	de·ka·fe
espresso	エスプレッソ	es·pres·so
latte	カフェラテ	ka·fe·ra·te

CULTURE TIP Chopstick Etiquette
Don't wave your chopsticks (ha·shi はし) around, rather put them down if you need to make hand gestures. Never leave them standing up in your food either – this position is associated with death because of the similarity with incense sticks offered to the dead. Also note that chopsticks are usually referred to with the honorific o (お), ie o·ha·shi (おはし).

Alcoholic Drinks

beer	ビール bī·ru
93a brandy	ブランデー bu·ran·dē
champagne	シャンペン sham·pen
chilled sake	冷酒 rē·shu
cocktail	カクテル ka·ku·te·ru
plum wine	梅酒 u·me·shu
sake	酒 sa·ke
shochu highball	酎ハイ chū·hai
shochu spirit	焼酎 shō·chū
warm sake	お燗 o·kan
a shot of rum	ラムをショットで ra·mu o shot·to de

a shot of vodka	ウォッカをショットで	wok·ka o shot·to de
93b a shot of (whisky)	ウィスキーをショットで	wis·kī o shot·to de
93c a bottle of (red) wine	(赤)ワインをボトルで	(a·ka)·wain o bo·to·ru de
93d a glass of (white) wine	(白)ワインをグラスで	(shi·ro)·wain o gu·ra·su de
dessert wine	デザートワイン	de·zā·to·wain
rosé	ロゼ	ro·ze
sparkling wine	スパークリング	spā·ku·rin·gu

あれをください。
a·re o ku·da·sai
I'll have that.

93e a bottle of beer	ビールをビンで	bī·ru o bin de
93f a glass of beer	ビールをグラスで	bī·ru o gu·ra·su de
a jug of beer	ビールをジャグで	bī·ru o ja·gu de
a large mug of beer	ビールを大ジョッキで	bī·ru o dai·jok·ki de
a small bottle of beer	ビールを中ビンで	bī·ru o chū·bin de

In the Bar

When going out, keep in mind that some bars impose a 'table charge' (tē·bu·ru·chā·ji テーブルチャージ). At the bar, if you fancy a bite with your drinks, check out which bar snacks (o·tsu·ma·mi おつまみ) are on offer.

Excuse me.	すみません。	su·mi·ma·sen
I'm next.	次は私です。	tsu·gi wa wa·ta·shi des
93g 🅠 **What would you like?**	何を飲みますか?	na·ni o no·mi·mas ka
93h 🅐 **I'll have (beer).**	（ビール）をお願いします。	(bī·ru) o o·ne·gai shi·mas
Same again, please.	同じのをお願いします。	o·na·ji no o o·ne·gai shi·mas
No ice, thanks.	氷なしでお願いします。	kō·ri·na·shi de o·ne·gai shi·mas
93i **I'll buy you a drink.**	1杯おごります。	ip·pai o·go·ri·mas
It's my round next.	次は私の番です。	tsu·gi wa wa·ta·shi no ban des
Do you serve meals here?	食事はできますか?	sho·ku·ji wa de·ki·mas ka
How much is the table charge?	テーブルチャージはいくらですか?	tē·bu·ru·chā·ji wa i·ku·ra des ka

> **CULTURE TIP**
>
> **Tea Ceremony**
> The sha·no·yu (茶の湯), or sa·do (茶道), as they're more commonly known, are quite elaborate tea ceremonies governed by a set of centuries-old rules and conventions. Guests are served the powdered green tea in a tea bowl that's larger than the standard tea cup, often a special piece of art in itself. Drink it by taking three or four large sips of tea, ensuring nothing remains in the bowl. You're allowed to make a slurping noise when drinking hot tea. Sweets are also served.

Drinking Up

93j Cheers!	乾杯! kam·pai
This is hitting the spot.	お腹に染みます。 o·na·ka ni shi·mi·mas
I feel fantastic!	気分がいいです。 ki·bun ga ī des
I think I've had one too many.	ちょっと飲みすぎました。 chot·to no·mi·su·gi·mash·ta
I'm feeling drunk.	酔いました。 yoy·mash·ta
I feel ill.	気分が悪いです。 ki·bun ga wa·ru·i des
Where's the toilet?	トイレはどこですか? toy·re wa do·ko des ka
I'm tired. I'd better go home.	疲れました。 うちに帰ります。 tsu·ka·re·mash·ta u·chi ni ka·e·ri·mas

🔊 **LISTEN FOR**

何にしますか?	nan ni shi·mas ka	What are you having?
もうじゅうぶん でしょう。	mō jū·bun de shō	I think you've had enough.
ラストオーダー です。	ras·to·ō·dā des	Last orders.

Can you call a taxi for me?	タクシーを呼んで くれますか? tak·shī o yon·de ku·re·mas ka
I don't think you should drive.	運転しないほうがいいと 思います。 un·ten shi·nai hō ga ī to o·moy·mas

Self-Catering

KEY PHRASES

What's the local speciality?	地元料理は何がありますか?	ji·mo·to·ryō·ri wa na·ni ga a·ri·mas ka
Where can I find the ... section?	…のコーナーはどこですか?	... no kō·nā wa do·ko des ka
I'd like ...	…ください。	... ku·da·sai

Buying Food

94a **What's the local speciality?**

地元料理は何が
ありますか?
ji·mo·to·ryō·ri wa na·ni ga
a·ri·mas ka

Do you sell locally produced food?

地元産の食べ物は
ありますか?
ji·mo·to·san no ta·be·mo·no wa
a·ri·mas ka

Do you sell organic produce?

オーガニックの食べ物は
ありますか?
ō·ga·nik·ku no ta·be·mo·no wa
a·ri·mas ka

94b **What's that?**

それは何ですか?
so·re wa nan des ka

Can I taste it?

味見してもいいですか?
a·ji·mi shi·te mo ī des ka

Can I have a bag, please?

1袋ください。
hi·to·fu·ku·ro ku·da·sai

🔊 LISTEN FOR

いらっしゃいませ。	i·ras·shai·ma·se
	Welcome./Can I help you?
なにをお探しですか?	na·ni o o·sa·ga·shi des ka
	What would you like?
他に何か	ho·ka ni na·ni ka o·sa·ga·shi des ka
お探しですか?	Anything else?
ございません。	go·zai·ma·sen.
	There isn't any.
(5千円)です。	(go·sen·en) des
	That's (5000 yen).

How much is a kilo of (rice)?	(米)1キロいくらですか? (ko·me) i·chi·ki·ro i·ku·ra des ka
How much?	いくら? i·ku·ra
I'd like this/that one.	これ/あれをください。 ko·re/a·re o ku·da·sai
94c I'd like ...	…ください。 ... ku·da·sai
95a I'd like (200) grams.	(200)グラムください。 (ni·hya·ku)·gu·ra·mu ku·da·sai
95b I'd like (two) kilos.	(2)キロください。 (ni)·ki·ro ku·da·sai
95c I'd like (three) pieces.	(3)個ください。 (san)·ko ku·da·sai
95d I'd like (six) slices.	(6)枚ください。 (ro·ku)·mai ku·da·sai
a dozen	1ダース i·chi·dās
a packet	1パック hi·to·pak·ku

(just) a little	（ほんの）少し
	(hon·no) su·ko·shi
some ...	…をいくらか
	... o i·ku·ra ka
95e Less.	少なく。
	su·ku·na·ku
95f More.	もっと。
	mot·to
95g Enough.	充分です。
	jū·bun des
Do you have anything cheaper?	安いものがありますか？
	ya·su·i mo·no ga a·ri·mas ka
Do you have other kinds?	他のものがありますか？
	ho·ka no mo·no ga a·ri·mas ka
Where can I find the ... section?	…のコーナーはどこですか？
	... no kō·nā wa do·ko des ka

dairy	乳製品	nyū·sē·hin
fish	魚	sa·ka·na
frozen goods	冷凍食品	rē·tō·sho·ku·hin
fruit and vegetable	果物と 野菜	ku·da·mo·no to ya·sai
meat	肉	ni·ku
poultry	鳥肉	to·ri·ni·ku

Cooking

Could I please borrow a (bottle opener)?	（栓抜き）を貸して もらえませんか？
	(sen·nu·ki) o ka·shi·te mo·ra·e·ma·sen ka
I need a (can opener).	（缶切り）が必要です。
	(kan·ki·ri) ga hi·tsu·yō des

bowl	ボール bō·ru
chopping knife	包丁 hō·chō
corkscrew	コークスクリュー kō·ku·sku·ryū
miso-soup bowl	お椀 o·wan
pair of chopsticks	箸 ha·shi
pair of disposable chopsticks	割り箸 wa·ri·ba·shi
rice cooker	炊飯器 su·i·han·ki
wok	中華鍋 chū·ka·na·be
cooked	火が通った hi ga tōt·ta
cured	保存 ho·zon
dried	乾燥 kan·sō
fresh	新鮮 shin·sen
frozen	冷凍 rē·tō
raw	なま na·ma
smoked	燻製 kun·sē

For more cooking implements, see the **dictionary**.

Vegetarian & Special Meals

KEY PHRASES

I'm a vegetarian.	私は ベジタリアンです。	wa·ta·shi wa be·ji·ta·ri·an des
Could you prepare a meal without ...?	…を使わない 料理をお願い できますか?	...o tsu·ka·wa·nai ryō·ri o o·ne·gai de·ki·mas ka
I'm allergic to ...	私は… にアレルギーが あります。	wa·ta·shi wa ... ni a·re·ru·gī ga a·ri·mas

Special Diets & Allergies

Halal and kosher food might be hard to come by, even in the big smoke, but you might want to try your luck with these phrases.

96a Is there a vegetarian restaurant (near here)?	(この近くに) ベジタリアンレストランは ありますか? (ko·no chi·ka·ku ni) be·ji·ta·ri·an res·to·ran wa a·ri·mas ka
Is there a kosher restaurant?	ユダヤ教徒のための コーシャーレストラン はありますか? yu·da·ya·kyō·to no ta·me no kō·shā res·to·ran wa a·ri·mas ka

Is there a halal restaurant?	イスラム教徒のための ハラルレストランは ありますか? i·su·ra·mu·kyō·to no ta·me no ha·ra·ru res·to·ran wa a·ri·mas ka
I'm on a special diet.	私は特殊な 食餌制限をしています。 wa·ta·shi wa to·ku·shu na sho·ku·ji·sē·gen o shi·te i·mas
I'm a vegan.	私は厳格な 菜食主義者です。 wa·ta·shi wa gen·ka·ku na sai·sho·ku·shu·gi·sha des
I'm a vegetarian.	私はベジタリアンです。 wa·ta·shi wa be·ji·ta·ri·an des
96b I'm allergic to dairy produce.	私は乳製品に アレルギーがあります。 wa·ta·shi wa nyū·sē·hin ni a·re·ru·gī ga a·ri·mas
96c I'm allergic to gluten.	私はグルテンに アレルギーがあります。 wa·ta·shi wa gu·ru·ten ni a·re·ru·gī ga a·ri·mas
96d I'm allergic to nuts.	私はナッツ類に アレルギーがあります。 wa·ta·shi wa nat·tsu·ru·i ni a·re·ru·gī ga a·ri·mas
96e I'm allergic to seafood.	私は海産物に アレルギーがあります。 wa·ta·shi wa kai·sam·bu·tsu ni a·re·ru·gī ga a·ri·mas

To explain your dietary restrictions with reference to religious beliefs, see **beliefs & culture** (p142).

Ordering Food

I don't eat ...	…は食べません。 ... wa ta·be·ma·sen
Could you prepare a meal without ...?	…を使わない料理をお願いできますか? ... o tsu·ka·wa·nai ryō·ri o o·ne·gai de·ki·mas ka
96f Could you prepare a meal without butter?	バターを使わない料理をお願いできますか? ba·tā o tsu·ka·wa·nai ryō·ri o o·ne·gai de·ki·mas ka
96g Could you prepare a meal without meat stock?	肉のだしを使わない料理をお願いできますか? ni·ku no da·shi o tsu·ka·wa·nai ryō·ri o o·ne·gai de·ki·mas ka
Is this ...?	これは…食品ですか? ko·re wa ... sho·ku·hin des ka

FOOD VEGETARIAN & SPECIAL MEALS

free of animal produce	動物性成分抜きの	dō·bu·tsu·sē·sē·bun·nu·ki no
free-range	放し飼いの	ha·na·shi·gai no
genetically modified	遺伝子組み替えの	i·den·shi·ku·mi·ka·e no
gluten-free	グルテン抜きの	gu·ru·ten·nu·ki no
low fat	脂肪分が低い	shi·bō·bun ga hi·ku·i
low in sugar	糖分が低い	tō·bun ga hi·ku·i
organic	オーガニックの	ō·ga·nik·ku no
salt-free	塩分抜きの	em·bun·nu·ki no

A

Menu
~ DECODER ~
料理読本

The Japanese dishes and ingredients in this menu decoder
are listed alphabetically, by pronunciation, so you can easily
understand what's on offer in Japanese eateries and ask for what
takes your fancy.

~ A ~

a·ba·ra あばら ribs

a·be·ka·wa·mo·chi 安倍川もち rice cakes covered with ki·na·ko & sugar (Shizuoka Prefecture)

a·bo·ga·do アボガド avocado

a·bu·ra 油 oil

a·bu·ra·a·ge 油揚げ deep-fried, thinly sliced tō·fu

... a·e …和え dishes dressed with ..., eg go·ma·a·e (dish dressed with sesame seeds)

a·e·mo·no 和え物 food blended with a dressing

...a·ge …揚げ fried ...

a·ge·da·shi·dō·fu 揚げだし豆腐 deep-fried tō·fu in fish stock

a·ge·mo·no 揚げ物 deep-fried food

a·hi·ru アヒル duck

ai·ga·mo 合鴨 Japanese duck

ai·na·me あいなめ green ling • ling cod (type of fish)

ais·ku·rī·mu アイスクリーム ice cream

a·ji アジ horse mackerel • scad (type of fish)

a·ka·a·ma·dai 赤アマダイ red a·ma·dai

a·ka·chi·ko·rī 赤チコリー radicchio

a·ka·gai 赤貝 ark shell • bearded clam • red clam

a·ka·ga·rē アカガレイ plaice

a·ka·in·gen 赤インゲン red kidney bean

a·ka·ji·so 赤じそ red shi·so

a·ka·kya·be·tsu 赤キャベツ red cabbage

a·ka·ren·zu·ma·me 赤レンズマメ red lentil

a·ka·ta·ma·ne·gi 赤たまねぎ red onion

a·ka·wain 赤ワイン red wine

a·ka·za·ke 赤酒 reddish wine made of rice, barley and/or wheat, to which wood ash is added (Kumamoto Prefecture)

a·ki·a·ji 秋味 see a·ra·ma·ki·za·ke

a·ki·ta·gai アキタ貝 north Japan term for scallop

a·ma·dai アマダイ blanquillo (type of fish) • ocean whitefish • tilefish (also called gu·ji)

a·ma·e·bi 甘エビ sweet prawn

a·mai 甘い sweet (taste)

a·ma·nat·tō 甘納豆 sugar-coated beans boiled in syrup

a·ma·za·ke 甘酒 sweet, warm sa·ke

B

ma·zu 甘酢 vinegar sweetened with ugar

m·bai 塩梅 literally 'salt-plum', mean-ng 'balance' – a term used by the der generation in reference to food

me 飴 candy • lolly

mi·ga·sa·ta·ke アミガサタケ morel ype of mushroom)

mi·ya·ki 網焼き cooked on a griddle

m·mi·tsu あんみつ a dessert made om fruit, boiled red peas, diced apanese gelatine & an·ko with syrup n top

m·pan アンパン baked bun filled ith an·ko

n あん sweet bean paste

na·kyū アナキュウ no·ri-rolled su·shi ith conger eel & cucumber

na·go アナゴ conger eel

n·cho·bi アンチョビ anchovy

n·ka·ke あんかけ dishes topped with sauce thickened with cornstarch

n·ko 杏子 a·zu·ki beans boiled with ugar

n·kō アンコウ angler • goosefish • onkfish

n·ko·ro·mo·chi あんころ餅 rice cake led with sweetened a·zu·ki beans

n·zu あんず apricot

n·zu·ta·ke アンズタケ chanterelle

o·ji·so 青じそ green beefsteak plant

o·no·ri あおのり a strong green type f no·ri seaweed, produced in flake orm & sprinkled on o·ko·no·mi·ya·ki & a·ki·so·ba

o·to あおと green peppers

o·ya·gi あおやぎ sunray surf clam • ough shell

o·yu あおゆ green yu·zu

ra アラ grouper • type of sea bass • ock cod that reaches up to 1m in ngth

ra あら left-over fish head, bones & fal used in hotpot, clear soups & stock

rai あらい a style of sa·shi·mi for hich raw, white-fleshed fish is thinly

sliced & washed in cold water to keep the meat firm

a·ra·ma·ki·za·ke 新巻鮭 salted whole salmon

a·ra·na·be アラ鍋 hotpot made with sea bass (Kyūshū)

a·ra·re あられ baked cracker made from mo·chi

a·sa no mi 麻の実 hemp seed

a·sa·ri あさり baby clam

a·sa·tsu·ki あさつき very thin spring onion

as·sa·ri あっさり general term for light (not greasy)

a·ta·ma·ryō·ri 頭料理 'head cuisine' using fish entrails (Taketa City)

ā·ti·chō·ku アーティチョーク artichoke

a·tsu·a·ge 厚揚げ fried tō·fu

a·wa アワ Italian millet • foxtail millet (rice substitute)

a·wa·bi あわび abalone

a·wa·bi no ka·su·zu·ke あわびの 粕漬け abalone pickled in sa·ke·ka·su (Iwate Prefecture)

a·wa·mo·ri 泡盛 alcoholic spirit made from rice (Okinawa Prefecture)

a·yu アユ sweetfish • smelt (salmo-noid food fish)

a·yu·ryō·ri アユ料理 sweetfish cuisine

a·zu·ki 小豆 red bean – ingredient for the sweet paste used as a filling in many Japanese cakes & confections

~ B ~

bai·gai バイ貝 bloody clam

ba·ka·gai バカ貝 see a·o·ya·gi

ban·cha 番茶 everyday tea made from the second tea harvest

ba·ni·ra バニラ vanilla

ba·ni·ku 馬肉 horse meat

ba·ra no mi·cha バラの実茶 rosehip tea

bas バス bass • sea perch

ba·sa·shi 馬刺し horse meat sa·shi·mi (Nagano Prefecture)

ba·tā バター butter
ba·tā·mi·ru·ku バターミルク buttermilk
bat·te·ra·zu·shi バッテラずし vinegared fish on pressed su·shi
be·bī·kōn ベビーコーン baby corn
bē·kon ベーコン bacon
bē·ku·do·po·te·to ベークドポテト baked potatoes
be·ni·ba·na·in·gen ベニバナインゲン runner bean
be·ni·shō·ga 紅しょうが red pickled ginger
be·ni·ta·de 紅たで water pepper, a dark red peppery garnish
ben·tō 弁当 lunch box normally containing rice with different vegetables, meat, fish & sometimes fruit
be·ra べら wrasse (type of fish)
be·rī ベリー berries
bet·ta·ra·zu·ke べったらづけ pickled dai·kon
bī·fu ビーフ beef
bī·fu·jā·kī ビーフジャーキー beef jerky
bī·fu·ka·tsu ビーフカツ beef cutlet
bi·fu·te·ki ビフテキ beef steak
bin·na·ga ビンナガ longfin tuna
bī·ru ビール beer • ale
bī·to·rū·to ビートルート beetroot
bi·wa びわ loquat (small yellow plum-like fruit)
bo·ra ボラ mullet
bo·ta·mo·chi 牡丹もち rice cake made from half sticky rice & half nonglutinous rice
bu·chin·gem·ma·me ブチインゲンマメ pinto bean
bu·dō ブドウ grapes
bu·na·shi·me·ji ぶなしめじ a small, yellow mushroom variety
bu·rak·ku·be·rī ブラックベリー blackberry
bu·rak·ku·pu·din·gu ブラックプディング black pudding
bu·ri ブリ amberjack • yellowtail (types of fish)

bu·ri·ko ブリコ ha·ta·ha·ta eggs (Akit Prefecture)
bu·rok·ko·rī ブロッコリー broccoli
bu·rū·be·rī ブルーベリー blueberry
bu·ta·ni·ku 豚肉 pork
bu·ta·ni·ku no shi·o·zu·ke 豚肉の塩漬け salted pork
bu·ta no shō·ga·ya·ki 豚の生姜焼き pork sautéed in ginger & shō·yu
bu·tsu·ji 仏事 Buddhist funerary cuisine

~ C ~

chā·han チャーハン fried rice
chai·bu チャイブ chive
cha·kai·se·ki 茶懐石 tea kai·se·ki
cham·pon チャンポン noodle soup
chan·ko·na·be ちゃんこ鍋 sumo wrestler's stew of meat & vegetables
cha no yu 茶の湯 tea ceremony
chā·shū·men チャーシュー麺 rā·men topped with sliced roast pork
cha·sō·men 茶そうめん noodles containing green tea
cha·wan·mu·shi 茶碗蒸 savoury steamed custard containing fish stock, chicken & gingko nuts
che·rī·to·ma·to チェリートマト cherry tomatoes • plum tomatoes
chi·dai チダイ 'blood tai' fish (smaller than the ma·dai)
chi·kin チキン chicken
chi·ko·rī チコリー chicory
chi·ku·wa ちくわ sausage-shaped minced fish meat
chi·ku·zen·ni 筑前煮 chicken, taro, carrots, go·bō, lotus root, kon·nya·ku, dried shī·ta·ke mushroom & snow peas stewed in a stock made of sugar shō·yu & mi·rin
chi·ma·ki ちまき nonglutinous-rice cake wrapped in large leaves
chim·pi 陳皮 citrus zest
chin·gen·sai チンゲンサイ bok choy
chip·pu チップ chips (crisps)

hi·ra·shi·zu·shi ちらしずし u·shi·me·shi topped with raw fish, ·bu·ra·a·ge & vegetables

hi·ri(·na·be) ちり(鍋) hotpot with white fish & vegetables

hi·ri·sō·su チリソース chilli sauce

hī·zu チーズ cheese

hō·ji チョウジ clove

ho·ko·rē·to チョコレート chocolate

hō·mi·ryō 調味料 seasoning

hop·pu チョップ chops

how·dā チャウダー chowder

hō·za·me チョウザメ sturgeon

hū·go·ku·cha 中国茶 Chinese tea

hū·hai 耐ハイ shō·chū served with various nonalcoholic mixers

hū·ka·so·ba 中華そば an old-fashioned term for rā·men – now suggests rā·men in a lighter, predominantly shō·yu-based da·shi

~ D ~

da·ga·shi 駄菓子 'no good' sweets – cheap and OK but a bit junky

dai·fu·ku·mo·chi 大福もち rice cake with an·ko inside

dai·gin·jō·shu 大吟醸酒 highest grade sa·ke – fruitier than gin·jō·shu

dai·kon 大根 Chinese radish (giant white radish)

dai·kon·o·ro·shi 大根おろし grated dai·kon

dai·ō ダイオウ rhubarb

dai·to·ku·ji·nat·tō 大徳寺納豆 soy beans fermented with yeast

dai·zu 大豆 soy bean

dan·go だんご round balls made from rice & flour

dan·sha·ku·i·mo 男爵芋 type of potato, especially common on Hokkaidō

da·ru·ma·ka·re·i ダルマカレイ turbot (type of fish)

da·shi だし stock, usually made from ka·tsu·o·bu·shi or kom·bu

da·shi·ji·ru だし汁 broth

da·te·ma·ki だて巻 sweetened rolled omelette, often served at New Year

de·be·ra でべら dried cinnamon flounder (Hiroshima Prefecture)

de·ka·fe no kō·cha デカフェの紅茶 decaffeinated tea

dem·bu でんぶ boiled & roasted snapper or cod flavoured with sugar & shō·yu & made into pink flakes that are used in su·shi rolls

den·ga·ku 田楽 dishes in which grilled fish, vegetables & tō·fu are topped with mi·so sauce

...·don …丼 rice with savoury topping

do·jō ドジョウ loach • oriental weatherfish (type of fish)

do·rai·bī·ru ドライビール 'dry beer' – it has a higher alcohol content & is more aerated than standard beer

do·rai·fu·rū·tsu ドライフルーツ dried fruit

do·ra·ya·ki どら焼き sweet a·zu·ki bean paste between two pancakes

do·te·na·be 土手鍋 hotpot with mi·so paste stock to which vegetables & seafood are added

~ E ~

e·bi エビ general term for prawn, shrimp, lobster & crayfish

e·bi·fu·rai エビフライ battered prawn

e·bi·sō·men エビそうめん shrimp sō·men

e·da·ma·me 枝豆 young soy bean – a favourite snack with beer

e·do·mi·so 江戸味噌 dark, fiery red & slightly sweet mi·so from Tokyo

e·i エイ ray fish

e·i·hi·re エイヒレ dried stingray fin served grilled as a snack with sa·ke

e·ki·ben 駅弁 station lunchbox

en·dai·bu エンダイブ endive

en·dō エンドウ field pea (type of green pea)

F

en·ga·wa えんがわ base of the dorsal fin of flounder & sole

e·no·ki·da·ke えのきだけ velvet shank mushroom • winter mushroom

e·ra えら gill

ē·ru エール ale

~ F ~

fen·ne·ru フェンネル fennel

fu 麩 shapes made from gluten flour used in clear soup

fu·cha·ryō·ri 普茶料理 Chinese Zen cuisine

fu·e·dai フエダイ snapper

fu·gu フグ puffer(fish) • globefish – famous fish that contains the deadly nerve toxin tetrodotoxin – its flesh is eaten as u·su·zu·ku·ri or in fu·gu·chi·ri & the milt (ie the testes of the fish) is regarded as a delicacy

fu·gu·chi·ri フグチリ hotpot with fu·gu

fu·gu·shi·ra·ko フグ白子 milt (ie the testes of the fish) of the fu·gu

fu·ka·ga·wa·na·be 深川鍋 hotpot with baby clam & spring onion

fu·ka·hi·re フカヒレ shark fin

fu·ki フキ Japanese butterbur (vegetable)

fu·ki·no·tō フキノトウ bud of fu·ki plant symbolising the beginning of spring

fu·ku·ro·ta·ke ふくろたけ paddy straw mushroom

fu·na フナ crucian carp – eaten as kan·ro·ni, tsu·ku·da·ni or a·rai

fu·na·zu·shi フナずし female crucian carp with eggs that are salted then pickled whole in fermented cooked rice (Shiga Prefecture)

fu·ri·ka·ke ふりかけ dried topping for rice

fu·rū·tsu·jū·su フルーツジュース fruit juice

fu·rū·tsu·kē·ki フルーツケーキ fruit cake

fu·rū·tsu·pan·chi フルーツパンチ fruit punch

fu·su·ma ふすま bran

fu·to·ma·ki 太巻き various ingredients rolled in no·ri seaweed (large su·shi rolls)

~ G ~

ga·chō ガチョウ goose

gai·mai 外米 foreign-produced rice

gam·mo·do·ki がんもどき minced tō·fu fried with finely chopped vegetables & seaweed – used in hotpots

gan ガン goose

ga·ri がり pickled pinkish-red ginger usually served as an accompaniment for su·shi

gek·kē·ju 月桂樹 bay

gem·mai 玄米 brown rice

gem·mai·cha 玄米茶 roasted tea with roasted & popped rice

ge·so げそ squid tentacles

gī ギー ghee

gin·jō 吟醸 sa·ke made of rice ground back to 60% of its weight before soaking and steaming

gin·jō·shu 吟醸酒 a type of sa·ke with a clean, fruity taste

gin·nan ぎんなん gingko nut

go·bō ごぼう burdock root

go·bu·zu·ki 五分づき mix of half white & half brown rice

go·ham·mo·no ご飯もの rice dishes

go·han ご飯 cooked rice • general term for 'a meal'

go·ma ごま sesame seeds

go·ma·a·bu·ra ごま油 sesame oil

go·ma·a·e ごま和え dishes mixed with sesame, salt & sugar sauce

go·ma·da·re ごまだれ sesame sauce

go·ma·dō·fu ごま豆腐 tō·fu-like food made of ground white sesame & starch

go·ma·me ゴマメ a small sardine cooked in shō·yu & sugar

go·mo·ku·so·ba 五目そば rā·men topped with vegetables, seafood & meat

go·ri·ryō·ri ゴリ料理 refers to dishes using ka·ji·ka (a type of fish) – a speciality of Kanazawa Prefecture

gu 具 filling • topping

gu·a·va グアヴァ guava

gu·ji ぐじ see a·ma·dai

gu·rap·pa グラッパ grappa (type of spirit)

gu·rē·pu·fu·rū·tsu グレープフルーツ grapefruit

gu·rīn·o·rī·bu グリーンオリーブ green olive

gu·ru·ta·min·san·sō·da グルタミン酸ソーダ MSG

gyo·ku·ro 玉露 highest-quality Japanese green tea

gyō·nyū 凝乳 curd

gyo·shō 魚醬 fish sauce

gyō·za ギョウザ Chinese-style dumplings, normally made from minced pork, cabbage, garlic, ginger & garlic chives

gyū·don 牛丼 thinly sliced beef simmered in sweetened shō·yu & served on rice

gyū·ni·ku 牛肉 beef

gyū·nyū 牛乳 milk

gyū·tan 牛タン beef tongue

~ H ~

ha 葉 leaf

hā·bu·tī ハーブティー herbal tea

ha·dok·ku ハドック haddock

hak·ka ハッカ mint • peppermint

ha·ku·mai 白米 plain, white rice

ha·ku·sai 白菜 Chinese cabbage

ha·ma·chi ハマチ yellowtail • amberjack (see bu·ri)

ha·ma·gu·ri ハマグリ clam

ha·mo ハモ conger • daggertooth (type of eel)

ham·pen はんぺん sponge-like fish cake made of ground shark meat mixed with grated yam & rice flour

ha·mu ハム ham

ha·na·dai·kon ハナダイコン rocket

ha·na·ma·me 花豆 flower bean

ha·na·sa·ki·ga·ni 花咲ガニ type of king crab • 'flower opening' crab that opens up when dipped into hot water

hap·pa 葉っぱ leaf

hap·pō·sai 八宝菜 stir-fry with assorted vegetables, meat & seafood & thickened with a Chinese-style sauce

ha·ra·pe·nyo ハラペニョ jalapeño chilli

ha·ra·wa·ta はらわた gizzards • offal

ha·ru·sa·me はるさめ bean-starch vermicelli

ha·sa·mi はさみ crab claws

ha·ta ハタ grouper (type of fish)

ha·ta·ha·ta ハタハタ sailfin sandfish used to make fermented fish sauce called shot·tsu·ru (Akita Prefecture)

ha·ta·ha·ta·zu·shi ハタハタずし pickled ha·ta·ha·ta

hat·chō·mi·so 八丁味噌 a dark mi·so originally created in Okazaki

ha·to 鳩 pigeon

ha·ya·shi·rai·su ハヤシライス stewed meat & vegetables with rice

ha·ya·to·u·ri ハヤトウリ chayote (fruit of a particular tropical climbing plant)

ha·ze ハゼ goby fish

hē·ku ヘイク hake

hē·ze·ru·nat·tsu ヘーゼルナッツ hazelnut

hi·bo·shi·to·ma·to 日干しトマト sun-dried tomatoes

hi·da·ra ヒダラ dried cod

hi·ga·shi 干菓子 dried sweets eaten during the tea ceremony

hi·ji·ki ひじき a type of seaweed

hi·ji·ki no ni·mo·no ひじきの煮物 hi·ji·ki simmered with shō·yu, sugar, fried tō·fu & boiled soy beans

hi·ki·ni·ku ひき肉 mince

hi·ki·wa·ri·mu·gi 挽き割り麦 cracked wheat

I

hi·ki·wa·ri·tō·mo·ro·ko·shi 挽き割りトウモロコシ hominy (boiled ground maize)

hi·ku·do·ri 肥育鶏 capon (castrated cock fowl fattened for eating)

hi·me·ma·su ヒメマス see ka·wa·ma·su

hi·mo·no 干物 dried fish

hi·ra·ki ひらき fully open ma·tsu·ta·ke mushroom

hi·ra·ma·sa ヒラマサ yellowtail • amberjack • kingfish

hi·ra·me ヒラメ bastard halibut • brill • flatfish • flounder • plaice • turbot

hi·ra·ta·ke ヒラタケ oyster mushroom

hi·re·ka·tsu ヒレカツ fried pork fillet

hi·to·ku·chi·to·ma·to 一口トマト cherry tomatoes • plum tomatoes

hi·tsu·ji 羊 sheep • lamb

hi·ya·mu·gi 冷麦 cold noodles dipped in cold sauce

hi·ya·shi·chū·ka 冷やし中華 cold noodles in sweet & sour soup with cucumber, chicken & egg on top

hi·ya·shi·u·don 冷やしうどん simple cold u·don

hi·ya·yak·ko 冷奴 cold tō·fu

hi·yo·ko·ma·me ヒヨコマメ chickpeas

hi·za·ni·ku ひざ肉 knuckle

hō·bō ホウボウ gurnard • bluefin • sea robin (types of fish)

hō·ji·cha ほうじ茶 parched ban·cha

hok·kai·dō·ryō·ri 北海道料理 Hokkaidō cuisine

hok·ke ホッケ atka mackerel

hok·ki·gai ホッキ貝 hen clam (also known as u·ba·gai)

ho·ko·ri·ta·ke ホコリタケ puffball (fungus)

hom·mi·rin 本みりん good quality mi·rin

hon·jō·zō·shu 本醸造酒 Japanese rice wine, ground back to 70% of its original size & blended with alcohol & water

hon·shi·me·ji 本しめじ type of mushroom

hō·ren·sō ホウレンソウ spinach

ho·shi·en·dō 干しエンドウ green split pea

ho·shi·ga·ki 干し柿 dried persimmon

ho·so·ma·ki 細まき thin su·shi roll

ho·ta·ru·i·ka ホタルイカ firefly squid

ho·ta·te(·gai) ホタテ (貝) scallop

ho·ta·te·ryō·ri ホタテ料理 scallop cuisine

ho·wai·to·pu·din·gu ホワイトプディング white pudding

ho·ya ホヤ sea squirt mixed with cucumber & vinegar & eaten raw

ho·zon·ryō 保存料 preservative

hya·ku·hi·ro 百尋 boiled whale intestine (Hakata City)

~ I ~

i·chi·go イチゴ strawberry

i·chi·ji·ku イチジク fig

ī·da·ko いいだこ 'rice octopus' – a small octopus with lots of eggs inside which look like rice

i·gai 貽貝 mussel (also known as mū·ru·gai)

i·ka イカ squid • cuttlefish

i·ki·zu·ku·ri 活き作り a method of presentation of fish & lobster, where the fish is served alive

i·ku·ra イクラ salted salmon eggs

i·na·go イナゴ rice locust – a type of rice-eating grasshopper, often eaten as tsu·ku·da·ni

i·na·ka·ryō·ri 田舎料理 rustic cuisine

i·na·man·jū いな饅頭 cleaned mullet stuffed with mi·so paste (Nagoya Prefecture) – also see bo·ra

i·na·ri·zu·shi 稲荷ずし vinegared rice in a fried tō·fu pouch

in·gem·ma·me インゲンマメ kidney bean

i·non·do イノンド dill

i·no·shi·shi いのしし wild boar

i·ri·do·ri 煎り鳥 stirfried chicken, dried shī·ta·ke, go·bō, ta·ro, kon·nya·ku, lotus

J

...pot, carrots & bamboo shoots stewed
... shō·yu & mi·rin
ri·ko いりこ sea cucumber • dried
...epang (sea cucumber) • dried sardine
se·e·bi イセエビ Japanese spiny
...lobster • crayfish
shi·ka·ri·na·be 石狩鍋 Hokkaidō
...almon & vegetable hotpot
so·be·ma·ki 磯辺巻き grilled rice
...akes dipped in shō·yu & wrapped
...f no·ri
. i·ta·me …炒め stir-fried …
ta·me·mo·no 炒め物 stir-fried dishes
ta·ya·gai いたや貝 a small scallop
...also known as sha·ku·shi·gai)
to·kon·nya·ku 糸こんにゃく thinly
...liced kon·nya·ku
to·na 糸菜 a pot-herb mustard, used
...s a leafy green vegetable
to·sō·men 糸そうめん thinnest type
...f sō·men
wa·na イワナ char (troutlike fish)
wa·shi いわし pilchard • sardine

~ J ~

a·ga·ba·tā ジャガバター baked
...otatoes with butter
a·ga·i·mo ジャガイモ potatoes
a·po·ni·ka·mai ジャポニカ米 short-
...grain rice
in·jā ジンジャー ginger
..ji·ru …汁 … juice • … soup
i·za·ke 地酒 local sa·ke
ō·ryū·shu 蒸留酒 spirits
ū·bu·zu·ki 十分づき plain white rice
um·mai·shu 純米酒 Japanese rice
wine made by grinding rice back to
...70% of its original weight
un·sai じゅんさい water shield (small
...water plant)

~ K ~

ka·ba·ya·ki 蒲焼 grilled fish or eel
...dipped in shō·yu-based sauce, eg
...u·na·gi no ka·ba·ya·ki

ka·bo·cha かぼちゃ Japanese
pumpkin
ka·bu かぶ turnip
ka·bu·na·me·ko かぶなめこ wild,
slightly larger variety of na·me·ko
mushroom
ka·bu·to·mu·shi かぶと蒸し steamed
head of large fish varieties
ka·bu·to·ni かぶと煮 stewed head of
large fish varieties
ka·e·ru カエル frog
ka·e·ru no a·shi カエルの足 frog legs
kai(·ru·i) 貝(類) shellfish
kai·sam·bu·tsu 海産物 seafood
kai·se·ki 懐石 see kai·se·ki·ryō·ri
kai·se·ki·ryō·ri 懐石料理 multicourse
set meal including many small
dishes – also known as kai·se·ki
kai·sō 海藻 generic term for edible
seaweed and sea vegetables
kai·wa·re·dai·kon 貝割れ大根 spicy
salad sprout from the mustard family
kai·zo·ku·ryō·ri 海賊料理 'pirate
food' – live seafood put on the BBQ
(Tokushima Prefecture)
ka·ji·ka カジカ similar to goby (freshwater fish) – dishes using ka·ji·ka are
called go·ri·ryō·ri & are a speciality of
Kanazawa Prefecture
ka·ji·ki カジキ marlin
ka·ke·so·ba かけそば buckwheat
noodles in broth
ka·ke·u·don かけうどん wheat flour
noodles in broth
ka·ki 柿 persimmon
ka·ki カキ oyster
ka·ki·a·ge かき揚げ finely chopped
seafood & vegetables fried in
tem·pu·ra batter
ka·ki·me·shi かき飯 oyster rice
ka·ki·mo·chi かきもち see a·ra·re
ka·ki·na·be カキ鍋 oyster hotpot
(Hiroshima Prefecture)
ka·ma·bo·ko かまぼこ minced whitefish meat that's steamed & sold in
blocks

K

ka·ma·su カマス barracuda • sea pike

ka·mi·re·ru·cha カミレル茶 chamomile tea

ka·mo 鴨 duck

kam·pa·chi カンパチ amberjack (type of fish best eaten in summer)

kam·pyō かんぴょう dried fruit of bottle gourd, flavoured with shō·yu

kam·pyō·ma·ki かんぴょう巻き su·shi rolls made using kam·pyō

ka·ni カニ crab

ka·ni·ba·sa·mi カニばさみ see ha·sa·mi

ka·ni·mi·so カニ味噌 crab reproductive organs, often eaten as an hors d'oeuvre

kan·ki·tsu·ru·i 柑橘類 citrus

kan·ko·ku·ryō·ri 韓国料理 Korean cuisine

kan·zō カンゾウ liquorice

kan·ro·ni 甘露煮 small fish boiled in & sweetly flavoured with shō·yu & mi·rin • chestnuts boiled in syrup

kan·to·da·ki かんと炊き the name used for o·den in the Kansai region

kap·pa·ma·ki かっぱ巻き cucumber su·shi rolled in no·ri seaweed

ka·ra 殻 shell

ka·ra·a·ge から揚げ meat or fish dusted in flour & deep-fried

ka·ra·me·ru カラメル caramel (baked sugar)

ka·ra·mi·mo·chi からみもち rice cake with grated dai·kon

ka·ra·shi からし mustard

ka·ra·shi· men·tai·ko 辛子明太子 salted cod roe pickled in chilli (Kyūshū) – also just men·tai·ko

ka·ra·shi·na からし菜 brown mustard

ka·ra·shi·zu·ke からし漬け pickled vegetables flavoured with mustard

ka·ra·su·mi からすみ dried mullet roe (Nagasaki & Kyūshū) – also see bo·ra

ka·rē カレー curry

ka·re·i カレイ dab • flatfish • flounder

ka·rē·nam·ban カレー南蛮 buckwhea noodles with chicken or pork curry

ka·rē·rai·su カレーライス Japanese-style curry & rice

ka·rē·u·don カレーうどん u·don noodles with curry roux sauce (ie sauce based on equal amounts of fat and flour)

ka·ri·fu·ra·wā カリフラワー cauliflower

ka·rin かりん Chinese quince

ka·rin·tō かりんとう sweet made of flour & baking powder, deep-fried & coated with brown sugar

ka·ru·da·mon カルダモン cardamom

ka·ru·don カルドン cardoon (thistle-like plant with edible stalks)

ka·ru·kan かるかん a confection mad from ya·ma·i·mo, rice powder & sugar (Kagoshima)

ka·shi·wa·mo·chi 柏もち rice cake wrapped in oak leaf – eaten on 5 May (Children's Day)

ka·su 粕 lees (sediment) from sa·ke

ka·su·ji·ru 粕汁 thick soup flavoured with lees (sediment) from sa·ke

ka·su·te·ra カステラ yellow sponge cake (Nagasaki Prefecture)

ka·su·zu·ke 粕漬け vegetables pickled in lees (sediment) from sa·ke

ka·ta·ku·chi·i·wa·shi カタクチイワシ anchovy • Japanese anchovy

ka·ta·ku·ri·ko 片栗粉 arrowroot flour

ka·ta·ya·ki·so·ba 固焼きそば crunchy fried noodles topped with vegetables

ka·ta·yu·de·ta·ma·go 固ゆで卵 hard-boiled egg

ka·tsu カツ cutlets

ka·tsu·don カツ丼 fried pork cutlet & egg on rice

ka·tsu·o カツオ bonito • skipjack (fish)

ka·tsu·o·bu·shi カツオ節 dried bonito (fish) flakes

ka·wa·ha·gi カワハギ leatherjacket • filefish

ka·wa·hi·me·ma·su カワヒメマス grayling (salmonoid fish)

ka·wa·ma·su 川マス freshwater red salmon • pike

ka·wa·za·ka·na 川魚 river fish • lake fish

ka·zu·no·ko かずのこ dried herring roe (also see o·se·chi·ryō·ri)

ke·chap·pu ケチャップ (tomato) ketchup

ke·ga·ni 毛がに bristly crab • horse-hair crab (best in winter)

kē·ki ケーキ cake(s)

ke·shi no mi ケシの実 poppy seed

kē·sho·ku 軽食 snacks

ki·dai キダイ yellowish tai, a cheap fish served as shi·o·ya·ki

ki·en·dō 黄エンドウ yellow split pea

ki·ha·da キハダ yellowfin tuna

ki·i·chi·go キイチゴ raspberry

ki·ji 雉 pheasant

ki·ku·i·mo キクイモ Jerusalem artichoke

ki·ku·ko きくこ cod milt (fish testes) used in hotpot

ki·ku·ra·ge きくらげ Jew's ear • Judas' ear • woody ear tree fungus

ki·mi·sō·men 黄身そうめん noodles with egg yolk

kim·ma キンマ betel (plant with edible leaves and nuts)

kim·me(·dai) キンメ（ダイ） redfish

ki·na·ko きなこ soy bean flour

ki·na·ko·mo·chi きなこもち rice cake covered with sweetened soy bean flour

kin·kan キンカン kumquat

kin·ko きんこ dried trepang (sea cucumber)

ki no mi 木の実 berries

kim·me(·dai) キンメ（ダイ） redfish • alfonsino

kim·pi·ra·go·bō きんぴらごぼう thinly cut go·bō, normally eaten flavoured with shō·yu

ki·no·ko きのこ mushroom

kin·to·ki 金時 large red bean

ki·nu·go·shi·dō·fu 絹ごし豆腐 smooth, soft tō·fu (see also mo·men·dō·fu)

ki·ri·mi 切り fish or meat fillet

ki·shi·men きしめん flat noodles (Nagoya)

ki·su キス whiting

ki·tsu·ne·so·ba きつねそば buck-wheat noodles with fried tō·fu

ki·tsu·ne·u·don きつねうどん wheat flour noodles with fried tō·fu

ki·yu·zu 黄ゆず yellow yu·zu

kō·be·gyū 神戸牛 beef from Kobe renowned as marble beef

ko·bu·cha 昆布茶 tea made of kom·bu seaweed (also called kom·bu·cha)

ko·bu·da·shi 昆布だし kelp stock

ko·bu·ma·ki 昆布巻 small fish or go·bō wrapped in kom·bu & boiled

kō·cha 紅茶 (black) tea

ko·chi·jan コチジャン a Korean sweet, spicy, pepper-mi·so paste

ko·e·bi 小エビ shrimp

ko·en·do·ro コエンドロ cilantro (also called Chinese parsley and coriander)

ko·ha·da こはだ threadfin shad • gizzard shad (herringlike types of fish also known as ko·no·shi·ro)

kō·hī コーヒー coffee

ko·hi·tsu·ji 子羊 lamb

ko·ko·a ココア cocoa

ko·ko·na·tsu ココナツ coconut

ko·ma·tsu·na 小松菜 mustard spinach (green leafy vegetable)

kom·bu 昆布 kelp (seaweed)

kom·bu·cha 昆布茶 see ko·bu·cha

ko·me 米 uncooked rice

ko·me·mi·so 米味噌 mi·so made from rice

kōm·mī·ru コーンミール cornmeal

ko·mu·gi 小麦 wheat

ko·mu·gi·ba·ku·ga 小麦麦芽 wheat germ

ko·na·go こうなご sand eel

ko·na·za·tō 粉砂糖 icing sugar

K

kon·nya·ku こんにゃく devil's tongue – a tuber used to make a gelatinous paste which is used in hotpots & stewed foods (Gunma, Tochigi & Fukushima Prefectures)

ko·no·ko このこ dried trepang roe eaten as a snack with sa·ke (Ishikawa Prefecture)

kō no mo·no 香の物 pickled vegetables, served during a cha·kai·se·ki

ko·no·shi·ro コノシロ see ko·ha·da

ko no wa·ta コノワタ salted trepang (sea cucumber) intestine

kon·sai 根菜 root vegetables

ko·ri·an·da コリアンダ coriander

kō·ri·dō·fu 凍り豆腐 freeze-dried tō·fu used in stewed dishes

kō·ri·mi·zu 氷水 ice water

ko·ro ころ young, fully closed ma·tsu·ta·ke

ko·ro·ha コロハ fenugreek

ko·rok·ke コロッケ croquette

ko·ro·mo ころも coating of deep-fried food · batter

kō·ryō·kyō コウリョウキョウ galangal

ko·shi·ni·ku 腰肉 loin

kō·shin·ryō 香辛料 condiments

ko·shō 胡椒 pepper

ko·shō·sō コショウソウ cress

ko·tsu·zui 骨髄 marrow

kot·te·ri こってり general term for rich or thick (see also as·sa·ri)

ko·u·shi no ni·ku 仔牛の肉 veal

koy コイ carp used for mi·so soup or a·rai

kō·ya·dō·fu こうや豆腐 see kō·ri·dō·fu

koy·cha 濃茶 thick tea

koy·ku·chi·shō·yu 濃い口しょう油 dark shō·yu

ku·chi·ko クチコ salted trepang roe

ku·da·mo·no くだもの fruit

ku·ji·ra くじら whale

ku·mi·a·ge·dō·fu くみ上げ豆腐 freshly made tō·fu

ku·min クミン cumin

kun·sē 燻製 smoked

kun·sē·sa·ke 燻製サケ kipper

ku·ra·ge クラゲ jellyfish

ku·rak·kā クラッカー cracker

ku·ram·be·rī クランベリー cranberry

ku·ram·be·rī·sō·su クランベリーソース cranberry sauce

ku·res クレス cress

ku·re·son クレソン watercress

ku·ri 栗 chestnut

ku·ri·jō·chū 栗焼酎 shō·chū made from chestnuts

ku·ri·kin·ton 栗きんとん chestnuts boiled in syrup & covered with mashed sweet potatoes

ku·ro·a·na·go クロアナゴ black conger eel

ku·ro·bī·ru 黒ビール stout (beer)

ku·rō·bu クローブ clove

ku·ro·dai クロダイ black bream or porgy

ku·ro·go·ma 黒ごま black sesame seed

ku·ro·ma·gu·ro クロマグロ bluefin tuna

ku·ro·ma·me 黒豆 black soy bean

ku·ro·o·rī·bu 黒オリーブ black olive

ku·ro·was·san クロワッサン croissant

ku·ru·ma·ba·sō クルマバソウ sweet woodruff (plant whose leaves are used to flavour wine and liqueurs)

ku·ru·ma·e·bi 車えび kuruma prawn · tiger prawn · scampi

ku·ru·mi クルミ walnut

ku·ru·zet·to クルゼット courgette · zucchini

ku·sa·mo·chi 草もち green rice cake mixed with mugwort (a herbal plant)

ku·sa·ya くさや strong-smelling dried fish (island of Niijima & Izu archipelago)

kū·sū 古酒 or クース aged a·wa·mo·ri alcohol

ku·wai クワイ arrowhead (water plant)

ku·wa no mi くわの実 mulberry

ku·zu 葛 the starch extracted from the root of the kudzu vine

M

ku·zu·ki·ri 葛きり thin, vermicelli-like noodles made from ku·zu

kya·be·tsu キャベツ (white) cabbage

kya·bya キャビア caviar

kya·ra·me·ru キャラメル caramel (lolly)

kya·ra·wē キャラウェー caraway seed

kyō·do·ryō·ri 郷土料理 regionalised speciality cuisine

kyō·na 京菜 a pot-herb mustard plant, used as leafy green vegetable

kyō·ri·ki·ko 強力粉 strong wheat flour

kyō·ryō·ri 京料理 Kyoto specialist cuisine

kyō·to·shi·ro·mi·so 京都白味噌 a delicate, sweet, white mi·so used in kyo·ryō·ri

kyū·ri キュウリ cucumber

kyū·ri·mo·mi キュウリもみ thinly sliced cucumber mixed & softened with salt

kyū·ri no pi·ku·ru·su キュウリのピクルス gherkin

kyū·shū·ryō·ri 九州料理 cuisine of the island of Kyūshū

kyū·tē·ryō·ri 宮廷料理 palace cuisine

~ M ~

ma·a·ji マアジ horse mackerel • jack mackerel • scad (type of fish)

ma·a·na·go マアナゴ conger eel

ma·dai マダイ red sea bream • silver sea bream • snapper

ma·ga·mo マガモ mallard (a duck)

ma·gu·ro マグロ tuna – caught mostly outside Japan

mai·ta·ke まいたけ hen-of-the-woods mushroom

ma·i·wa·shi まいわし sardine • pilchard

ma·ki·zu·shi 巻きずし general term for no·ri-rolled su·shi

ma·me 豆 beans, including pea & soy beans

ma·me·mi·so 豆味噌 mi·so made from soy beans

ma·me·ru·i 豆類 legume

man·gō マンゴー mango

man·jū 饅頭 steamed bun filled with sweet a·zu·ki beans

ma·ri·ne マリネ marinade

ma·ru·me·ro マルメロ quince

mas·shu·po·te·to マッシュポテト mashed potatoes

mas·tā·do マスタード mustard

ma·su マス pink salmon • generic term for trout

mat·cha 抹茶 powdered green tea

mat·cha·ai·su 抹茶アイス green tea ice cream

mat·cha·shi·o 抹茶塩 salt & powdered green tea, used for dipping tem·pu·ra

ma·tō·dai マトウダイ John Dory (fish)

ma·ton マトン mutton

ma·tsu·ka·wa·zu·ku·ri 松皮づくり a type of sa·shi·mi made from un-skinned tai – the skin is tasty & looks like pine bark

ma·tsu no mi 松の実 pine nut

ma·tsu·ta·ke マツタケ expensive & highly fragrant mushroom variety

ma·yo·nē·zu マヨネーズ mayonnaise

me·ba·chi メバチ bigeye tuna

me·ba·ru メバル brown rockfish

me·bō·ki メボウキ sweet basil

me·da·ma·ya·ki 目玉焼き fried egg

men 麺 noodles

men·chi·ka·tsu メンチカツ crumbed & fried mince meat patties

men·ru·i 麺類 generic term for noodles

men·tai·ko 明太子 see ka·ra·shi·men·tai·ko

me·ron メロン melon • cantaloupe

mēs メース mace (a spice)

mi 身 generic term for flesh (of fish & shellfish)

mi·ga·ki·ni·shin 身欠きにしん dried herring

mi·kan みかん mandarin orange

mi·na·mi·ma·gu·ro ミナミマグロ southern bluefin tuna

M

min·to ミント mint
mi·rin みりん sweet rice wine used for cooking
mi·ru·gai みる貝 otter shell
mi·ru·ku ミルク milk
mi·ru·ku·tī ミルクティー milk tea
mi·so 味噌 fermented soy-bean paste – can also be made from rice or barley
mi·so·ni 味噌煮 fish simmered in mi·so stock
mi·so·rā·men 味噌ラーメン rā·men with mi·so-flavoured broth
mi·so·shi·ru 味噌汁 soup made from mi·so paste with fish stock – often includes vegetables, tō·fu & wa·ka·me
mi·so·zu·ke 味噌漬 meat, fish & vegetables pickled in mi·so
mi·tsu·ba みつば Japanese wild chervil, used to add flavour to hotpots, cha·wan·mu·shi & o·ya·ko·don
mi·tsu·ma·me みつまめ Japanese dessert made from boiled red peas, diced Japanese gelatine (agar-agar) & fruit topped with syrup – similar to am·mi·tsu, but does not include an·ko
mi·zu 水 water
mi·zu·na ミズナ a pot-herb mustard plant, used as leafy green vegetable
mi·zu·ta·ki 水炊き hotpot with chicken & vegetables boiled in their own stock – eaten with dipping sauce made from shō·yu & pon·zu
mi·zu·yō·kan 水羊羹 mild, sweet yō·kan jelly
mo·chi もち rice cake made from glutinous rice
mo·chi·go·me もち米 glutinous rice, used to make mo·chi
mo·dan·ya·ki モダン焼き Japanese-style savoury pancake with noodles
mo·men·dō·fu 木綿豆腐 rough, firm tō·fu (see also ki·nu·go·shi·dō·fu)
mo·mi·ji·o·ro·shi もみじおろし relish from grated dai·kon & chilli
mo·mo 桃 peach

mo·na·ka 最中 a sweet made of an·ko inside a thin wafer shell
mo·ri·so·ba もりそば cold buckwheat noodles served in a bamboo steamer & dipped into a cold sauce before eating
mo·tsu モツ chicken, pork, or beef offal
mo·tsu·na·be モツ鍋 hotpot made of chicken, pork or beef offal
mo·tsu·ni モツ煮 simmered chicken, pork or beef offal
mo·ya·shi モヤシ bean sprouts
mo·zu·ku モズク type of seaweed served mixed with vinegar
mo·zu·ku·ga·ni モズクガニ small freshwater crab
mu·gi 麦 general term for wheat, oat, barley & rye
mu·gi·cha 麦茶 cold tea made of roasted barley
mu·gi·jō·chū 麦焼酎 shō·chū made from wheat (Oita Prefecture)
mu·gi·mi·so 麦味噌 barley mi·so popular in Kyūshū
mu·gi·to·ro 麦とろ cooked rice & wheat with grated yam on top
mu·ne·ni·ku 胸肉 brisket (meat from the breast of a four-legged animal, especially beef)
mu·ni·e·ru ムニエル meunière (describes a dish fried lightly in butter)
mū·ru·gai ムール貝 mussel (also known as i·gai)
mu·shi·gyō·za 蒸しギョウザ steamed gyō·za dumpling
mu·shi·mo·no 蒸し物 steamed dishes
mu·tsu·go·rō ムツゴロウ a kind of goby • mud skipper
myō·ga ミョウガ Japanese ginger
myū·zu·rī ミューズリー muesli

~ N ~

na 菜 leaf vegetables (also see nap·pa)
...·na·be …鍋 hotpot made of ...
na·be(·mo·no) 鍋(物) general term for hotpot – the diner selects the

N

raw ingredients & cooks them in the na·be pot

na·be·ya·ki·u·don 鍋焼きうどん u·don noodles, seafood, meat & vegetables cooked in a small pot

na·ma·ga·shi 生菓子 uncooked sweet paste confections filled with red an

na·ma·ko ナマコ trepang (sea cucumber)

na·ma·su なます thinly cut, raw seafood or uncooked vegetables steeped in vinegar

na·ma·ta·ma·go 生卵 raw egg

na·ma·za·ke 生酒 sa·ke that has not been pasteurised

na·ma·zu ナマズ catfish

na·me·ko なめこ a small, golden-brown mushroom related to the ma·tsu·ta·ke

nam·ban·zu·ke 南蛮漬け fried fish marinated in vinegar with sliced onions & chilli

na·no·ha·na·zu·ke 菜の花漬け rape shoot pickle (Kyoto)

nap·pa 菜っ葉 leaf vegetables (also see na)

na·re·zu·shi なれずし salted a·yu pickled in vinegar & cooked rice

na·ru·to·ma·ki なると巻き thinly sliced fish cakes served in noodles, such as rā·men & u·don – contains the same ingredients as ka·ma·bo·ko

na·su ナシ Japanese pear

na·su ナス eggplant • aubergine

na·ta·ne 菜種 rape seed

na·ta·ne·fu·gu 菜種フグ end-of-season fu·gu, at its tastiest & most poisonous

na·tsu·me なつめ date

na·tsu·me·gu ナツメグ nutmeg

na·tsu·me·ya·shi ナツメヤシ date (fruit)

nat·tō 納豆 sticky, fermented soy beans

ne·gi ねぎ spring onion • scallion • welsh onion

ne·gi·ma ねぎま tuna & spring onion stewed in a hotpot (Tokyo) • grilled spring onion & chicken meat on skewers served in ya·ki·to·ri restaurants

ne·ku·ta·rin ネクタリン nectarine

ni·bo·shi 煮干 dried anchovies used to make stock

ni·ga·u·ri にがうり balsam pear • bitter melon

ni·gi·ri·zu·shi にぎりずし hand-pressed su·shi

ni·go·ri·za·ke にごり酒 cloudy sa·ke

ni·hon·cha 日本茶 Japanese tea

ni·hon·ryō·ri 日本料理 Japanese cuisine

ni·hon·shu 日本酒 another word for sa·ke

ni·ji·ma·su ニジマス see ka·wa·ma·su

ni·ki·ri·mi·rin 煮きりみりん mi·rin with alcohol that is burned off prior to use

nik·kē 肉桂 see nik·ki

nik·ki ニッキ cinnamon

nik·ko·ro·ga·shi 煮っころがし potatoes or ta·ro stewed in shō·yu-based stock

ni·ku 肉 meat

ni·ku·dan·go 肉団子 meatball

ni·ku·ja·ga 肉じゃが potato & meat stew

ni·ku·ji·ru 肉汁 gravy

ni·ku·zu·ku ニクズク nutmeg

ni·mai·gai 二枚貝 clam

ni·mo·no 煮物 simmered dishes

nin·jin ニンジン carrot

nin·ni·ku ニンニク garlic

ni·ra にら Chinese chives • garlic chives

ni·shin にしん herring (best in spring)

ni·tsu·ke 煮つけ fish or vegetables simmered in savoury stock until almost all the liquid evaporates

ni·wa·to·ri にわとり chicken

no·bu·ta 野豚 wild boar

no·mi·ya 飲み屋 Japanese-style bar

O

no·ri 海苔 sea laver (particular type of seaweed) • type of seaweed formed into sheets & used to wrap su·shi
no·ri·ma·ki 海苔巻 su·shi rolled in seaweed
no·shi·i·ka のしいか dried, hand-rolled squid
no·u·sa·gi 野ウサギ hare
nu·ka 糠 (rice) bran
nu·ka·mi·so 糠味噌 fermented rice bran used as a base to make pickles
nu·ka·zu·ke 糠漬け vegetables pickled in nu·ka·mi·so
nu·ta ぬた clam or tuna with spring onion covered in vinegared mi·so
nyū·men にゅうめん sō·men noodles in hot soup

~ O ~

o·a·ge おあげ thinly sliced, thick tō·fu fried in sesame oil
o·ben·tō お弁当 see ben·tō
o·cha お茶 Japanese green tea
o·cha·zu·ke お茶漬け white rice with green tea poured onto it
o·den おでん hotpot with tō·fu, kon·nya·ku, fish-cake meatballs & potato stewed in stock
o·do·ri·gu·i おどり食い shrimps or small fish eaten live & dipped in vinegar or shō·yu
ō·gi·gai 扇貝 scallop
o·ha·gi おはぎ see bo·ta·mo·chi
o·hi·ta·shi おひたし boiled green-leaf vegetables served cold with shō·yu
o·kan お燗 warm sa·ke
o·ka·ra おから lees from soy milk eaten with finely chopped vegetables
o·ka·shi お菓子 sweets • lollies
o·ka·shi·ra·tsu·ki 尾頭付き dish consisting of a whole fish
o·ka·yu おかゆ rice porridge • congee (gruel of boiled rice and water)
o·ka·zu おかず a dish accompanying rice, mi·so, soup & pickles

o·ko·no·mi·ya·ki お好み焼き Japanese-style savoury pancake
o·ku·ra オクラ okra
ō·mu·gi 大麦 barley
o·mu·rai·su オムライス dish consisting of omelette with a rice filling
o·mu·re·tsu オムレツ omelette
o·ni·ga·ra·ya·ki 鬼殻焼き prawns in the shell, grilled over hot coals
o·ni·gi·ri おにぎり rice ball
on·sen·ta·ma·go 温泉たまご egg boiled in a natural hot spring
o·re·ga·no オレガノ oregano
o·ren·ji オレンジ orange
o·rī·bu オリーブ olive
o·rī·bu·oy·ru オリーブオイル olive oil
···o·ro·shi …おろし grated …
o·ro·shi·shō·ga おろししょうが grated ginger
ō·ru·spais オールスパイス allspice
o·se·chi·ryō·ri おせち料理 various preserved dishes stored in layered lacquerware dishes & served at New Year
o·sa·ke お酒 Japanese wine (also see sa·ke)
o·shi·ru·ko お汁粉 grilled rice cake served with sweet, stewed a·zu·ki bean
o·shi·zus·hi 押しずし su·shi made by pressing vinegared rice into a square box & layering su·shi ingredients on top (Kansai region)
ō·to·mī·ru オートミール oatmeal
o·ya·ko·don 親子丼 chicken & egg on rice

~ P ~

pā·chi パーチ perch
pai パイ pie
pai·nap·pu·ru パイナップル pineapple
pan パン bread • bread roll
pan·ga·ta パン型 loaf
pan·ko パン粉 breadcrumbs
pa·pa·i·ya パパイヤ papaya
pa·pu·ri·ka パプリカ paprika

pa·se·ri パセリ parsley

pās·nip·pu パースニップ parsnip

pas·ta パスタ pasta

pas·to·ra·mi パストラミ pastrami

pe·kan ペカン pecan

pe·pā·min·to ペパーミント peppermint

pe·pā·min·to·tī ペパーミントティー peppermint tea

pe·pa·rō·ni ペペローニ pepperoni

pes·to·rī ペストリー pastry

pī·man ピーマン capsicum (usually green) • bell pepper

pī·nats ピーナツ groundnut • peanut

pis·ta·chi·o ピスタチオ pistachio

pō·chi·do·eg·gu ポーチド・エッグ poached egg

pō·ku ポーク pork (also called bu·ta·ni·ku)

pō·ku·sō·sē·ji ポークソーセージ pork sausages

pō·ku·so·tē ポークソテー sautéed pork

pon·kan ポンカン a large type of citrus fruit

pon·zu ポン酢 juice from citrus fruits • a mix of shō·yu, da·shi, citrus juices & sometimes vinegar used as a dipping sauce & in salad dressings

pop·pu·kōn ポップコーン popcorn

po·te·to ポテト potatoes

po·te·to·fu·rai ポテトフライ fried potatoes • French fries

pō·to·wain ポートワイン port

pu·ra·mu·to·ma·to プラムトマト plum tomatoes

pu·rūn プルーン prune

~ R ~

ra·dis·shu ラディッシュ radish

rā·do ラード lard

ra·gā·bī·ru ラガービール lager

rak·kyō ラッキョウ scallion • baker's garlic

rā·men ラーメン yellow wheat noodles

ra·mu ラム lamb

rā·yu ラー油 chilli oil

re·ba·sa·shi レバ刺し liver sa·shi·mi

re·mon レモン lemon

re·mon·tī レモンティー lemon tea

ren·kon れんこん lotus root

ren·zu·ma·me レンズマメ lentil

rē·shi レイシ lychee

rē·shu 冷酒 chilled sa·ke

re·tas レタス lettuce

rē·tō 冷凍 frozen

rē·zun レーズン raisin • sultana

ri·kyū·ru リキュール liqueur

rin·go りんご apple

ro·bus·tā ロブスター lobster

rō·ru·do·ō·to ロールドオート rolled oats

rō·ru·kya·be·tsu ロールキャベツ cabbage rolls

rō·ru·pan ロールパン bread roll

rōs(·to) ロース(ト) roast

rōz·ma·rī ローズマリー rosemary

ryō·chō 猟鳥 game (birds)

ryō·jū 猟獣 game (other animals)

ryo·ku·cha 緑茶 green tea

(...) ryō·ri (…)料理 (...-style) cuisine

~ S ~

sa·ba サバ chub mackerel • Pacific mackerel

sa·ba no mi·so·ni サバの味噌煮 mackerel simmered with mi·so

sa·ba no ni·tsu·ke サバの煮付け mackerel simmered with shō·yu

sa·dō 茶道 tea ceremony

sa·fu·ran サフラン saffron

sa·go サゴ sago

sa·ka·na 魚 fish

sa·ka·na no pē·sto 魚のペースト fish paste

sa·ka·na no ta·ma·go 魚の卵 fish roe

sa·ke 酒 alcohol made from a fermenting process that uses grain (known in the West as rice wine) • general term for alcoholic drinks (also called o·sa·ke & ni·hon·shu)

S

sa·ke 鮭 salmon • chum salmon • dog salmon (also known as sha·ke)

sa·ke·a·te 酒あて accompaniments to sa·ke & beer

sa·ke·ka·su 酒粕 lees (sediment) from rice wine

sa·ku·ra·ma·su 桜マス/琵琶マス cherry salmon

sa·ku·ra·mo·chi 桜もち pink rice cake wrapped in a cherry leaf

sa·ku·ram·bo さくらんぼ cherry

sa·ku·ra·ni·ku さくら肉 horse meat

sam·ma さんま Pacific saury • saury pike (types of fish)

san·do·rai·to·ma·to サンドライトマト sun-dried tomatoes

san·jin·ryō·ri 山人料理 'mountain man food' (Fukushima Prefecture & Tohoku region)

san·sai 山菜 edible, wild mountain vegetables

san·sai·ryō·ri 山菜料理 mountain vegetable cuisine

san·shō 山椒 Japanese prickly ash pod • Sichuan pepper

sa·ra·shi·ne·gi さらしねぎ Welsh onion, soaked in water, drained & thinly sliced

sā·ro·in サーロイン sirloin

sa·sa·ge ささげ black-eyed peas

sa·shi·mi 刺身 raw fish or meat

sa·tō 砂糖 sugar

sa·to·i·mo サトイモ taro

sa·tsu·ma·a·ge さつま揚げ minced fish meat mixed with finely chopped vegetables, then fried in sesame oil – used in ni·mo·no & o·den

sa·tsu·ma·i·mo サツマイモ sweet potato

sa·wa·chi·ryō·ri 皿鉢料理 celebratory cuisine with vegetables, seafood, ni·mo·no & a·ge·mo·no piled on one large platter (Kōchi Prefecture & island of Shikoku)

sa·wa·ga·ni 沢がに freshwater crab, often served deep-fried in ka·ra·a·ge

sa·wā·ku·rī·mu サワークリーム sour cream

sa·wa·ra さわら spotted mackerel • Spanish mackerel

sa·ya·en·dō サヤエンドウ snow pea

sa·ya·in·gen サヤインゲン string beans

sa·yo·ri サヨリ garfish • halfbeak • snipe fish

sa·za·e サザエ whelk (mollusc)

sa·za·e no tsu·bo·ya·ki サザエのつぼ焼き whelk (mollusc) grilled in the shell

sē·ji セージ sage

se·ki·han 赤飯 'red rice' with a·zu·ki beans

sem·bē せんべい rice cracker

sem·mai·zu·ke 千枚漬け large turnips pickled in sweet vinegar (Kyoto)

sen·cha 煎茶 a typical Japanese green tea

sen·dai·mi·so 仙台味噌 salty mi·so (Miyagi Prefecture)

sen·gi·ri 千切 vegetables thinly sliced lengthways • julienne

se·ri せり water dropwort (type of plant) – used in su·ki·ya·ki, soups & salads

se·ro·ri セロリ celery

sē·shu 清酒 sa·ke • generic term for clear rice wine

sha·bu·sha·bu しゃぶしゃぶ thinly sliced beef dipped into a boiling hotpot, then into sesame or pon·zu sauces

sha·ko しゃこ mantis shrimp • squilla (type of mantis shrimp)

sha·ku·shi·gai 杓子貝 see i·ta·ya·gai

sham·pen シャンペン sparkling wine

shan·dī シャンディー shandy

she·rī シェリー sherry

shi·ba·e·bi 芝エビ shiba shrimp • prawn

shi·bō 脂肪 fat

shi·bo·ri·ta·te jū·su しぼりたてジュース fresh juice

shi·chi·bu·zu·ki 七分づき a mixture of 70% white & 30% brown rice

shi·chi·men·chō 七面鳥 turkey

shi·chi·mi·tō·ga·ra·shi 七味唐辛子 a blend of seven spices used as a condiment for noodle dishes & na·be·mo·no

shi·chū シチュー stew

shī·fū·do シーフード seafood

shi·ka 鹿 deer

shi·ka·ni·ku 鹿肉 venison

shi·ki·mi シキミ star anise

shi·ma·a·ji シマアジ crevalle jack (type of fish)

shi·ma·dō·fu しまどうふ hard tō·fu suited to frying (Okinawa Prefecture)

shi·me·ji しめじ a type of mushroom

shi·me·sa·ba しめサバ vinegared mackerel

shi·mo·fu·ri(·gyū·ni·ku) 霜降り (牛肉) marbled (beef)

shi·na·chi·ku シナチク pickled Chinese bamboo sprouts

shi·na·mon シナモン cinnamon

shin·cha 新茶 new-season green tea – usually available in stores in early summer

shin·shū·mi·so 信州味噌 mi·so from Nagano Prefecture

shi·o 塩 salt

shi·o·bo·shi·wa·ka·me 塩干しワカメ wa·ka·me washed in salt water, then dried

shi·o·ka·ra 塩辛 seafood pickled with salt

shi·o·nu·ki·wa·ka·me 塩抜きワカメ wa·ka·me washed in plain, unsalted water & dried

shi·o·ya·ki 塩焼き salted & grilled food

shi·o·zu·ke 塩漬け vegetables, meat or seafood pickled in salt

ship·po·ku·ryō·ri 卓袱料理 a refined banquet cuisine from Nagasaki Prefecture

shi·ra·ko 白子 milt (testes from fish)

shi·ra·shi·me·yu 白絞め油 salad oil, normally rape seed oil

shi·ra·su シラス whitebait

shi·ra·su·bo·shi しらす干し boiled & dried young anchovies or pilchards

shi·ra·ta·ki しらたき kon·nya·ku in noodle form

shi·ra·u·o しらうお a type of fish eaten live & known in English as ice goby or icefish (Fukuoka Prefecture)

shi·ri·ni·ku 尻肉 rump

shi·ro·a·e 白和え vegetables mixed with sauce made from tō·fu

shi·ro·a·ma·dai 白アマダイ white a·ma·dai

shi·ro·go·ma 白ごま white sesame seed

shi·ro·ke·shi no mi 白ケシの実 white poppy seed

shi·ro·mi·so 白味噌 white mi·so

shi·ro·mi·za·ka·na 白身魚 white-fleshed fish

shi·ro·wain 白ワイン white wine

shi·ro·za·ke 白酒 white, cloudy rice wine

shi·rya·ru シリアル cereal

shi·sha·mo ししゃも capelin • longfin smelt • night smelt (types of fish)

shi·so しそ beefsteak plant • perilla (a member of the mint family) – used as a condiment, a colouring or as a flavouring for pickles

shi·ta 舌 tongue

shi·ta·bi·ra·me シタビラメ sole

shī·ta·ke しいたけ shiitake mushroom

shō·chū 焼酎 distilled spirit made from sweet potato, rice, millet or lees (sediment) from rice wine

shō·ga しょうが ginger

shō·ga·su しょうが酢 ginger vinegar

shō·ga·ya·ki しょうが焼き grilled meat or fish flavoured with ginger & shō·yu

shō·ga·yu しょうが湯 ginger & hot water – a traditional cure

shō·jin·a·ge 精進揚げ vegetarian tem·pu·ra

shō·jin·ryō·ri 精進料理 traditional vegetarian food

S

MENU DECODER

S

sho·ku·bu·tsu·yu 植物油 vegetable oil

sho·ku·pan 食パン square-shaped loaf of bread

sho·ku·ryō 食料 stock (food)

shop·pai しょっぱい salty

shot·tsu·ru しょっつる fermented fish sauce made from ha·ta·ha·ta (Akita Prefecture)

shō·yu しょう油 soy sauce made from fermented soy bean & wheat

shō·yu·ya·ki しょう油焼き grilled with shō·yu

shō·yu·zu·ke しょう油漬け vegetables pickled in shō·yu

shū·mai シュウマイ steamed, round Chinese dumplings

shun·gi·ku 春菊 crown daisy • garland chrysanthemum – eaten as o·hi·ta·shi, a·e·mo·no & na·be

shu·tō 酒盗 salted & fermented ka·tsu·o intestine – a good accompaniment for drinking sa·ke

skam·pi スカンピ scampi

skas·shu スカッシュ squash

skā·to スカート skirt (a cut of beef from the flank)

snak·ku スナック snacks

so·ba そば buckwheat • noodles made of buckwheat

so·ba·cha そば茶 buckwheat tea

so·ba·ga·ki そばがき dough made of buckwheat flour mixed with boiled water

sō·da ソーダ soda water

sō·men そうめん fine wheat noodles eaten cold & dipped in sauce

so·ra·ma·me そら豆 broad bean

sō·sē·ji ソーセージ sausage

sō·su ソース sauce • Worcester sauce

so·tē ソテー sauté

su 酢 vinegar

su·ga·ta·mu·shi 姿蒸し steamed whole fish

su·gu·ki 酢茎 turnip pickle (Kyoto Prefecture)

su·gu·ri スグリ currant • gooseberry

spair·ri·bu スペアリブ sparerib

spā·ku·rin·gu·wain スパークリングワイン sparkling wine

su·i·ka すいか watermelon

su·i·ku·chi 吸い口 topping for clear soup

su·i·mo·no 吸い物 clear Japanese soup made of fish stock (also called su·ma·shi or su·ma·shi·ji·ru)

su·i·to·kōn スウィートコーン sweetcorn

su·ī·to·ba·ji·ru スウィートバジル sweet basil

su·i·ton すいとん balls made of wheat flour & boiled with vegetables in soup

su·ji スジ sinew • tendon of pork or beef (term used in ya·ki·to·ri restaurants)

su·ji·ko すじこ salted salmon roe

su·ki·ya·ki すき焼き beef, tō·fu, vegetables & shi·ra·ta·ki cooked in an iron pan with shō·yu, sugar & sa·ke & served with raw egg dip

su·ma·shi(·ji·ru) 澄まし(汁) see su·i·mo·no

su·me·shi 酢飯 vinegared rice used for su·shi

su·mi·bi·ya·ki 炭火焼き charcoal-grilled food

su·mi·so 酢味噌 sauce made of vinegar & mi·so

su·mo·mo スモモ plum

su·ne·ni·ku すね肉 shank

su·no·mo·no 酢の物 vinegared food

sup·pon スッポン snapping turtle

sup·pon·na·be スッポン鍋 hotpot of sup·pon

sup·pon·ryō·ri スッポン料理 snapping turtle served as na·be·mo·no, sa·shi·mi, or deep-fried

sū·pu スープ soup

su·ri·ba·chi すり鉢 mortar (as in mortar & pestle)

su·ri·go·ma すりごま ground sesame

su·ru·me スルメ dried squid

su·shi すし any food served on or rolled in vinegared rice

T

su·shi·da·ne すし種 su·shi topping

su·shi·me·shi すし飯 vinegared rice for su·shi

su·ya·ke 素焼き plainly grilled without salt

su·zu·ke 酢漬け vinegared pickles

su·zu·ki スズキ common sea bass • Japanese sea perch

su·zu·ki no hō·sho·ya·ki スズキの奉書焼き grilled sea bass served wrapped in traditional Japanese paper (city of Matsue & Shimane Prefecture)

su·zu·me すずめ sparrow – served at ya·ki·to·ri restaurants

~ **T** ~

ta·chi·u·o タチウオ cutlass fish • hairtail (fish)

tai タイ snapper • bream

tai·mu タイム thyme

tai·ra·gai タイラ貝 fan shell • sea pen (invertebrate sea creature)

tai·ra·gi タイラギ see tai·ra·gai

tai·ryō·ri 鯛料理 sea bream cuisine

tai·shō·e·bi 大正エビ fleshy prawn

ta·ka·na 高菜 broad-leafed mustard

ta·ka·na·zu·ke 高菜漬け mustard leaf pickles

ta·ka no tsu·me 鷹の爪 red-hot peppers

ta·ke·no·ko タケノコ bamboo shoots

ta·ki·ko·mi·go·han 炊き込み御飯 rice cooked together with vegetables & seasonings

ta·ko タコ octopus

ta·ko·ya·ki タコ焼き balls made of flour with octopus inside, fried (Osaka)

ta·ku·an たくあん pickled dai·kon

ta·ma·go 卵 egg

ta·ma·go·to·ji 卵とじ cooked vegetables or meat covered with whisked egg

ta·ma·go·ya·ki 卵焼き Japanese-style fried egg • omelette

ta·ma·ne·gi たまねぎ onion

ta·ma·ne·gi no su·zu·ke たまねぎの酢漬け pickling onion

ta·ma·ri·dō·fu たまりどうふ tō·fu infused with egg

ta·ma·ri·jō·yu たまりじょう油 wheat-free shō·yu

tan タン tongue

ta·ra タラ cod • Pacific cod • grey cod

ta·ra·ba·ga·ni タラバガニ Alaskan crab • king crab

ta·ra·gon タラゴン tarragon

ta·ra·ko タラコ salted cod • collack roe

ta·ra·no·me タラノメ angelica tree sprout (available only in early spring)

ta·re たれ sauce – usually made from shō·yu, mi·rin & sugar

ta·ro·i·mo タロイモ taro

ta·ta·ki たたき minced raw fish flesh • meat or fish seared on the outside & served sliced, with the inside remaining rare

ta·tsu·ta·a·ge 竜田揚げ meat or fish dipped in shō·yu & seasoned flour, then deep-fried

te·kī·ra テキーラ tequila

tek·ka·don 鉄火丼 tuna sa·shi·mi on a large bowl of steamed rice

tek·ka·ma·ki 鉄火巻き tuna su·shi roll

te·ma·ki·zu·shi 手巻きずし do-it-yourself su·shi roll

tem·pu·ra てんぷら seafood, meat & vegetables deep-fried in light batter & eaten dipped in a light sauce with ginger & grated dai·kon

tem·pu·ra·so·ba てんぷらそば buckwheat noodles in broth with tem·pu·ra pieces on top

tem·pu·ra·u·don てんぷらうどん wheat flour noodles in broth with tem·pu·ra pieces on top

ten·don 天丼 battered prawn on rice

te·ri·ya·ki 照り焼き meat or fish, brushed with marinade made of shō·yu, mi·rin & sugar, then grilled

tē·sho·ku 定食 set menu

U

tes·sa てっさ fu·gu sa·shi·mi

te·u·chi·so·ba 手打ちそば traditional, handmade so·ba

to·bi·u·o トビウオ flying fish

tō·fu とうふ soy-bean curd (tofu)

tō·ga·ra·shi とうがらし red chilli pepper • cayenne

to·ki·shi·ra·zu ときしらず see a·ra·ma·ki·za·ke

to·ma·to トマト tomato

to·ma·to·sō·su トマトソース tomato sauce

tō·mo·ro·ko·shi トウモロコシ corn

ton·ko·tsu とんこつ pork broth

ton·ko·tsu·rā·men とんこつラーメン rā·men with white pork broth

ton·ka·tsu·sō·su とんかつソース sauce to go with ton·ka·tsu (pork cutlet)

to·nik·ku トニック tonic water

tō·nyū 豆乳 soy milk

top·pin·gu トッピング topping

to·ra·fu·gu トラフグ tiger fu·gu

to·rai·pu トライプ tripe

to·ra·ma·me とら豆 tiger beans

to·ri·ni·ku 鶏肉 chicken (meat)

to·ri·ni·ku 鳥肉 poultry

to·ro とろ the fattiest (and also considered the tastiest) meat of tuna fish ma·gu·ro

to·ro·ro とろろ grated yam

to·ro·ro·ji·ru とろろ汁 grated yam mixed with stock

to·ryu·fu トリュフ truffle

to·shō·shi·yu 杜松子油 juniper berry oil

tōs·to トースト toast

tsu·ba·me·u·o ツバメ魚 swallow fish • a type of batfish

tsu·bo·ya·ki つぼ焼き shellfish (normally whelks) grilled in its own shell

tsu·ke·mo·no 漬物 pickles

tsu·ki·mi·so·ba 月見そば buckwheat noodles in broth with a raw egg

tsu·ki·mi·u·don 月見うどん wheat flour noodles in broth with a raw egg

tsu·ku·da·ni 佃煮 seafood or vegetables simmered in a thick sauce made from salt, sugar & shō·yu until all moisture is reduced

tsu·ku·ne つくね minced fish or chicken balls eaten fried or boiled

tsu·ku·ri 造り slices of raw fish, another term for sa·shi·mi

tsu·ma つま garnish

tsu·me·mo·no 詰め物 stuffing

tsu·mi·re つみれ fish-cake balls – used in o·den & stew

tsu·no·ga·rē ツノガレイ plaice

tsu·yu つゆ dipping sauce

tu·ke·a·wa·se 付け合せ garnish • relish

~ U ~

u·ba·gai ウバ貝 hen clam

u·do ウド mountain vegetable eaten fresh, stewed or pickled

u·don うどん thick noodles made of wheat flour

u·kon ウコン turmeric

u·me 梅 Japanese plum

u·me·bo·shi 梅干 dried & pickled Japanese plum

u·me·zu 梅酢 sour-plum vinegar

u·mi·u·o 海魚 fish from the ocean

u·na·don うな丼 grilled eel on rice

u·na·gi うなぎ eel

u·na·gi no ka·ba·ya·ki うなぎの蒲焼 grilled eel flavoured with soy-based sauce

u·na·jū うな重 grilled eel served on rice in a lacquered box

u·ni ウニ sea urchin

u·no·ha·na 卯の花 see o·ka·ra

u·ro·ko うろこ fish scales

ū·ron·cha 烏龍茶 oolong tea

u·ru·chi·mai うるち米 non-glutinous rice

u·ru·ka ウルカ salted innards of a·yu

u·ru·me·i·wa·shi ウルメイワシ Japanese sardine

·shi no o 牛の尾 oxtail

·shi·o·ji·ru うしお汁 delicately flavoured clear soup made from fish & shellfish

·su·a·ji 薄味 light-tasting or lightly seasoned

·su·cha 薄茶 thinner tea than koy·cha

·su·ku·chi·shō·yu 薄口しょう油 light shō·yu

·su·tā·sō·su ウスターソース Worcester sauce

·su·zu·ku·ri 薄作り raw, thinly sliced 'u·gu flesh

·zu·ra ウズラ quail

·zu·ra no ta·ma·go ウズラの卵 quail egg

~ **W** ~

wa·ga·shi 和菓子 Japanese sweets

wa·gyū 和牛 Japanese beef

wai·ru·do·rai·su ワイルドライス wild rice

wa·ka·me ワカメ type of seaweed

wa·ka·sa·gi わかさぎ pond smelt (a freshwater fish)

wa·ke·gi ワケギ shallots

wa·ni ワニ shark meat (Chūgoku region) • crocodile

wan·tan·men ワンタン麺 rā·men noodles in broth, with meat dumplings

wa·ra·bi 蕨 a kind of fern of which the tender young shoots are eaten

wa·ra·ma·ki·bu·ri 藁巻きブリ salted & dried bu·ri, which is then rolled in straw (Toyama Prefecture)

wa·ri·shi·ta 割り下 sauce of shō·yu, mi·rin & sugar, used in su·ki·ya·ki

wa·sa·bi ワサビ very hot Japanese horseradish

wa·sa·bi·ma·ki ワサビ巻き su·shi roll containing wa·sa·bi

wa·sa·bi·zu·ke ワサビ漬け vegetables pickled in a wa·sa·bi base

wa·ta わた see ha·ra·wa·ta

wa·ta·ri·ga·ni ワタリガニ blue swimmer crab

wi·kyō ウイキョウ fennel

wi·kyō no mi ウイキョウの実 fennel seed

wi·rō ういろう a steamed sweet made of rice flour & arrowroot (Nagoya)

~ **Y** ~

...·ya …屋 ... shop • ... restaurant, eg su·shi·ya, sha·bu·sha·bu·ya

ya·e·na·ri ヤエナリ mung bean

...·ya·ki/ya·ki... …焼き/焼き… food that is grilled, baked, barbecued or pan fried

ya·ki·dō·fu 焼き豆腐 grilled tō·fu used for hotpot

ya·ki·gyō·za 焼きギョウザ grilled gyō·za dumpling

ya·ki·me·shi 焼き飯 fried rice

ya·ki·mo·chi 焼きもち toasted rice cake

ya·ki·mo·no 焼きもの broiled, grilled or pan-fried dishes

ya·ki·na·su 焼きナス grilled eggplant

ya·ki·ni·ku 焼肉 cook-it-yourself, Korean-style barbecue

ya·ki·no·ri 焼き海苔 lightly toasted no·ri

ya·ki·o·ni·gi·ri 焼きおにぎり grilled rice ball

ya·ki·so·ba 焼きそば fried so·ba noodles with vegetables, meat & sauce

ya·ki·to·ri 焼きとり grilled meat on skewers served with ta·re or salt

ya·ki·za·ka·na 焼き魚 grilled fish

ya·ku·mi 薬味 condiment • relish • seasoning

ya·ma·i·mo 山芋 yam

ya·ma·ka·ke 山かけ grated yam with seasoning

ya·ma·ku·ji·ra 山鯨 'mountain whale' – the renamed i·no·shi·shi (wild boar)

ya·ma·me ヤマメ freshwater salmon

ya·ma no mo·no 山のもの mountain dishes

Z

ya·na·ga·wa·na·be 柳川鍋 boiled loach or weatherfish with whisked eggs on top

ya·sai 野菜 vegetables

ya·sai·i·ta·me 野菜炒め fried vegetables

ya·sē 野生 wild

ya·sō 野草 wild greens

ya·tsu·ga·shi·ra 八ッ頭 most sought-after type of taro

ya·tsu·ha·shi 八橋 sweet cinnamon-flavoured hard crackers (Kyoto Prefecture)

yō·kan ようかん sweet jelly made of ground a·zu·ki beans

yo·mo·gi ヨモギ mugwort

yō·na·shi 洋ナシ pear

yo·se·na·be 寄せ鍋 hotpot with seafood, chicken & vegetables in a light stock

yō·sho·ku 洋食 Japanese versions of Western dishes

yu·ba ゆば thin layers of skin skimmed from boiled soy milk

yu·de·gyō·za ゆでギョウザ boiled gyō·za dumpling

yu·de·ta·ma·go ゆで卵 boiled eggs

yu·dō·fu 湯豆腐 tō·fu boiled in a weak kom·bu broth

yū·ga·o ユウガオ white-flower gourd • bottle gourd

yū·han 夕飯 dinner

yu·shi·dō·fu ゆし豆腐 a soft variety of tō·fu from Okinawa

yu·zu ゆず a type of citrus fruit

~ Z ~

zak·ko·ku 雑穀 millet

za·ku·ro ざくろ pomegranate

za·ru·gai ザルガイ cockle

za·ru·so·ba ざるそば cold buckwheat noodles served with no·ri, spring onion & wa·sa·bi

zem·mai ゼンマイ osmund • royal fern (mountain vegetable)

zen·ryū·ko·mu·gi 全粒小麦 whole-wheat

zen·ryū·ko·mu·gi·ko 全粒小麦粉 wholewheat flour

zen·zai ぜんざい sweet a·zu·ki bean soup with rice cakes

ze·ra·chin ゼラチン gelatine

ze·rī ゼリー jelly

zo·me·ki·ryō·ri ぞめき料理 cuisine of local vegetables & seafood from Tokushima Prefecture

zō·mo·tsu 臓物 offal • giblets

zō·ni 雑煮 rice cake in soup

zō·su·i 雑炊 rice gruel • soup with vegetables & seafood flavoured with mi·so or shō·yu

zu·i·ki ずいき taro stem

zu·wai·ga·ni ズワイガニ red crab • snow crab

Dictionary

ENGLISH *to* JAPANESE
英語 – 日本語

Verbs in this dictionary are in their ·mas (ます) form (for more information on this, see **grammar**). The symbols ⓝ, ⓐ and ⓥ (indicating noun, adjective and verb) have been added for clarity where an English term could be either. Basic food terms have been included – for a more extensive list of ingredients and dishes, see the **menu decoder**.

A

aboard 乗って not·te
abortion 中絶 chū·ze·tsu
about だいたい dai·tai
above 上に u·e ni
abroad 海外 kai·gai
accident 事故 ji·ko
accommodation 宿泊 shu·ku·ha·ku
(bank) account 口座 kō·za
across 横切って yo·ko·git·te
actor 俳優 hai·yū
acupuncture 鍼 ha·ri
adaptor アダプター a·da·pu·tā
addiction 中毒 chū·do·ku
address 住所 jū·sho
administration 管理 kan·ri
admission (price) 入場料 nyū·jō·ryō
adult ⓐ 大人 o·to·na
adventure 冒険 bō·ken
advertisement 広告 kō·ko·ku
advice 意見 i·ken
aerobics エアロビクス air·ro·bi·kus
aeroplane 飛行機 hi·kō·ki
Africa アフリカ a·fu·ri·ka

after あと a·to
afternoon 午後 go·go
(this) afternoon (今日の)午後 (kyō no) go·go
aftershave アフターシェーブ af·tā·shē·bu
again また ma·ta
age ⓝ 年齢 nen·rē
(three days) ago (3日)前 (mik·ka) ma·e
aggressive 攻撃的な kō·ge·ki·te·ki na
agree 賛成します san·sē shi·mas
agriculture 農業 nō·gyō
ahead 向うに mu·kō ni
AIDS エイズ ē·zu
air 空気 kū·ki
air-conditioned エアコン付きの air·kon·tsu·ki no
air-conditioning エアコン air·kon
airline 航空 kō·kū
airmail 航空便 kō·kū·bin
airplane 飛行機 hi·kō·ki
airport 空港 kū·kō
airport tax 空港税 kū·kō·zē
aisle (eg, on plane) 通路 tsū·ro

B

alarm clock 目覚し時計 me·za·ma·shi·do·kē
alcohol アルコール a·ru·kō·ru
alcove (in house) 床の間 to·ko·no·ma
all 全部 zem·bu
allergy アレルギー a·re·ru·gī
almond アーモンド ā·mon·do
almost ほとんど ho·ton·do
alone ひとりで hi·to·ri de
already もう mō
also また ma·ta
altar 祭壇 sai·dan
altitude 標高 hyō·kō
always いつも i·tsu·mo
ambassador 大使 tai·shi
ambulance 救急車 kyū·kyū·sha
America アメリカ a·me·ri·ka
amount (money) 総計 sō·kē
anaemia 貧血 hin·ke·tsu
anaesthetic 麻酔 ma·su·i
anchovy アンチョビ・カタクチイワシ an·cho·bi · ka·ta·ku·chi·i·wa·shi
ancient 大昔の ō·mu·ka·shi no
and そして so·shi·te
angry 怒ります o·ko·ri·mas
animal 動物 dō·bu·tsu
ankle 足首 a·shi·ku·bi
annual 年一回の nen·ik·kai no
another もう一つの mō·hi·to·tsu no
answer ⓝ 答 ko·ta·e
ant アリ a·ri
antibiotics 抗生剤 kō·sē·zai
antihistamines 抗ヒスタミン剤 kō·hi·su·ta·min·zai
antinuclear 反核の han·ka·ku no
antique ⓝ アンティーク an·tī·ku
antiseptic ⓝ 消毒剤 shō·do·ku·zai
any いくらか i·ku·ra·ka
apartment マンション・アパート man·shon · a·pā·to
apéritif 食前酒 sho·ku·zen·shu
appendix (organ) 盲腸 mō·chō
appetiser 前菜 zen·sai
apple りんご rin·go
appointment 予約 yo·ya·ku
apricot あんず an·zu

archaeological 考古学的な kō·ko·ga·ku·te·ki na
architect 建築家 ken·chi·ku·ka
architecture 建築 ken·chi·ku
argue 反論します han·ron shi·mas
arm 腕 u·de
aromatherapy アロマテラピー a·ro·ma·te·ra·pī
arrest ⓥ 逮捕します tai·ho shi·mas
arrivals 到着 tō·cha·ku
arrive 到着します tō·cha·ku shi·mas
art 美術 bi·ju·tsu
art gallery 美術館 bi·ju·tsu·kan
artist 芸術家 gē·ju·tsu·ka
ashtray 灰皿 hai·za·ra
Asia アジア a·jya
ask (a question) たずねます ta·zu·ne·mas
ask (for something) たのみます ta·no·mi·mas
asparagus アスパラガス as·pa·ra·gas
aspirin アスピリン as·pi·rin
assault 暴行 bō·kō
asthma 喘息 zen·so·ku
at で de
athletics 運動 un·dō
atmosphere 雰囲気 fun·i·ki
aubergine ナス na·su
aunt おばさん o·ba·san
Australia オーストラリア ō·sto·ra·rya
automatic ⓐ オートマチック ō·to·ma·chik·ku
automated teller machine (ATM) ATM ē·tī·e·mu
autumn 秋 a·ki
avenue 大通り ō·dō·ri
avocado アボガド a·bo·ga·do
awful ひどい hi·doy

B

B&W (film) 白黒（フィルム） shi·ro·ku·ro (fi·ru·mu)
baby 赤ちゃん a·ka·chan
baby food 離乳食 ri·nyū·sho·ku
baby powder ベビーパウダー be·bī·pow·dā

B

babysitter ベビーシッター be·bi·shit·tā
back (body part) 背中 se·na·ka
back (position) うしろ u·shi·ro
backpack バックパック bak·ku·pak·ku
bacon ベーコン bē·kon
bad 悪い wa·ru·i
bag (general) かばん ka·ban
bag (shopping) 袋 fu·ku·ro
baggage 手荷物 te·ni·mo·tsu
baggage allowance 手荷物許容量 te·ni·mo·tsu·kyo·yō·ryō
baggage claim バッゲージクレーム bag·gē·ji·ku·rē·mu
bakery パン屋 pan·ya
balance (account) 残高 zan·da·ka
balcony バルコニー ba·ru·ko·nī
ball (sport) ボール bō·ru
ballet バレエ ba·rē
banana バナナ ba·na·na
band (music) バンド ban·do
bandage 包帯 hō·tai
Band-Aids バンドエイド ban·do·ēdo
bank (money) 銀行 gin·kō
bank account 銀行口座 gin·kō·kō·za
banknote 紙幣 shi·hē
bar バー bā
bar fridge ミニバー mi·ni·bā
bar work バーテンダー bā·ten·dā
barber 床屋 to·ko·ya
baseball 野球 ya·kyū
basketball バスケット(ボール) bas·ket·to (bōru)
bath ⓝ お風呂 o·fu·ro
bath house 銭湯 sen·tō
bathing suit 水着 mi·zu·gi
bathroom 風呂場 fu·ro·ba
batter バター ba·tā
battery (general) 電池 den·chi
battery (for car) バッテリー bat·te·rī
be です des
beach ビーチ bī·chi
beach volleyball ビーチバレー bī·chi·ba·rē
beans 豆 ma·me
beansprouts もやし mo·ya·shi

bear ⓝ クマ ku·ma
beautiful 美しい u·tsu·ku·shī
beauty salon 美容室 bi·yō·shi·tsu
because だから da·ka·ra
bed ベッド bed·do
bed linen シーツ shī·tsu
bedding 寝具 shin·gu
bedroom 寝室 shin·shi·tsu
bee 蜂 ha·chi
beef 牛肉 gyū·ni·ku
beer ビール bī·ru
beetroot ビートルート bī·to·rū·to
before 前 ma·e
beggar 乞食 ko·ji·ki
behind うしろ u·shi·ro
Belgium ベルギー be·ru·gī
below 下 shi·ta
belt 帯 o·bi
berries 木の実・ベリー ki·no·mi・be·rī
beside 横 yo·ko
best 最高 sai·kō no
bet ⓥ 賭け ka·ke
better より良い yo·ri yoy
between あいだ ai·da
bicycle 自転車 ji·ten·sha
big 大きい ō·kī
bigger より大きい yo·ri ō·kī
biggest いちばん大きい i·chi·ban ō·kī
bike ⓝ 自転車 ji·ten·sha
bike chain 自転車のチェーン ji·ten·sha no chēn
bike lock 自転車の鍵 ji·ten·sha no ka·gi
bike path 自転車道 ji·ten·sha·dō
bike shop 自転車屋 ji·ten·sha·ya
bill (restaurant etc) ⓝ 勘定 kan·jō
binoculars 双眼鏡 sō·gan·kyō
bird 鳥 to·ri
birth certificate 出生証明書 shus·sē·shō·mē·sho
birthday 誕生日 tan·jō·bi
biscuit ビスケット bis·ket·to
bite (dog) ⓝ かみ傷 ka·mi·ki·zu
bite (insect) ⓝ 虫刺され mu·shi·sa·sa·re
bitter ⓐ 苦い ni·gai

B

black 黒い ku·roy
black (coffee) ブラック bu·rak·ku
bladder 膀胱 bō·kō
blanket 毛布 mō·fu
blind 目が見えない me ga mi·e·nai
blister 水疱 su·i·hō
blocked つまります tsu·ma·ri·mas
blood 血 chi
blood group 血液型 ke·tsu·e·ki·ga·ta
blood pressure 血圧 ke·tsu·a·tsu
blood test 血液検査 ke·tsu·e·ki·ken·sa
blue 青い a·oy
board (a plane, ship etc) ⓥ 乗ります
no·ri·mas
boarding house 下宿屋 ge·shu·ku·ya
boarding pass 搭乗券 tō·jō·ken
boat ⓝ 船 fu·ne
boat-trip ボートツアー bō·to·tsu·ā
bok choy チンゲンサイ chin·gen·sai
body 体 ka·ra·da
boil (in hot water) ゆでます
yu·de·mas
boil (in stock) 煮ます ni·mas
bone 骨 ho·ne
book ⓝ 本 hon
book (make a booking) ⓥ 予約
します yo·ya·ku shi·mas
booked out 満席 man·se·ki
bookshop 本屋 hon·ya
boots (footwear) ブーツ bū·tsu
border ⓝ 境界 kyō·kai
boring 退屈な tai·ku·tsu na
borrow 借ります ka·ri·mas
botanic garden 植物園
sho·ku·bu·tsu·en
both 両方 ryō·hō
bottle ビン bin
bottle opener 栓抜き sen·nu·ki
bottle shop 酒屋 sa·ka·ya
bottom (body) お尻 o·shi·ri
bottom (position) 最後 sai·go
bowl ⓝ ボール bō·ru
  rice bowl 茶碗 cha·wan
  soup bowl お椀 o·wan
box 箱 ha·ko
boxing ⓝ ボクシング bo·ku·shin·gu

boy 男の子 o·to·ko no ko
boyfriend ボーイフレンド
bōy·fu·ren·do
bra ブラジャー bu·ra·jā
Braille ブレール式点字
bu·rē·ru·shi·ki·ten·ji
brakes ブレーキ bu·rē·ki
brandy ブランデー bu·ran·dē
brave 勇敢な yū·kan na
bread パン pan
bread rolls ロールパン rō·ru·pan
break ⓥ 壊します ko·wa·shi·mas
break down ⓥ 壊れます
ko·wa·re·mas
breakfast 朝食・朝ごはん chō·sho·ku
· a·sa·go·han
breast (body) 乳房 chi·bu·sa
breathe 息をします i·ki o shi·mas
bribe ⓥ わいろ wai·ro
bridge ⓝ 橋 ha·shi
briefcase ブリーフケース bu·rī·fu·kē·su
bring 持ってきます mot·te·ki·mas
brochure パンフレット pan·fu·ret·to
broken 壊れた ko·wa·re·ta
broken down 故障した ko·shō·shi·ta
bronchitis 気管支炎 ka·kan·shi·en
broth だし汁 da·shi·ji·ru
brother 兄弟 kyō·dai
brown 茶色い chai·roy
brown rice 玄米 gem·mai
bruise あざ a·za
brush ⓝ ブラシ bu·ra·shi
bucket バケツ ba·ke·tsu
Buddhist ⓝ 仏教徒 buk·kyō·to
budget 予算 yo·san
buffet (meal) ビュッフェ byuf·fe
bug ⓝ 虫 mu·shi
building 建物 ta·te·mo·no
bullet train 新幹線 shin·kan·sen
bum お尻 o·shi·ri
bumbag ウエストポーチ wes·to·pō·chi
burn ⓝ やけど ya·ke·do
burnt 焼けた ya·ke·ta
bus (city) (市)バス (shi) bas
bus (intercity) (長距離)バス
(chō·kyo·ri) bas

C

ous station バスターミナル bas·tā·mi·na·ru

ous stop バス停 bas·tē

ousiness ビジネス bi·ji·nes

ousiness card 名刺 mē·shi

ousiness class ビジネスクラス bi·ji·nes·ku·ras

ousiness man サラリーマン sa·ra·rī·man

ousiness person ビジネスマン bi·ji·nes·man

ousiness trip 出張 shut·chō

ousiness woman ビジネスウーマン bi·ji·nes·ū·man

ousker 大道芸人 dai·dō·gē·nin

ousy 忙しい i·so·ga·shī

out しかし shi·ka·shi

outcher's shop 肉屋 ni·ku·ya

outter バター ba·tā

outterfly 蝶 chō

outton ボタン bo·tan

ouy ⓥ 買います kai·mas

C

cabbage キャベツ kya·be·tsu

cabin 船室 sen·shi·tsu

cable car ケーブルカー kē·bu·ru·kā

café カフェ ka·fe

cake ケーキ kē·ki

cake shop ケーキ屋 kē·ki·ya

calculator 計算機 kē·san·ki

calendar カレンダー ka·ren·dā

call ⓥ 呼びます yo·bi·mas

calligraphy 書道 sho·dō

camera カメラ ka·me·ra

camera shop カメラ屋 ka·me·ra·ya

camp site キャンプ場 kyam·pu·jō

camping store キャンプ用品店 kyam·pu·yō·hin·ten

can (be able) できます de·ki·mas

can (have permission) してもいいです shi·te·mo ī des

can (tin) 缶 kan

can opener 缶切 kan·ki·ri

Canada カナダ ka·na·da

cancel キャンセル kyan·se·ru

cancer (illness) 癌 gan

candle ろうそく rō·so·ku

candy キャンディー kyan·dī

cantaloupe メロン me·ron

capsicum ピーマン pī·man

capsule hotel カプセルホテル ka·pu·se·ru·ho·te·ru

car 自動車 ji·dō·sha

car deck 車両甲板 sha·ryō·kam·pan

car hire レンタカー ren·ta·kā

car lights ヘッドライト hed·do·rai·to

car owner's title 自動車所有権 ji·dō·sha·sho·yū·ken

car park 駐車場 chū·sha·jō

car registration 自動車登録 ji·dō·sha·tō·ro·ku

caravan キャンピングカー kyam·pin·gu·kā

cardiac arrest 心拍停止 shim·pa·ku·tē·shi

cards (playing) トランプ to·ram·pu

care (for someone) ⓥ 面倒を見ます men·dō o mi·mas

carpark 駐車場 chū·sha·jō

carpenter 大工 dai·ku

carrot ニンジン nin·jin

carry 運びます ha·ko·bi·mas

carry-on luggage 機内持込の手荷物 ki·nai·mo·chi·ko·mi no te·ni·mo·tsu

carton カートン ka·ton

cartoons 漫画 man·ga

cash ⓝ 現金 gen·kin

cash (a cheque) ⓥ 現金化します gen·kin·ka shi·mas

cash register レジ re·ji

cashew カシューナッツ ka·shū·nat·tsu

cashier レジ re·ji

casino カジノ ka·ji·no

cassette カセット ka·set·to

castle 城 shi·ro

casual work 臨時の仕事 rin·ji no shi·go·to

cat ネコ ne·ko

cathedral 大聖堂 dai·sē·dō

Catholic ⓝ カトリック ka·to·rik·ku

DICTIONARY

cauliflower カリフラワー ka·ri·fu·ra·wā

cave 洞窟 dō·ku·tsu

caviar キャビア kya·bya

CD CD shī·dī

celebration お祝い oy·wai

cell phone 携帯電話 kē·tai·den·wa

cemetery 墓地 bo·chi

centimetre センチ sen·chi

central 中央の chū·ō no

centre 中央 chū·ō

ceramics セラミックス se·ra·mik·ku·su

cereal シリアル shi·ri·a·ru

certificate 証明書 shō·mē·sho

chain 鎖 ku·sa·ri

chair 椅子 i·su

chair (legless) 座椅子 za·i·su

chairlift (skiing) リフト ri·fu·to

champagne シャンペン sham·pen

championships 選手権 sen·shu·ken

change ⓝ 変化 hen·ka

change (coins) 小銭 ko·ze·ni

change (money) ⓥ 換金します kan·kin shi·mas

changing room (in shop) 試着室 shi·cha·ku·shi·tsu

changing room (for sport) 更衣室 kōy·shi·tsu

charming チャーミングな chā·min·gu·na

cheap 安い ya·su·i

cheat ⓝ ずる zu·ru

check (banking) ⓝ 小切手 ko·git·te

check (bill) ⓝ 確認 ka·ku·nin

check ⓥ 点検します ten·ken shi·mas

check-in (desk) ⓝ チェックイン chek·ku·in

checkpoint チェックポイント chek·ku·poyn·to

cheese チーズ chī·zu

chef シェフ she·fu

chemist (shop) 薬局 yak·kyo·ku

chemist (person) 薬剤師 ya·ku·zai·shi

cheque (banking) 小切手 ko·git·te

cheque (bill) 手形 te·ga·ta

cherry さくらんぼ sa·ku·ram·bo

cherry blossom 桜 sa·ku·ra

chess (Japanese) 将棋 shō·gi

chess (Western) チェス ches

chest (body) 胸 mu·ne

chestnut 栗 ku·ri

chewing gum チューインガム chū·in·ga·mu

chicken (animal) にわとり ni·wa·to·ri

chicken (meat) 鶏肉 to·ri·ni·ku

chicken pox 水ぼうそう mi·zu·bō·sō

chickpeas ヒヨコマメ hi·yo·ko·ma·me

child 子供 ko·do·mo

child seat チャイルドシート chai·ru·do·shī·to

childminding 子守り ko·mo·ri

children 子供 ko·do·mo

chilli 唐辛子 tō·ga·ra·shi

chilli oil ラー油 rā·yu

chilli sauce チリソース chi·ri·sō·su

China 中国 chū·go·ku

Chinese ⓐ 中国の chū·go·ku no

Chinese cabbage 白菜 ha·ku·sai

Chinese food 中華料理 chū·ka·ryō·ri

Chinese radish 大根 dai·kon

Chinese tea 中国茶 chū·go·ku·cha

chips チップ chip·pu

chiropractor カイロプラクター kai·ro·pu·ra·ku·tā

chocolate チョコレート cho·ko·rē·to

choose 選びます e·ra·bi·mas

chopping board まな板 ma·nai·ta

chopping knife 包丁 hō·chō

chopsticks はし ha·shi

chopsticks (disposable) 割り箸 wa·ri·ba·shi

chopstick holder はし置き ha·shi·o·ki

Christian ⓝ キリスト教徒 ki·ri·su·to·kyō·to

Christian name 洗礼名 sen·rē·mē

Christmas クリスマス ku·ri·su·mas

church 教会 kyō·kai

cider サイダー sai·dā

cigar 葉巻 ha·ma·ki

cigarette タバコ ta·ba·ko

cigarette lighter ライター rai·tā

cinema 映画館 ē·ga·kan

circus サーカス sā·kas

citizenship 市民権 shi·min·ken

city 市 shi

city centre 市の中心 shi no chū·shin

civil rights 公民権 kō·min·ken

class (category) 種類 shu·ru·i

class system 階級 kai·kyū

classical クラシックの ku·ra·shik·ku no

classical art 古典芸術 ko·ten·gē·ju·tsu

classical music クラシック音楽 ku·ra·shik·ku·on·ga·ku

classical theatre 古典演劇 ko·ten·en·ge·ki

clean @ きれいな ki·rē·na

clean @ 掃除をします sō·ji o shi·mas

cleaning @ クリーニング ku·rī·nin·gu

client 顧客 ko·kya·ku

cliff がけ ga·ke

climb @ 登ります no·bo·ri·mas

cloakroom クローク ku·rō·ku

clock 時計 to·kē

close (nearby) 近く chi·ka·ku

close @ 閉めます shi·me·mas

closed @ 閉店した hē·ten·shi·ta

cloth フキン fu·kin

clothes 衣類 i·ru·i

clothesline 物干し mo·no·ho·shi

clothing 衣類 i·ru·i

clothing store 衣料店 i·ryō·ten

cloud 雲 ku·mo

cloudy 曇りの ku·mo·ri·no

clutch (car) クラッチ ku·rat·chi

coach (bus) バス bas

coach (sport) コーチ kō·chi

coast 海岸 kai·gan

coat コート kō·to

cocaine コカイン ko·kain

cockroach ゴキブリ go·ki·bu·ri

cocktail カクテル ka·ku·te·ru

cocoa ココア ko·ko·a

coconut ココナツ ko·ko·na·tsu

coffee コーヒー kō·hī

coins コイン ko·in

cold @ 風邪 ka·ze

have a cold 風邪を引いています ka·ze o hī·te i·mas

cold (atmosphere) @ 寒い sa·mu·i

cold (to the touch) @ 冷たい tsu·me·ta·i

colleague 同僚 dō·ryo

collect call コレクトコール ko·re·ku·to·kō·ru

college カレッジ ka·rej·ji

colour 色 i·ro

comb くし ku·shi

come 来ます ki·mas

comedy コメディー ko·me·dī

comfortable 心地よい ko·ko·chi·yoy

comics 漫画 man·ga

commission 手数料 te·sū·ryo

communist @ 共産主義者 kyō·san·shu·gi·sha

companion コンパニオン kom·pa·ni·on

company (firm) 会社 kai·sha

compass 方位磁石 hōy·ji·sha·ku

complaint 苦情 ku·jō

complimentary (free) 無料の mu·ryō no

computer コンピュータ kom·pyū·ta

computer game コンピュータゲーム kom·pyū·ta·gē·mu

concert コンサート kon·sā·to

concussion 脳しんとう nō·shin·tō

conditioner (hair) コンディショナー kon·di·sho·nā

condom コンドーム kon·dō·mu

conference (big) コンファレンス kon·fa·ren·su

conference (small) ミーティング mī·tin·gu

confirm (a booking) 確認する ka·ku·nin su·ru

conjunctivitis 結膜炎 ke·tsu·ma·ku·en

connection 接続 se·tsu·zo·ku

conservative @ 保守 ho·shu

constipation 便秘 bem·pi

consulate 領事館 ryō·ji·kan

contact lens solution コンタクトレンズの洗浄液 kon·ta·ku·to·ren·zu no sen·jō·e·ki

D

contact lenses コンタクトレンズ kon·ta·ku·to·ren·zu
contraceptives (devices) 避妊具 hi·nin·gu
contraceptives (medicine) 避妊薬 hi·nin·yaku
contract 契約 kē·ya·ku
convenience store コンビニ kom·bi·ni
cook ⓝ コック kok·ku
cook ⓥ 料理します ryō·ri shi·mas
cooked 火が通った hi ga tōt·ta
cookie クッキー kuk·kī
cooking ⓝ 料理 ryō·ri
cool (temperature) 涼しい su·zu·shī
corkscrew コークスクリュー kō·ku·su·ku·ryū
corn とうもろこし tō·mo·ro·ko·shi
corner 角 ka·do
cornflakes コーンフレーク kōn·fu·rē·ku
corrupt 腐敗した fu·hai shi·ta
cost ⓥ 費用がかかります hi·yō ga ka·ka·ri·mas
cotton 綿 men
cotton balls 脱脂綿 das·shi·men
cotton buds 綿棒 mem·bō
cough ⓥ せきが出ます se·ki ga de·mas
cough medicine せき止め se·ki·do·me
count ⓥ かぞえます ka·zo·e·mas
counter (at bar) カウンター ka·un·tā
country (nation) 国 ku·ni
countryside 田舎 i·na·ka
coupon クーポン kū·pon
course (class) コース kōs
court (legal) 裁判所 sai·ban·sho
court (tennis) コート kō·to
cover charge カバーチャージ ka·bā·chā·ji
cow 牛 u·shi
crab カニ ka·ni
cracker クラッカー ku·rak·kā
crafts 工芸品 kō·gē·hin
crash ⓝ 衝突 shō·to·tsu

crazy きちがいの ki·chi·gai no
cream クリーム ku·rī·mu
crèche 託児所 ta·ku·ji·sho
credit 預金 yo·kin
credit card クレジットカード ku·re·jit·to·kā·do
cricket (sport) クリケット ku·ri·ket·
crime 犯罪 han·zai
crowded 混雑している kon·za·tsu shi·te·i·ru
cucumber キュウリ kyū·ri
cup カップ kap·pu
cupboard 食器棚 shok·ki·da·na
currency exchange 為替 ka·wa·se
current (electricity) 電流 den·ryū
current affairs 時事問題 ji·ji·mon·dai
curry カレー ka·rē
cushion 座布団 za·bu·ton
custom 習慣 shū·kan
customs 税関 zē·kan
cut (wound) ⓝ 切り ki·ri·ki·zu
cut ⓥ 切りま ki·ri·mas
cutlery ナイフとフォーク nai·fu to fō·ku
CV 履歴書 ri·re·ki·sho
cycling ⓝ サイクリング sai·ku·rin·gu
cyclist サイクリスト sai·ku·ris·to
cystitis ぼうこう炎 bō·kō·en

D

dad お父さん o·tō·san
daily 毎日 mai·ni·chi
dairy 乳製品 nyū·sē·hin
damage 被害 hi·gai
dance ⓥ 踊ります o·do·ri·mas
dancing ⓝ ダンス dan·su
dangerous 危ない a·bu·nai
dark 暗い ku·rai
date (appointment) 予約 yo·ya·ku
date (day) ⓝ 日付 hi·zu·ke
date (fruit) ⓝ ナツメヤシ na·tsu·me·ya·shi
date (with a person) ⓝ デート dē·to
date (a person) ⓥ デートします dē·to shi·mas
date of birth 誕生日 tan·jō·bi

D

daughter 娘 mu·su·me

dawn 夜明け yo·a·ke

day 日中 nit·chū

(the) day after tomorrow あさって a·sat·te

(the) day before yesterday おととい o·to·toy

day trip 1日観光 i·chi·ni·chi kan·kō

dead 死んでいる shin·de iru

deaf 耳が聞こえない mi·mi ga ki·ko·e·nai

decaffeinated デカフェ de·ka·fe

deck (ship) 甲板 kam·pan

decide 決めます ki·me·mas

deep 深い fu·kai

deep-fried 揚げて a·ge·te

deforestation 森林伐採 shin·rin·bas·sai

degrees (temperature) 度 do

delay 遅れ o·ku·re

delicatessen デリカテッセン de·ri·ka·tes·sen

deliver 配達します hai·ta·tsu shi·mas

democracy 民主主義 min·shu·shu·gi

demonstration (protest) デモ de·mo

Denmark デンマーク dem·mā·ku

dental floss デンタルフロス den·ta·ru·fu·ros

dentist 歯医者 ha·i·sha

deodorant 消臭剤 shō·shū·zai

depart (leave) 出発します shup·pa·tsu shi·mas

department store デパート de·pā·to

departure 出発 shup·pa·tsu

departure gate 出発ゲート shup·pa·tsu gē·to

deposit (bank) 預金 yo·kin

deposit (refundable) 預かり金 a·zu·ka·ri·kin

desert ⓝ 砂漠 sa·ba·ku

design ⓝ デザイン de·za·in

dessert デザート de·zā·to

destination 目的地 mo·ku·te·ki·chi

details 詳細 shō·sai

diabetes 糖尿病 tō·nyō·byō

dial tone ダイアルトーン dai·a·ru·tōn

diaper オムツ o·mu·tsu

diaphragm 腹膜 fu·ku·ma·ku

diarrhoea 下痢 ge·ri

diary 日記 nik·ki

dictionary 辞書 ji·sho

die ⓥ 死にます shi·ni·mas

diesel ディーゼル dī·ze·ru

diet ダイエット dai·et·to

different 違う chi·ga·u

difficult 難しい mu·zu·ka·shī

digital デジタルの de·ji·ta·ru no

dining car 食堂車 sho·ku·dō·sha

dinner 夕食・晩ごはん yū·sho·ku・ban·go·han

direct 直接に cho·ku·se·tsu ni

direct-dial ⓝ 直通 cho·ku·tsū

direction 方向 hō·kō

director ディレクター di·re·ku·tā

dirty 汚い ki·ta·nai

disabled ⓐ 障害をもつ shō·gai o mo·tsu

discount ⓝ 割引 wa·ri·bi·ki

discrimination 差別 sa·be·tsu

disease 病気 byō·ki

dish (food) 皿 sa·ra

disk (CD-ROM) CD-ROM shī·dī·ro·mu

disposable 使い捨ての tsu·kai·su·te no

disposable chopsticks 割り箸 wa·ri·ba·shi

diving ダイビング dai·bin·gu

diving equipment ダイビング用具 dai·bin·gu·yō·gu

divorced 離婚した ri·kon shi·ta

dizzy めまいがする me·mai ga su·ru

do します shi·mas

doctor 医者 i·sha

documentary ドキュメンタリー do·kyu·men·ta·rī

dog 犬 i·nu

dole 失業手当 shi·tsu·gyō·te·a·te

doll 人形 nin·gyō

dollar ドル do·ru

domestic 国内 ko·ku·nai

door ドア do·a

E

door (Japanese-style) ふすま fu·su·ma
dope (drugs) マリファナ ma·ri·fa·na
double 2倍の ni·bai no
double bed ダブルベッド da·bu·ru·bed·do
double room ダブルルーム da·bu·ru·rū·mu
down 下へ shi·ta e
downhill 下り坂の ku·da·ri·za·ka no
dozen ダース dās
drama ドラマ do·ra·ma
dream ⓝ 夢 yu·me
dress ⓝ ドレス do·res
dried 乾いた ka·wai·ta
dried fruit ドライフルーツ do·rai·fu·rū·tsu
drink ⓝ 飲み物 no·mi·mo·no
drink (alcoholic) ⓝ 酒・アルコール sa·ke・a·ru·kō·ru
drink ⓥ 飲みます no·mi·mas
drive ⓥ 運転します un·ten·shi·mas
driver 運転手 un·ten·shu
drivers licence 運転免許証 un·ten·men·kyo·shō
drug (medicine) 薬 ku·su·ri
drug (narcotic) 麻薬 ma·ya·ku
drug addiction 麻薬中毒 ma·ya·ku·chū·do·ku
drug dealer 麻薬の密売人 ma·ya·ku no mi·tsu·bai·nin
drug trafficking 麻薬の輸送 ma·ya·ku no yu·sō
drug user 麻薬使用者 ma·ya·ku·shi·yō·sha
drum (music) ⓝ ドラム do·ra·mu
drunk ⓐ 酔った yot·ta
dry ⓐ 乾いた ka·wai·ta
dry ⓥ 乾きます ka·wa·ki·mas
dry (clothes) ⓥ 乾かします ka·wa·ka·shi·mas
duck アヒル a·hi·ru
dummy (pacifier) おしゃぶり o·sha·bu·ri
dumplings ギョウザ gyō·za
during あいだ ai·da

duty-free 免税店 men·zē·ten
DVD DVD dī·bī·dī

E

each それぞれ so·re·zo·re
ear 耳 mi·mi
early 早く ha·ya·ku
earn 稼ぎます ka·se·gi·mas
earplugs 耳栓 mi·mi·sen
earrings イヤリング i·ya·rin·gu
earthquake 地震 ji·shin
east 東 hi·ga·shi
Easter イースター ī·stā
easy 簡単な kan·tan na
eat 食べます ta·be·mas
economy class エコノミークラス e·ko·no·mī·ku·ras
ecstacy (drug) エクスタシー e·kus·ta·shī
eczema 湿疹 shis·shin
education 教育 kyōy·ku
eel うなぎ u·na·gi
egg 卵 ta·ma·go
　boiled egg ゆで卵 yu·de·ta·ma·go
　fried egg 目玉焼き me·da·ma·ya·ki
　hard-boiled egg 固ゆで卵 ka·ta·yu·de·ta·ma·go
　poached egg ポーチドエッグ pō·chi·do·eg·gu
　scrambled egg 卵焼き ta·ma·go·ya·k
　raw egg 生卵 na·ma·ta·ma·go
eggplant ナス na·su
election 選挙 sen·kyo
electrical store 電化製品店 den·ka·se·hin
electrician 電気技師 den·ki·gi·shi
electricity 電気 den·ki
elevator エレベータ e·re·bē·ta
email Eメール ī·mē·ru
embarrassed 恥ずかしい ha·zu·ka·sʰ
embassy 大使館 tai·shi·kan
emergency 救急 kyū·kyū
emotional 感情的な kan·jō·te·ki na
Emperor (Japanese) 天皇 ten·nō
Emperor (non-Japanese) 皇帝 kō·tē
Empress 皇后 kō·gō

employee 従業員 jū·gyō·in
employer 雇用者 ko·yō·sha
empty 空の ka·ra no
end ⓝ おわり o·wa·ri
endangered species 絶滅に瀕した生物
ze·tsu·me·tsu ni hin shi·ta sē·bu·tsu
engaged (phone) お話中
o·ha·na·shi·chū
engaged (to be married) 婚約した
kon·ya·ku shi·ta
entrée アントレー an·to·rē
engine エンジン en·jin
engineer 技術者 gi·ju·tsu·sha
engineering 工学 kō·ga·ku
England イギリス i·gi·ri·su
English 英語 ē·go
enjoy (oneself) 楽しみます
a·no·shi·mi·mas
enough 充分な jū·bun na
enter 入ります hai·ri·mas
entertainment guide エンターテイ
メントガイド en·tā·tē·men·to·gai·do
entry 入場 nyū·jō
envelope 封筒 fū·tō
environment 環境 kan·kyō
epilepsy てんかん ten·kan
equality 平等 byō·dō
equipment 道具 dō·gu
escalator エスカレータ es·ka·rē·ta
estate agency 不動産屋 fu·dō·san·ya
euro ユーロ yū·ro
Europe ヨーロッパ yō·rop·pa
euthanasia 安楽死 an·ra·ku·shi
evening 晩 ban
every 毎 mai
everyone みんな min·na
everything 全部 zem·bu
exactly ちょうど chō·do
example 例 rē
excellent 素晴らしい su·ba·ra·shī
excess (baggage) 超過 chō·ka
exchange ⓝ 交換 kō·kan
exchange ⓥ 交換します kō·kan
shi·mas
exchange rate 為替レート
ka·wa·se·rē·to

excluded 抜きで nu·ki de
exhaust (car) 排気 hai·ki
exhibition 展覧会 ten·ran·kai
exit ⓝ 出口 de·gu·chi
expensive 高い ta·kai
experience 経験 kē·ken
exploitation 開発 kai·ha·tsu
express ⓐ 明白な mē·ha·ku na
express (mail) 速達 so·ku·ta·tsu
express train 急行 kyū·kō
extension (visa) 延長 en·chō
eye 目 me
eye drops 目薬 me·gu·su·ri

F

F

fabric 布 nu·no
face ⓝ 顔 ka·o
face cloth 洗面タオル sen·men·tow·ru
factory 工場 kō·jō
factory worker 工員 kō·in
fall (autumn) ⓝ 秋 a·ki
fall (down) ⓥ 倒れます tow·re·mas
family 家族 ka·zo·ku
family name 名字 myō·ji
family ticket 家族チケット
ka·zo·ku·chi·ket·to
famous 有名な yū·mē na
fan (machine) 扇風機 sem·pū·ki
fan (made of paper) 扇子 sen·su
fan (sport, etc) ファン fan
fanbelt ファンベルト fan·be·ru·to
far 遠い tōy
fare 料金 ryō·kin
farm 農場 nō·jō
farmer 農民 nō·min
fashion ファッション fas·shon
fast ⓐ 速い ha·yai
fat ⓐ 太った fu·tot·ta
father お父さん o·tō·san
father-in-law 義理のお父さん gi·ri no
o·tō·san
faucet 蛇口 ja·gu·chi
fault (someone's) 間違い ma·chi·gai
faulty 欠点のある ket·ten no a·ru
favourite 好きな su·ki na
fax (document) ⓝ ファックス fak·kus

fax (machine) ⓝ ファックス fak·kus

fee 料金 ryō·kin

feed ⓥ 餌をやります e·sa o ya·ri·mas

feeling (physical) 感触 kan·sho·ku

feelings 感情 kan·jō

female 女性 jo·sē

fence フェンス fen·su

fencing (sport) ⓝ フェンシング fen·sin·gu

ferry ⓝ フェリー fe·rī

festival 祭 ma·tsu·ri

fever 熱 ne·tsu

few (2 or 3) 2,3の ni, san no

few (more than 2 or 3) いくつかの i·ku·tsu·ka no

fiancé(e) 婚約者 kon·ya·ku·sha

fiction フィクション fik·shon

fig イチジク i·chi·ji·ku

fight ⓝ 戦い ta·ta·kai

fill いっぱいにします ip·pai ni shi·mas

fillet ⓝ フィレ fi·re

film (cinema) ⓝ 映画 ē·ga

film (for camera) ⓝ フィルム fi·ru·mu

film speed フィルムの感度 fi·ru·mu no kan·do

filtered フィルターを通した fi·ru·tā o tō·shi·ta

find ⓥ 見つけます mi·tsu·ke·mas

fine (penalty) ⓝ 罰金 bak·kin

fine ⓐ 元気な gen·ki na

finger 指 yu·bi

finish ⓝ 終わり o·wa·ri

finish ⓥ 終わります o·wa·ri·mas

Finland フィンランド fin·ran·do

fire 火 hi

firewood 薪 ma·ki

first 最初の sai·sho no

first-aid kit 救急箱 kyū·kyū·ba·ko

first class ⓝ ファーストクラス fā·sto·ku·ras

first name 名前 na·ma·e

first name (Christian only) 洗礼名 sen·rē·mē

fish ⓝ 魚 sa·ka·na

fish paste 魚のペースト sa·ka·na no pē·sto

fish sauce 魚醤 gyo·shō

fish shop 魚屋 sa·ka·na·ya

fishing ⓝ 釣り tsu·ri

flag ⓝ 旗 ha·ta

flannel フランネル fu·ran·ne·ru

flashlight (torch) 懐中電灯 kai·chū·den·tō

flat (apartment) フラット fu·rat·to

flat ⓐ 平らな tai·ra na

flea のみ no·mi

fleamarket フリーマーケット fu·rī·mā·ket·to

flight 航空便 kō·kū·bin

flood ⓝ 洪水 kō·zu·i

floor (ground) 床 yu·ka

floor (storey) 階 kai

florist 花屋 ha·na·ya

flour 小麦粉 ko·mu·gi·ko

flower 花 ha·na

flower arranging 生け花 i·ke·ba·na

flu インフルエンザ in·fu·ru·en·za

fly ⓝ ハエ ha·e

fly ⓥ 飛びます to·bi·mas

foggy 霧がかかった ki·ri ga ka·kat·ta

follow ついていきます tsu·i·te i·ki·mas

food 食べ物 ta·be·mo·no

food poisoning 食中毒 sho·ku·chū·do·ku

food supplies 食料 sho·ku·ryō

foot 足 a·shi

football (soccer) サッカー sak·kā

footpath 歩道 ho·dō

foreign 外国の gai·ko·ku no

forest 森 mo·ri

forever 永遠に ēn ni

forget 忘れます wa·su·re·mas

forgive 許します yu·ru·shi·mas

fork フォーク fō·ku

fortnight 2週間 ni·shū·kan

foul ⓝ ファウル fow·ru

foyer ロビー ro·bī

fragile 壊れやすい ko·wa·re·ya·su·i

France フランス fu·ran·su

free (gratis) 無料の mu·ryō no

free (not bound) 自由に ji·yū ni

freeze 凍ります kō·ri·mas

fresh 新鮮な shin·sen na

fridge 冷蔵庫 rē·zō·ko

fried 揚げた a·ge·ta

fried noodles 焼きそば ya·ki·so·ba

fried rice チャーハン・焼き飯 chā·han · ya·ki·me·shi

fried vegetables 野菜炒め ya·sai·i·ta·me

friend 友達 to·mo·da·chi

frog カエル ka·e·ru

from から ka·ra

frost 霜 shi·mo

frozen 凍った kōt·ta

fruit 果物 ku·da·mo·no

fruit juice フルーツジュース fu·rū·tsu·jū·su

fry 揚げます a·ge·mas

frying pan フライパン fu·rai·pan

full いっぱいの ip·pai no

full-time work 正社員の仕事 sē·shain no shi·go·to

fun 楽しい ta·no·shī

have fun 楽しみます ta·no·shi·mi·mas

funeral 葬式 sō·shi·ki

funny おかしい o·ka·shī

furniture 家具 ka·gu

futon ふとん fu·ton

future ⓝ 未来 mi·rai

G

game (computer) ゲーム gē·mu

game (sport) 試合 shi·ai

garage ガレージ ga·rē·ji

garbage ごみ go·mi

garbage can ごみ箱 go·mi·ba·ko

garden 庭 ni·wa

gardening ⓝ 庭仕事 ni·wa·shi·go·to

garlic ニンニク nin·ni·ku

gas (for cooking) ガス gas

gas (petrol) ガソリン ga·so·rin

gas cartridge ガスカートリッジ gas·kā·to·rij·ji

gastroenteritis 胃腸炎 i·chō·en

gate (airport, etc) ゲート gē·to

gauze ガーゼ gā·ze

gay (homosexual) ⓐ ゲイの gē no

gears (bicycle) ギア gya

geisha 芸者 gē·sha

Germany ドイツ doy·tsu

get 手に入れます te ni i·re·mas

get off (a train, etc) 降ります o·ri·mas

geyser 間欠泉 kan·kets·sen

gift 贈物 o·ku·ri·mo·no

gig ギグ gi·gu

gin ジン jin

ginger しょうが・ジンジャー shō·ga · jin·jā

girl 女の子 on·na no ko

girlfriend ガールフレンド gā·ru·fu·ren·do

give あげます a·ge·mas

given name 名前 na·ma·e

given name (Christian only) 洗礼名 sen·rē·mē

glandular fever 腺熱 sen·ne·tsu

glass (drinking) グラス gu·ra·su

glasses (spectacles) 眼鏡 me·ga·ne

gloves 手袋 te·bu·ku·ro

glue 糊 no·ri

go 行きます i·ki·mas

go out 出かけます de·ka·ke·mas

go out with 付き合います tsu·ki·ai·mas

goal ゴール gō·ru

goalkeeper ゴールキーパー gō·ru·kī·pā

goat ヤギ ya·gi

god (general) 神 ka·mi

goggles (skiing) ゴーグル gō·gu·ru

goggles (swimming) 水中眼鏡 su·i·chū·me·ga·ne

gold 金 kin

golf ball ゴルフボール go·ru·fu·bō·ru

golf course ゴルフコース go·ru·fu·kō·su

good いい ī

government 政府 sē·fu

gram グラム gu·ra·mu

grandchild 孫 ma·go

grandfather おじいさん o·jī·san

H

grandmother おばあさん o·bā·san

grapefruit グレープフルーツ gu·rē·pu·fu·rū·tsu

grapes ブドウ bu·dō

grass 草 ku·sa

grateful 感謝している kan·sha shi·te i·ru

grave 墓 ha·ka

gray 灰色の hai·ro no

great (fantastic) 素晴らしい su·ba·ra·shī

green 緑の mi·do·ri no

greengrocer 八百屋 ya·o·ya

greens 野菜 ya·sai

grey 灰色の hai·ro no

grilled グリルして gu·ri·ru shi·te

grocery 食料品 sho·ku·ryō·hin

groundnut ピーナツ pī·na·tsu

group グループ gu·rū·pu

grow 育ちます so·da·chi·mas

guaranteed 保証された ho·shō sa·re·ta

guess ⓥ 言い当てます ī·a·te·mas

guesthouse ゲストハウス ges·to·how·su

guide (audio) ⓝ 案内 an·nai

guide (person) ⓝ ガイド gai·do

guidebook ガイドブック gai·do·buk·ku

guide dog 盲導犬 mō·dō·ken

guided tour ガイド付きツアー gai·do·tsu·ki·tsu·ā

guilty 有罪の yū·zai no

guitar ギター gi·tā

gum (chewing) ガム ga·mu

gums (of mouth) 歯茎 ha·gu·ki

gun 銃 jū

gym (place) ジム ji·mu

gymnastics 体操 tai·sō

gynaecologist 婦人科医 fu·jin·ka·i

H

hair 毛 ke

hairbrush ヘアブラシ hair·bu·ra·shi

haircut ヘアカット hair·kat·to

hairdresser 美容師 bi·yō·shi

halal ハラルの ha·ra·ru no

half ⓝ 半分 ham·bun

hallucination 幻覚 gen·ka·ku

ham ハム ha·mu

hammer ハンマー ham·mā

hammock ハンモック ham·mok·ku

hand 手 te

handbag ハンドバッグ han·do·bag·[gu]

handball ハンドボール han·do·bō·[ru]

handicrafts 手芸品 shu·gē·hin

handkerchief ハンカチ han·ka·chi

handlebars ハンドル han·do·ru

handmade 手作りの te·zu·ku·ri no

handsome ハンサムな han·sa·mu na

happy 幸せな shi·a·wa·se na

harassment いやがらせ i·ya·ga·ra·se

harbour 港 mi·na·to

hard (not soft) かたい ka·tai

hard (not easy) たいへんな tai·hen

hard-boiled 固ゆでの ka·ta·yu·de n[o]

hardware store ホームセンター hō·mu·sen·tā

hash こま切れ ko·ma·gi·re·ni·ku

hat 帽子 bō·shi

have 持っています mot·te i·mas

have a cold 風邪を引いています ka[·ze] o hī·te i·mas

have fun 楽しみます ta·no·shi·mi·m[as]

hay fever 花粉症 ka·fun·shō

hazelnut ヘーゼルナッツ hē·ze·ru·nat·tsu

he 彼は ka·re wa

head 頭 a·ta·ma

headache 頭痛 zu·tsū

headlights ヘッドライト hed·do·rai[·to]

health 健康 ken·kō

hear 聞きます ki·ki·mas

hearing aid 補聴器 ho·chō·ki

heart 心臓 shin·zō

heart attack 心臓麻痺 shin·zō·ma·h[i]

heart condition 心臓病 shin·zō·byō

heat 熱 ne·tsu

heated 熱くなった a·tsu·ku nat·ta

heater ヒーター hī·tā

heavy 重い o·moy

helmet ヘルメット he·ru·met·to

help ⊙ たすけ tas·ke
help ⊙ たすけます tas·ke·mas
hepatitis 肝炎 kan·en
her (ownership) 彼女の ka·no·jo no
her (object of sentence) 彼女を ka·no·jo o
herb ハーブ hā·bu
herbalist ハーバリスト hā·ba·ris·to
here ここで ko·ko de
heroin ヘロイン he·royn
high 高い ta·kai
high school 高校 kō·kō
highchair ベビーチェア be·bī·che·a
highway 幹線道路 kan·sen·dō·ro
hike ⊙ ハイキングをします hai·kin·gu o shi·mas
hiking ⊙ ハイキング hai·kin·gu
hiking boots ハイキングブーツ hai·kin·gu·bū·tsu
hiking route ハイキングルート hai·kin·gu·rū·to
hill 丘 o·ka
him 彼を ka·re o
Hindu ⊙ ヒンズー教 hin·zū·kyō
hire ⊙ 賃貸します chin·tai shi·mas
his 彼の ka·re no
historical 歴史的な re·ki·shi·te·ki na
history 歴史 re·ki·shi
hitchhike ヒッチハイク hit·chi·hai·ku
HIV HIV et·chi·ai·vī
hobby 趣味 shu·mi
hockey ホッケー hok·kē
holiday 休日 kyū·ji·tsu
holidays 休暇 kyū·ka
home ⊙ うち u·chi
homeless ホームレス hō·mu·res
homemaker (female) 主婦 shu·fu
homemaker (male) 主夫 shu·fu
homeopathy ホメオパシー ho·me·o·pa·shī
homosexual ⊙ ホモ ho·mo
honey 蜂蜜 ha·chi·mi·tsu
honeymoon ハネムーン ha·ne·mūn
horoscope 星占い ho·shi·u·ra·nai
horse 馬 u·ma
horseradish わさび wa·sa·bi

horse riding 乗馬 jō·ba
hospital 病院 byō·in
hospitality もてなし mo·te·na·shi
hot 熱い a·tsu·i
hot water お湯 o·yu
hotel ホテル ho·te·ru
hotpot 鍋・鍋もの na·be・na·be·mo·no
hour 時間 ji·kan
house 家 i·e
housework 家事 ka·ji
how どのように do·no yō ni
how much どのくらい do·no ku·rai
how much (money) いくら i·ku·ra
hug ⊙ 抱きます da·ki·mas
huge 巨大な kyo·dai na
human resources 人的資源 jin·te·ki·shi·gen
human rights 人権 jin·ken
humanities 人文科学 jim·bun·ka·ga·ku
hundred 百 hya·ku
hungry (to be) ⊙ お腹がすいた o·na·ka·ga su·i·ta
hunting ⊙ 猟 ryō
hurt ⊙ 傷つけます ki·zu·tsu·ke·mas
(to be in a) hurry ⊙ 急ぎます i·so·gi·mas
husband 夫 ot·to

I

I 私は wa·ta·shi wa
ice 氷 kō·ri
ice axe ピッケル pik·ke·ru
ice cream アイスクリーム ais·ku·rī·mu
ice hockey アイスホッケー ais·hok·kē
identification 身分証明 mi·bun·shō·mē
identification card (ID) 身分証明書 mi·bun·shō·mē·sho
idiot ばか ba·ka
if もし mo·shi
ill 病気の byō·ki no
illegal 違法の i·hō no
immigration 移民 i·min
important 大切 tai·se·tsu na

J

impossible 不可能な fu·ka·nō na
in なか na·ka
in a hurry 急いで i·soy de
in front of 前 ma·e
incense 香 kō
included 含んで fu·kun·de
income tax 所得税 sho·to·ku·zē
India インド in·do
indicator 標識 hyō·shi·ki
indigestion 消化不良 shō·ka·fu·ryō
indoor 室内の shi·tsu·nai no
industry 産業 san·gyō
infection 感染 kan·sen
inflammation 発火 hak·ka
influenza インフルエンザ
in·fu·ru·en·za
information 情報 jō·hō
information office 案内所 an·nai·jo
ingredient 成分 sē·bun
inhaler 吸入器 kyū·nyū·ki
injection 注射 chū sha
injury けが ke·ga
inn (traditional Japanese) 旅館
ryo·kan
inner tube チューブ chū·bu
innocent 潔白な kep·pa·ku na
insect 虫 mu·shi
inside 内部 nai·bu
instructor インストラクター
in·sto·rak·tā
insurance 保険 ho·ken
interesting おもしろい o·mo·shi·roy
intermission 中止 chū·shi
international 国際的な
ko·ku·sai·te·ki na
internet インターネット in·tā·net·to
internet cafe インターネットカフェ
in·tā·net·to·ka·fe
interpreter 通訳 tsū·ya·ku
intersection 交差点 kō·sa·ten
interview 面接 men·se·tsu
invite ⓥ 招待します shō·tai shi·mas
Ireland アイルランド ai·ru·ran·do
iron (for clothes) ⓝ アイロン ai·ron
island 島 shi·ma
Israel イスラエル i·su·ra·e·ru

it それ so·re
IT IT ai·tī
Italy イタリア i·ta·rya
itch かゆみ ka·yu·mi
itemised 箇条書きの ka·jō·ga·ki no
itinerary 旅行日程 ryo·kō·nit·tē

J

jacket ジャケット ja·ket·to
jail 牢屋 rō·ya
jam ジャム ja·mu
Japan 日本 ni·hon • nip·pon
Japanese ⓐ 日本の ni·hon no
Japanese doll 日本人形
ni·hon·nin·gyō
Japanese food 和食 wa·sho·ku
Japanese garden 日本庭園 ni·hon·tēn
jar ジャー jā
jaw あご a·go
jealous 嫉妬深い shit·to·bu·kai
jeans ジーンズ jīn·zu
jeep ジープ jī·pu
jet lag 時差ぼけ ji·sa·bo·ke
jewellery 宝石 hō·se·ki
Jewish ユダヤ教の yu·da·ya·kyō no
job 仕事 shi·go·to
jogging ジョギング jo·gin·gu
joke 冗談 jō·dan
journalist ジャーナリスト jā·na·ris·to
journey 旅 ta·bi
judge ⓝ 裁判官 sai·ban·kan
judo 柔道 jū·dō
juice ジュース jū·su
jumper (sweater) セーター sē·tā
jumper leads ブースターケーブル
bū·stā·kē·bu·ru

K

kelp 昆布 kom·bu
ketchup ケチャップ ke·chap·pu
key 鍵 ka·gi
keyboard キーボード kī·bō·do
kick ⓥ けります ke·ri·mas
kill 殺します ko·ro·shi·mas
kidney 腎臓 jin·zō

kilo(gram) キロ（グラム）ki·ro(·gu·ra·mu)

kilometre キロメートル ki·ro·mē·to·ru

kimono (bath robe) 浴衣 yu·ka·ta

kind (nice) 親切 shin·se·tsu na

kindergarten 幼稚園 yō·chi·en

king 王 ō

kiosk キヨスク ki·yos·ku

kiss ⓝ キス kis

kiss ⓥ キスします kis shi·mas

kitchen 台所 dai·do·ko·ro

kiwifruit キウィ ki·wi

knee ひざ hi·za

knife ナイフ nai·fu

know 知っています shit·te i·mas

kosher コーシャー kō·shā

L

labourer 労働者 rō·dō·sha

lake 湖 mi·zū·mi

lamb 子羊 ko·hi·tsu·ji

land 陸 ri·ku

landlady 女主人 on·na·shu·jin

landlord 地主 ji·nu·shi

language 言語 gen·go

laptop ラップトップ rap·pu·top·pu

laquerware 漆器 shik·ki

large 大きい ō·kī

last (final) 最後の sai·go no

last (previous) 前の ma·e no

last (week) 先（週）sen(·shū)

late 遅い o·soy

later あとで a·to de

laugh ⓥ 笑います wa·rai·mas

launderette コインランドリー ko·in·ran·do·rī

laundry (clothes) 洗濯物 sen·ta·ku·mo·no

laundry (place) 洗濯場 sen·ta·ku·ba

laundry (room) 洗濯室 sen·ta·ku·shi·tsu

law 法律 hō·ri·tsu

law (study, professsion) 法学 hō·ga·ku

lawyer 弁護士 ben·go·shi

laxative 下剤 ge·zai

lazy 怠け者の na·ma·ke·mo·no no

leader リーダー rī·dā

leaf 葉 ha

learn 習います na·rai·mas

leather 皮 ka·wa

ledge 岩礁 gan·shō

leek リーキ rī·ki

left (direction) ⓐ 左 hi·da·ri

left luggage (office) 手荷物預かり所 te·ni·mo·tsu·a·zu·ka·ri·sho

left-wing 左翼の sa·yo·ku no

leg (body part) 脚 a·shi

legal 法的な hō·te·ki na

legume 豆類 ma·me·ru·i

lemon レモン re·mon

lemonade レモネード re·mo·nē·do

lens レンズ ren·zu

lentil レンズマメ ren·zu·ma·me

lesbian ⓝ レズ re·zu

less 少ない su·ku·nai

letter (mail) 手紙 te·ga·mi

lettuce レタス re·tas

liar うそつき u·so·tsu·ki

library 図書館 to·sho·kan

lice 虱 shi·ra·mi

licence ライセンス rai·sen·su

license plate number ナンバープレート nam·bā·pu·rē·to

lie (not stand) 横になります yo·ko ni na·ri·mas

life 命 i·no·chi

life boat 救命艇 kyū·mē·tē

life jacket 救命胴衣 kyū·mē·dōy

lift (elevator) エレベータ e·re·bē·ta

light ⓝ 電気 den·ki

light (not heavy) 軽い ka·ru·i

light (of colour) 明るい a·ka·ru·i

light bulb 電球 den·kyū

light meter 照度計 shō·do·kē

lighter (cigarette) ライター rai·tā

lights (on car) ヘッドライト hed·do·rai·to

like ⓥ 好きです su·ki des

lime ライム rai·mu

linen (material) リンネル rin·ne·ru

linen (sheets etc) リネン ri·nen

lip balm リップクリーム rip·pu·ku·rī·mu

M

lips 唇 ku·chi·bi·ru
lipstick 口紅 ku·chi·be·ni
liquor store 酒屋 sa·ka·ya
list ⓝ リスト ris·to
listen (to) 聴きます ki·ki·mas
litre リットル rit·to·ru
little (not much) ⓐ 少し su·ko·shi
little ⓐ 小さい chī·sai
live (somewhere) 住みます
su·mi·mas
liver 肝臓 kan·zō
lizard トカゲ to·ka·ge
lobster ロブスター ro·bus·tā
local ⓐ 地元 ji·mo·to
local train 各駅停車 ka·ku·e·ki·tē·sha
lock ⓝ 錠 jō
lock ⓥ 鍵をかけます ka·gi o ka·ke·mas
locked 鍵をかけた ka·gi o ka·ke·ta
lollies キャンデー kyan·dē
long 長い na·gai
look ⓥ 見ます mi·mas
look after 面倒を見ます men·dō o
mi·mas
look for 探します sa·ga·shi·mas
lookout 見晴台 mi·ha·ra·shi·dai
loose ⓐ 緩んだ yu·run·da
loose change 小銭 ko·ze·ni
lost (item) なくした na·ku·shi·ta
lost property office 遺失物取扱所
i·shi·tsu·bu·tsu·to·ri·a·tsu·kai·jo
(a) lot たくさん tak·san
loud うるさい u·ru·sai
love ⓝ 愛 ai
love ⓥ 愛します ai shi·mas
love hotel ラブホテル ra·bu·ho·te·ru
lover 恋人 koy·bi·to
low 低い hi·ku·i
lubricant 潤滑油 jun·ka·tsu·yu
lucky 幸運な kō·un·na
luggage 手荷物 te·ni·mo·tsu
luggage lockers ロッカー rok·kā
luggage tag 手荷物札
te·ni·mo·tsu·fu·da
lump こぶ ko·bu
lunch 昼食・昼ごはん chū·sho·ku・
hi·ru·go·han

lung 肺 hai
luxury ⓐ 豪華な gō·ka na
lychee レイシ rē·shi

M

machine ⓝ 機械 ki·kai
made of (cotton) (コットン)製の
(kot·ton)·sē no
Mafia (Japanese) ヤクザ ya·ku·za
magazine 雑誌 zas·shi
mail (letters) 郵送 yū·sō
mail (postal system) 郵便 yū·bin
mailbox 郵便ポスト yū·bin·pos·to
main 主な o·mo·na
main course メインコース mēn·kō·s
main road 幹線道路 kan·sen·dō·ro
make ⓥ 作ります tsu·ku·ri·mas
make-up メーキャップ mē·kyap·pu
mammogram マンモグラム
mam·mo·gu·ra·mu
man (human) 人 hi·to
man (male) 男の人 o·to·ko no hi·to
manager (company) 支配人
shi·hai·nin
manager (restaurant, hotel)
マネージャー ma·nē·jā
mandarin マンダリン man·da·rin
mango マンゴー man·gō
monorail モノレール mo·no·rē·ru
manual マニュアルの ma·nyu·a·ru no
manual worker 肉体労働者
ni·ku·tai·rō·dō·sha
many たくさんの ta·ku·san no
map 地図 chi·zu
marble 大理石 dai·ri·se·ki
margarine マーガリン mā·ga·rin
marijuana マリファナ ma·ri·fa·na
marital status 配偶関係 hai·gū·kan·k
market ⓝ 市場 i·chi·ba
marmalade マーマレード
mā·ma·rē·do
married 既婚 ki·kon
marry 結婚します kek·kon shi·mas
martial arts 武道 bu·dō
mass (Catholic) ミサ mi·sa
massage マッサージ mas·sā·ji

M

masseur マッサージ師 mas·sâ·ji·shi
masseuse マッサージ師 mas·sâ·ji·shi
mat マット mat·to
mat (reed) たたみ ta·ta·mi
match (sports) 試合 shi·ai
matches (for lighting) マッチ mat·chi
mattress マットレス mat·to·res
maybe たぶん ta·bun
mayonnaise マヨネーズ ma·yo·nê·zu
me 私を wa·ta·shi o
meal 食事 sho·ku·ji
measles はしか ha·shi·ka
meat 肉 ni·ku
mechanic 機械工 ki·kai·kô
media メディア me·dya
medicine (medication) 薬 ku·su·ri
medicine (study, profession) 医学 i·ga·ku
meditation 瞑想 mê·sô
meet 会います ai·mas
meeting ミーティング mî·tin·gu
melon メロン me·ron
member メンバー mem·bâ
menstruation 月経 gek·kê
menu メニュー me·nyû
message 伝言 den·gon
metal ⑩ 金属 kin·zo·ku
metre メートル mê·to·ru
meter (in taxi) メーター mê·tâ
metro (train) 地下鉄 chi·ka·te·tsu
metro station 地下鉄の駅 chi·ka·te·tsu no eki
microwave (oven) 電子レンジ den·shi·ren·ji
midday 正午 shô·go
midnight 真夜中 ma·yo·na·ka
migraine 偏頭痛 hen·zu·tsû
military ⑩ 軍 gun
military service 軍役 gun·e·ki
milk ミルク mi·ru·ku
millimetre ミリ（メートル) mi·ri(·mê·to·ru)
million 百 hya·ku·man
mince ⑩ ひき肉 hi·ki·ni·ku
mineral hot-spring spa 温泉 on·sen

mineral water ミネラルウォーター mi·ne·ra·ru·wô·tâ
mini-bar ミニバー mi·ni·bâ
minute 分 fun
mirror ⑩ 鏡 ka·ga·mi
miscarriage 流産 ryû·zan
miso-soup 味噌汁 mi·so·shi·ru
miso-soup bowl お椀 o·wan
miss (feel absence of) ⑰ 懐かしがります na·tsu·ka·shi·ga·ri·mas
mistake 間違い ma·chi·gai
mix ⑰ 混ぜます ma·ze·mas
mobile phone 携帯電話 kê·tai·den·wa
modem モデム mo·de·mu
modern モダンな mo·dan na
moisturiser 保湿剤 ho·shi·tsu·zai
monastery 修道院 shû·dô·in
money お金 o·ka·ne
monk 僧 sô
month 月 ga·tsu
monument 記念碑 ki·nen·hi
moon 月 tsu·ki
more もっと mot·to
morning 朝 a·sa
morning sickness つわり tsu·wa·ri
mosque モスク mos·ku
mosquito 蚊 ka
mosquito coil 蚊取り線香 ka·to·ri·sen·kô
mosquito net 蚊帳 ka·ya
motel モーテル mô·te·ru
mother お母さん o·kâ·san
mother-in-law 義理のお母さん gi·ri no o·kâ·san
motorbike オートバイ ô·to·bai
motorboat モーターボート mô·tâ·bô·to
motorcycle オートバイ ô·to·bai
motorway (tollway) 高速道路 kô·so·ku·dô·ro
mountain 山 ya·ma
mountain bike マウンテンバイク ma·un·ten·bai·ku
mountain path 登山道 to·zan·dô
mountain range 山脈 sam·mya·ku
mountaineering 登山 to·zan

mouse ネズミ ne·zu·mi
mouth 口 ku·chi
movie 映画 e·ga
Mr/Mrs/Ms/Miss さん ·san
MSG グルタミン酸ソーダ
gu·ru·ta·min·san·sō·da
mud 泥 do·ro
muesli ミューズリー myū·zu·rī
mum お母さん o·kā·san
mumps おたふく風邪 o·ta·fu·ku·ka·ze
murder ⑩ 殺人 sa·tsu·jin
muscle 筋肉 kin·ni·ku
museum 博物館 ha·ku·bu·tsu·kan
mushroom キノコ ki·no·ko
music 音楽 on·ga·ku
music shop レコード店 re·kō·do·ten
musician 音楽家 on·gak·ka
Muslim ⑪ イスラム教徒
i·su·ra·mu·kyō·to
mussel ムール貝 mū·ru·gai
mustard マスタード mas·tā·do
mute ⓐ 口のきけない ku·chi no
ki·ke·nai
my 私の wa·ta·shi no

N

nail clippers 爪切り tsu·me·ki·ri
name 名前 na·ma·e
napkin ナプキン na·pu·kin
nappy オムツ o·mu·tsu
nappy rash オムツかぶれ
o·mu·tsu·ka·bu·re
national 国の ku·ni no
national park 国立公園
ko·ku·ri·tsu·kō·en
nationality 国籍 ko·ku·se·ki
nature 自然 shi·zen
naturopathy 自然療法 shi·zen·ryō·hō
nausea 吐き気 ha·ki·ke
near 近く chi·ka·ku
nearby 近くの chi·ka·ku no
nearest いちばん近くの i·chi·ban
chi·ka·ku no
necessary 必要な hi·tsu·yō na
neck 首 ku·bi
nectarine ネクタリン ne·ku·ta·rin

need ⓥ 必要があります hi·tsu·yō ga
a·ri·mas
needle (sewing) 針 ha·ri
needle (syringe) 注射針 chū·sha·ba·ri
negative 否定的な hi·tē·te·ki na
net 網 a·mi
Netherlands オランダ o·ran·da
never 決してない kes·shi·te nai
new 新しい a·ta·ra·shī
New Year's Day 元旦 gan·tan
New Year's Eve 大晦日 ō·mi·so·ka
New Zealand ニュージーランド
nyū·jī·ran·do
news ニュース nyū·su
news stand 新聞販売店
shim·bun·ham·bai·ten
newsagency 通信社 tsū·shin·sha
newspaper 新聞 shim·bun
next つぎ tsu·gi
next (month) 来(月) rai(·ge·tsu)
next to となり to·na·ri
nice いい ī
nickname あだ名 a·da·na
night 夜 yo·ru
night out 夜遊び yo·a·so·bi
nightclub ナイトクラブ
nai·to·ku·ra·bu
no いいえ ī·e
no vacancy 満室 man·shi·tsu
noisy うるさい u·ru·sai
none なにもない na·ni·mo nai
nonsmoking 禁煙の kin·en no
noodles 麺類 men·ru·i
noon (lunchtime) 昼 hi·ru
noon (midday) 正午 shō·go
north 北 ki·ta
Norway ノルウェー no·ru·wē
nose 鼻 ha·na
not ない nai
notebook (paper) ノート nō·to
nothing 何もない na·ni·mo nai
not yet まだ ma·da
now 今 i·ma
nuclear energy 核エネルギー
ka·ku·e·ne·ru·gī
nuclear testing 核実験 ka·ku·jik·ken

nuclear waste 核廃棄物
ka·ku·hai·ki·bu·tsu
number 数字 sū·ji
numberplate ナンバープレート
nam·bā·pu·rē·to
nun 修道女 shū·dō·jo
nurse 看護婦 kan·go·fu
nut ナッツ nat·tsu

O

oats オート麦 ō·to·mu·gi
occupation (work) 職業 sho·ku·gyō
ocean 海 u·mi
octopus タコ ta·ko
off (spoiled) いたんだ i·tan·da
office 事務所 ji·mu·sho
office worker 事務員 ji·mu·in
often しばしば shi·ba·shi·ba
oil (food) 油 a·bu·ra
oil (petrol) 石油 se·ki·yu
old 古い fu·ru·i
olive オリーブ o·rī·bu
olive oil オリーブオイル o·rī·bu·o·yu
Olympic Games オリンピック
o·rim·pik·ku
omelette オムレツ o·mu·re·tsu
on 上に u·e·ni
on time 時間どおり ji·kan·dō·ri
once 1度 i·chi·do
one 1 i·chi
one-way (ticket) 片道(切符)
ka·ta·mi·chi(·kip·pu)
onion タマネギ ta·ma·ne·gi
only たった tat·ta no
open ⓐ 開いている hi·rai·te i·ru
open ⓥ 開きます hi·ra·ki·mas
open-air baths 露天風呂 ro·tem·bu·ro
opening hours 営業時間 kai·ten·ji·kan
opera オペラ o·pe·ra
opera house オペラ劇場
o·pe·ra·ge·ki·jō
operation (medical) 手術 shu·ju·tsu
operator オペレーター o·pe·rē·tā
opinion 意見 i·ken
opposite 反対の han·tai no
optometrist 検眼医 ken·gan·i

or または ma·ta wa
orange (colour) オレンジ o·ren·ji
orange (fruit) オレンジ o·ren·ji
orange juice オレンジジュース
o·ren·ji·jū·su
orchestra オーケストラ ō·kes·to·ra
order ⓝ 命令 mē·rē
order ⓥ 命令します mē·rē shi·mas
ordinary 普通の fu·tsū no
orgasm オーガズム ō·ga·zu·mu
original オリジナルの o·ri·ji·na·ru no
other ほかの ho·ka no
our 私たちの wa·ta·shi·ta·chi no
out of order 故障中 ko·shō·chū
outside 外側の so·to·ga·wa no
ovarian cyst 卵巣のう腫
ran·sō·nō·shu
ovary 卵巣 ran·sō
oven オーブン ō·bun
overcoat オーバー ō·bā
overdose 薬の飲みすぎ ku·su·ri no
no·mi·su·gi
overnight 一晩 hi·to·ban
overseas 海外 kai·gai
owe 借りがあります ka·ri ga a·ri·mas
owner 所持者 sho·ji·sha
oxygen 酸素 san·so
oyster カキ ka·ki
ozone layer オゾン層 o·zon·sō

O

P

pacemaker ペースメーカー
pēs·mē·kā
pacifier (dummy) おしゃぶり
o·sha·bu·ri
package 包み tsu·tsu·mi
packet (general) 小包 ko·zu·tsu·mi
padlock 南京錠 nan·kin·jō
page ページ pē·ji
pain 痛み i·ta·mi
painkiller 鎮痛剤 chin·tsū·zai
painter 画家 ga·ka
painting (a work) ⓝ 絵 e
painting (the art) ⓝ 絵画 kai·ga
pair ⓝ ペア pair
pair of chopsticks 箸 ha·shi

P

palace 宮殿 kyū·den
pan 鍋 na·be
pants (trousers) ズボン zu·bon
panty liners 生理用ナプキン
sē·ri·yō·na·pu·kin
pantyhose パンティーストッキング
pan·tī·stok·kin·gu
pap smear 子宮癌塗抹検査
shi·kyū·gan·to·ma·tsu·ken·sa
paper 紙 ka·mi
papers (documents) 書類 sho·ru·i
paperwork 事務処理 ji·mu·sho·ri
paraplegic ⑥ 下半身不随
ka·han·shin·fu·zu·i
parcel 小包 ko·zu·tsu·mi
parents 両親 ryō·shin
park ⑥ 公園 kō·en
park (a car) ⑫ 駐車します chū·sha
shi·mas
parliament 国会 kok·kai
part (component) 部分 bu·bun
partner (intimate) パートナー pā·to·nā
part-time アルバイトな a·ru·bai·to
party (night out) ⑥ パーティー pā·tī
party (politics) ⑥ 党 tō
pass (document) ⑥ 許可証
kyo·ka·shō
pass (mountain) ⑥ 山道
ya·ma·mi·chi
pass (sport) ⑥ パス pas
pass ⑫ 通過します tsū·ka shi·mas
passenger 乗客 jō·kya·ku
passionfruit パッションフルーツ
pas·shon·fu·rū·tsu
passport パスポート pas·pō·to
passport number パスポート番号
pas·pō·to·ban·gō
past ⑥ 過去 ka·ko
pasta パスタ pas·ta
pastry ペストリー pes·to·rī
path 小道 ko·mi·chi
pay ⑫ 支払います shi·a·rai·mas
payment 支払い shi·ha·rai
pea 豆 ma·me
peace 平和 hē·wa
peach 桃 mo·mo

peak (mountain) ⑥ 峰 mi·ne
peanut ピーナツ pī·na·tsu
pear 洋ナシ yō·na·shi
pedal ⑥ ペダル pe·da·ru
pedestrian 歩行者 ho·kō·sha
pedestrian crossing 横断歩道
ō·dan·ho·dō
pegs (camping) ペグ pe·gu
pen (ballpoint) ペン pen
pencil エンピツ em·pi·tsu
penis ペニス pe·nis
penicillin ペニシリン pe·ni·shi·rin
penknife ペナイフ pen·nai·fu
pensioner 年金者 nen·kin·sha
people 人びと hi·to·bi·to
pepper コショウ koshō
pepper (bell) ピーマン pī·man
per (eg day) 毎 mai
per cent パーセント pā·sen·to
perfect 完璧な kam·pe·ki na
performance パフォーマンス
pa·fō·man·su
perfume 香水 kō·su·i
period 時代 ji·dai
period (menstruation) 月経 gek·kē
period pain 生理痛 sē·ri·tsū
permanent 永久の ē·kyū no
permission 許可 kyo·ka
permit 許可証 kyo·ka·shō
persimmon 柿 ka·ki
person 人 hi·to
personal 個人的な ko·jin·te·ki na
petition 嘆願書 tan·gan·sho
petrol ガソリン ga·so·rin
petrol station ガソリンスタンド
ga·so·rin·stan·do
pharmacy 薬局 yak·kyo·ku
phone book 電話帳 den·wa·chō
phone box 電話ボックス
den·wa·bok·kus
phone call 電話 den·wa
phone card テレフォンカード
te·re·fon·kā·do
phone number 電話番号
den·wa·ban·gō
photo 写真 sha·shin

P

photographer 写真家 sha·shin·ka
photography 写真 sha·shin
phrasebook フレーズブック fu·rē·zu·buk·ku
pickaxe つるはし tsu·ru·ha·shi
picnic ピクニック pi·ku·nik·ku
pie パイ pai
piece かけら ka·ke·ra
pig 豚 bu·ta
pigeon 鳩 ha·to
pill 錠剤 jō·zai
the Pill ピル pi·ru
pillow 枕 ma·ku·ra
pillowcase 枕カバー ma·ku·ra·ka·bā
pinball ピンボール pin·bō·ru
pineapple パイナップル pai·nap·pu·ru
pink ピンクの pin·ku·no
pistachio ピスタチオ pis·ta·chi·o
place 場所 ba·sho
place of birth 出身地 shus·shin·chi
plane ⓝ 飛行機 hi·kō·ki
planet 惑星 wa·ku·sē
plant ⓝ 植物 sho·ku·bu·tsu
plastic ⓐ プラスチックの pu·ras·chik·ku no
plate (big) 皿 sa·ra
plate (small) 小皿 ko·za·ra
plateau 高原 kō·gen
platform プラットフォーム pu·rat·to·fō·mu
play (cards, game) ⓥ します shi·mas
play (instrument) ⓥ 弾きます hi·ki·mas
play (theatre) ⓝ 劇 ge·ki
playground 遊び場 a·so·bi·ba
plug (bath) 栓 sen
plug (electricity) プラグ pu·ra·gu
plum スモモ su·mo·mo
poached ポーチした pō·chi shi·ta
pocket ポケット po·ket·to
pocket knife ポケットナイフ po·ket·to·nai·fu
poetry 詩 shi
point ⓝ 点 ten
point ⓥ 示します shi·me·shi·mas
poisonous 毒の do·ku no

police 警察 kē·sa·tsu
police box 交番 kō·ban
police officer 警官 kē·kan
police station 警察署 kē·sa·tsu·sho
policy 方針 hō·shin
politician 政治家 sē·ji·ka
politics 政治 sē·ji
pollen 花粉 ka·fun
pollution 公害 kō·gai
pool (game) ビリヤード bi·ri·yā·do
pool (swimming) プール pū·ru
poor 貧しい ma·zu·shī
popular 人気がある nin·ki ga a·ru
pork 豚肉 bu·ta·ni·ku
porridge おかゆ o·ka·yu
port (sea) 港 mi·na·to
portion 部分 bu·bun
possible 可能な ka·nō na
postcode 郵便番号 yū·bin·ban·gō
post office 郵便局 yū·bin·kyo·ku
poste restante 局留め kyo·ku·do·me
postage 郵送料 yū·sō·ryō
postcard はがき ha·ga·ki
poster ポスター pos·tā
pot (ceramics) つぼ tsu·bo
pot (dope) マリファナ ma·ri·fa·na
potato ジャガイモ ja·ga·i·mo
pottery 陶器 tō·ki
poultry 鳥肉 to·ri·ni·ku
pound (money, weight) ポンド pon·do
poverty 貧困 hin·kon
powder 粉 ko·na
power 力 chi·ka·ra
prawn エビ e·bi
prayer 祈り i·no·ri
prefer ... …のほうがすきです ... no hō ga su·ki·des
pregnancy test kit 妊娠テストキット nin·shin·tes·to·kit·to
pregnant 妊娠している nin·shin shi·te·i·ru
premenstrual tension 月経前緊張症 gek·kē·zen·kin·chō·shō
prepare 準備します jum·bi shi·mas

Q

prescription 処方箋 sho·hō·sen

present (gift) ⓝ プレゼント pu·re·zen·to

present (time) ⓝ 現在 gen·zai

president 大統領 dai·tō·ryō

pretty かわいい ka·wa·ī

previous 前の ma·e no

price 値段 ne·dan

priest (Christian) 牧師 bo·ku·shi

priest (Shinto) 神主 kan·nu·shi

prime minister 総理大臣 sō·ri·dai·jin

prince 王子 ō·ji

princess 姫 hi·me

printer (computer) プリンタ prin·ta

prison 牢屋 rō·ya

prisoner 囚人 shū·jin

private ⓐ 個人的な ko·jin·te·ki na

produce ⓥ 生産します sē·san shi·mas

profit ⓝ 利益 ri·e·ki

program ⓝ プログラム pu·ro·gu·ra·mu

projector 映写機 ē·sha·ki

promise ⓥ 約束します ya·ku·so·ku shi·mas

prostitute 売春 bai·shun

protect 保護します ho·go shi·mas

protected (species) 保護された (生物) ho·go sa·re·ta (sē·bu·tsu)

protest ⓝ 反対 han·tai

provisions 食料 sho·ku·ryō

prune プルーン pu·rūn

pub (bar) パブ pa·bu

public baths 銭湯 sen·tō

public gardens 公園 kō·en

public holiday 祭日 sai·ji·tsu

public telephone 公衆電話 kō·shū·den·wa

public toilet 公衆トイレ kō·shū·toy·re

pufferfish フグ fu·gu

pull 引きます hi·ki·mas

pump ⓝ ポンプ pom·pu

pumpkin カボチャ ka·bo·cha

puncture パンク pan·ku

puppet 人形 nin·gyō

puppet theatre 人形劇 nin·gyō·ge·ki

pure 純粋な jun·su·i na

purple 紫の mu·ra·sa·ki no

purse 財布 sai·fu

push ⓥ 押します o·shi·mas

put 置きます o·ki·mas

Q

quadriplegic ⓝ 四肢麻痺 shi·shi·ma·hi

qualifications 資格 shi·ka·ku

quality 品質 hin·shi·tsu

quarantine ⓝ 検疫 ken·e·ki

quarter ⓝ 4分の1 yon·bun no i·chi

queen 女王 jō

question ⓝ 質問 shi·tsu·mon

queue ⓝ 列 re·tsu

quick すばやい su·ba·yai

quiet 静かな shi·zu·ka na

quilt 掛け布団 ka·ke·bu·ton

quit 辞めます ya·me·mas

R

rabbit ウサギ u·sa·gi

race (sport) レース rē·su

racetrack 競走場 kyō·gi·jō

racing bike レーシングバイク rē·shin·gu·bai·ku

racism 人種差別 jin·shu·sa·be·tsu

racquet ラケット ra·ket·to

radiator ラジエーター ra·ji·ē·tā

radio ラジオ ra·ji·o

radish ラディッシュ ra·dis·shu

railway station 駅 e·ki

rain ⓝ 雨 a·me

raincoat レインコート re·in·kō·to

raisin レーズン rē·zun

rally ⓝ 集会 shū·kai

rape ⓝ レイプ rē·pu

rapid train 快速 kai·so·ku

rare (food) レアの rair no

rare (uncommon) 珍しい me·zu·ra·shī

rash 発疹 has·shin

raspberry ラズベリー ra·zu·be·rī

rat ネズミ ne·zu·mi

rave ⓝ レイブ rē·bu
raw 生の na·ma no
razor 剃刀 ka·mi·so·ri
razor blade 剃刀の刃 ka·mi·so·ri no ha
read 読みます yo·mi·mas
ready 準備ができた jum·bi ga de·ki·ta
real estate agent 不動産屋
fu·dō·san·ya
rear (seat etc) ⓐ 後ろの u·shi·ro no
reason 理由 ri·yū
receipt レシート re·shī·to
recently 最近 sai·kin
recommend 勧めます su·su·me·mas
record ⓥ 記録します ki·ro·ku shi·mas
recording ⓝ レコーディング
re·kō·din·gu
recyclable リサイクルできる
ri·sai·ku·ru de·ki·ru
recycle リサイクルします ri·sai·ku·ru
shi·mas
red 赤い a·kai
red wine 赤ワイン a·ka·wain
referee 審判 shim·pan
reference 参照 san·shō
reflexology リフレクソロジー
ri·fu·re·ku·so·ro·jī
refrigerator 冷蔵庫 rē·zō·ko
refugee 難民 nam·min
refund ⓝ 払い戻し ha·rai·mo·do·shi
refuse ⓥ 拒絶します kyo·ze·tsu
shi·mas
regional 地方の chi·hō no
registered mail/post 書留 ka·ki·to·me
regular ⓐ 通常の tsū·jō no
rehydration salts 経口補水塩
kē·kō·ho·su·i·en
relationship 関係 kan·kē
relax リラックスします ri·rak·ku·su
shi·mas
relic 遺物 i·bu·tsu
religion 宗教 shū·kyo
religious 宗教的な shū·kyo·te·ki na
remote 遠い tōy
remote control リモコン ri·mo·kon
rent 貸します ka·shi·mas
repair 修理します shū·ri shi·mas

republic 共和国 kyō·wa·ko·ku
reservation (booking) 予約 yo·ya·ku
rest ⓥ 休みます ya·su·mi·mas
restaurant レストラン res·to·ran
résumé (CV) ⓝ 履歴書 ri·re·ki·sho
retired 退職した tai·sho·ku shi·ta
return (come back) ⓥ もどります
mo·do·ri·mas
return ticket 往復切符 ō·fu·ku·kip·pu
review ⓝ 評論 hyō·ron
rhythm リズム ri·zu·mu
rib 肋骨 rok·ko·tsu
rice (cooked) ごはん go·han
rice (uncooked) 米 ko·me
rice bowl 茶碗 cha·wan
rice cake もち mo·chi
rice cooker 炊飯器 su·i·han·ki
rice cracker せんべい sen·bē
rich (wealthy) お金持ちの
o·ka·ne·mo·chi no
ride ⓝ 乗ること no·ru·ko·to
ride (horse) ⓥ 乗ります no·ri·mas
right (correct) 正しい ta·da·shī
right (direction) 右 mi·gi
right-wing 右翼 u·yo·ku
ring (on finger) ⓝ 指 yu·bi·wa
ring (by phone) ⓥ 電話します
den·wa shi·mas
rip-off ⓝ ぼられること bo·ra·re·ru
ko·to
risk ⓝ リスク ris·ku
river 川 ka·wa
road 道 mi·chi
road map ロードマップ rō·do·map·pu
rob 強盗します gō·tō shi·mas
robbery 強奪 gō·da·tsu
rock 岩 i·wa
rock (music) ⓝ ロック rok·ku
rock climbing ロッククライミング
rok·ku·ku·rai·min·gu
rock group ロックバンド
rok·ku·ban·do
rockmelon メロン me·ron
roll (bread) ⓝ ロール rō·ru
rollerblading ⓝ ローラーブレード
rō·rā·bu·rē·do

S

romantic ロマンチックな ro·man·chik·ku na

room 部屋 he·ya

room number ルームナンバー rū·mu·nam·bā

rope ロープ rō·pu

round まるい ma·ru·i

roundabout ロータリー rō·ta·rī

route ルート rū·to

rowing ⓝ ローイング rō·in·gu

rubbish ごみ go·mi

rubella 風疹 fū·shin

rug じゅうたん jū·tan

rugby ラグビー ra·gu·bī

ruins 廃墟 hai·kyo

rum ラム ra·mu

run ⓥ 走ります ha·shi·ri·mas

running (sport) ランニング ran·nin·gu

S

sad 悲しい ka·na·shī

saddle サドル sa·do·ru

safe ⓝ 金庫 kin·ko

safe ⓐ 安全な an·zen na

safe sex セーフセックス sē·fu·sek·kus

saint 聖人 sē·jin

salad サラダ sa·ra·da

salary サラリー sa·ra·rī

sale セール sē·ru

sales tax 消費税 shō·hi·zē

salmon サケ sa·ke

salt 塩 shi·o

same 同じ o·na·ji

sand 砂 su·na

sandal サンダル san·da·ru

sandwich サンドイッチ san·do·it·chi

sanitary napkin 生理用ナプキン sē·ri·yō·na·pu·kin

sardine イワシ i·wa·shi

sauce ソース sō·su

saucepan 鍋 na·be

sauna サウナ sow·na

sausage ソーセージ sō·sē·ji

say ⓥ 言います ī·mas

scallop ホタテ ho·ta·te

scalp 頭皮 tō·hi

scampi スカンピ・クルマエビ skam·pi · ku·ru·ma·e·bi

scarf スカーフ skā·fu

school 学校 gak·kō

science 科学 ka·ga·ku

scientist 科学者 ka·ga·ku·sha

scissors ハサミ ha·sa·mi

scooter スクーター skū·tā

score ⓥ 得点します to·ku·ten shi·mas

scoreboard スコアボード sko·a·bō·do

Scotland スコットランド skot·to·ran·do

scrambled かき混ぜた ka·ki·ma·ze·ta

screen (room) ついたて tsu·i·ta·te

screen (sliding) 障子 shō·ji

sculpture 彫刻 chō·ko·ku

sea 海 u·mi

seafood 海産物・シーフード kai·sam·bu·tsu · shī·fū·do

seasick 船酔い fu·na·yoy

seaside 海辺 u·mi·be

season 季節 ki·se·tsu

seat (place) 席 se·ki

seatbelt シートベルト shī·to·be·ru·to

sea urchin ウニ u·ni

sea vegetables 海藻 kai·sō

seaweed 海藻 kai·sō

second ⓝ 秒 byō

second ⓐ 2番目の ni·bam·me no

secondhand 中古の chū·ko no

secondhand shop 中古品店 chū·ko·hin·ten

second class ⓝ セカンドクラス se·kan·do·ku·ras

secretary 秘書 hi·sho

see 見ます mi·mas

self service ⓐ セルフサービスの se·ru·fu·sā·bis no

self-employed 自営業 ji·ē·gyō

sell 売ります u·ri·mas

send 送ります o·ku·ri·mas

sensible 分別のある fum·be·tsu no a·ru

sensual 官能的な kan·nō·te·ki na

separate 別々の be·tsu·be·tsu no

serious まじめな ma·ji·me na

service ⓝ サービス sā·bis

S

service charge サービス料 sā·bis·ryō

service station ガソリンスタンド ga·so·rin·stan·do

serviette ナプキン na·pu·kin

sesame oil ごま油 go·ma·a·bu·ra

sesame seed ごま go·ma

several いくつかの i·ku·tsu·ka no

sew 縫います nu·i·mas

sex セックス sek·kus

sexism 性差別 sē·sa·be·tsu

sexy セクシーな sek·shī na

shade 日陰 hi·ka·ge

shadow 影 ka·ge

shallot (onion) ワケギ wa·ke·gi

shampoo ⓝ シャンプー sham·pū

shape ⓝ 形 ka·ta·chi

share (a dorm etc) ⓥ シェアします she·a shi·mas

share (with) ⓥ 分け合います wa·ke·ai·mas

shave ⓝ シェービング shē·bin·gu

shaving cream シェービングクリーム hē·bin·gu·ku·rī·mu

she 彼女は ka·no·jo wa

sheep 羊 hi·tsu·ji

sheet (bed) シーツ shī·tsu

shelf 棚 ta·na

shellfish 貝 kai

shingles (illness) 帯状疱疹 ai·jō·hō·shin

ship ⓝ 船 fu·ne

shirt シャツ sha·tsu

shoe 靴 ku·tsu

shoe shop 靴屋 ku·tsu·ya

shoot 撃ちます u·chi·mas

shop ⓝ 店 mi·se

shop ⓥ 買い物をします kai·mo·no o shi·mas

shopping ⓝ 買い物 kai·mo·no

shopping centre ショッピング センター shop·pin·gu·sen·tā

short (height) 低い hi·ku·i

short (length) 短い mi·ji·kai

shortage 不足 fu·so·ku

short-grain rice ジャポニカ米 a·po·ni·ka·mai

shorts 半ズボン han·zu·bon

shoulder 肩 ka·ta

shout ⓥ 怒鳴ります do·na·ri·mas

show ⓝ ショー shō

show ⓥ 見せます mi·se·mas

shower シャワー sha·wā

shrine 神社 jin·ja

shrimp 小エビ ko·e·bi

shut ⓐ 閉まった shi·mat·ta

shy 恥ずかしがり屋の ha·zu·ka·shi·ga·ri·ya no

sick 病気の byō·ki no

sick bag 乗り物酔いの袋 no·ri·mo·no·yoy no fu·ku·ro

side 側 ga·wa

sign 標識 hyō·shi·ki

side plate 小皿 ko·za·ra

signature サイン sain

silk ⓝ 絹 ki·nu

silver ⓝ 銀 gin

SIM card SIMカード shi·mu·kā·do

similar よく似た yo·ku ni·ta

simple 単純な tan·jun·na

since ... (time) …から ... ka·ra

sing 歌います u·tai·mas

singer 歌手 ka·shu

single (for person) ⓐ 独身 do·ku·shin

single room シングルルーム shin·gu·ru·rū·mu

singlet アンダーシャツ an·dā·sha·tsu

sister 姉妹 shi·mai

sit 座ります su·wa·ri·mas

size (general) サイズ sai·zu

skate ⓥ スケート skē·to

skateboarding ⓝ スケートボード skē·to·bō·do

ski ⓝ スキー skī

ski ⓥ スキーをします skī o shi·mas

skiing ⓝ スキー skī

skim milk スキムミルク ski·mu·mi·ru·ku

skin 皮膚 hi·fu

skirt スカート skā·to

skull 頭蓋骨 zu·gai·ko·tsu

sky 空 ka·ra

S

sleep ⓥ 眠ります ne·mu·ri·mas
sleeping bag 寝袋 ne·bu·ku·ro
sleeping berth 寝台 shin·dai
sleeping car 寝台車 shin·dai·sha
sleeping pills 睡眠薬 su·i·min·ya·ku
sleepy 眠い ne·mu·i
slice ⓝ スライス su·rai·su
slide (film) ⓝ スライド su·rai·do
sliding screen 障子 shō·ji
slow 遅い o·soy
slowly ゆっくり yuk·ku·ri
small 小さい chī·sai
smaller より小さい yo·ri chī·sai
smallest いちばん小さい i·chi·ban
chī·sai
smell ⓝ におい ni·oy
smile ⓝ 笑顔 e·ga·o
smoke ⓥ タバコを吸います ta·ba·ko
o su·i·mas
smoked (food) ⓐ 燻製 kun·sē
smoking ⓐ 喫煙 kits·en
snack 軽食 kē·sho·ku
snail カタツムリ ka·ta·tsu·mu·ri
snake ヘビ he·bi
snorkelling ⓝ シュノーケリング
shu·nō·ke·rin·gu
snow 雪 yu·ki
snowboarding ⓝ スノーボード
su·nō·bō·do
snow pea サヤエンドウ sa·ya·en·dō
soap 石鹸 sek·ken
soap opera メロドラマ
me·ro·do·ra·ma
soccer サッカー sak·kā
social welfare 社会福祉
sha·kai·fu·ku·shi
socialist 社会主義者
sha·kai·shu·gi·sha
socks 靴下 ku·tsu·shi·ta
soft やわらかい ya·wa·ra·kai
soft drink ソフトドリンク
so·fu·to·do·rin·ku
soft-boiled 半熟の han·ju·ku no
soldier 兵士 hē·shi
some いくらかの i·ku·ra ka no
someone 誰か da·re ka

something 何か na·ni ka
sometimes ときどき to·ki·do·ki
son 息子 mu·su·ko
song 歌 u·ta
soon すぐに su·gu ni
sore ⓐ 痛い i·tai
soup スープ sū·pu
soup bowl お椀 o·wan
sour cream サワークリーム
sa·wā·ku·rī·mu
south 南 mi·na·mi
souvenir お土産 o·mi·ya·ge
souvenir shop お土産店 o·mi·ya·ge·ya
soy bean 大豆 dai·zu
soy milk 豆乳 tō·nyū
soy sauce しょう油 shō·yu
space スペース su·pē·su
Spain スペイン spe·in
sparkling wine スパークリングワイン
spā·ku·rin·gu·wain
speak 話します ha·na·shi·mas
special ⓐ 特別な to·ku·be·tsu na
specialist 専門家 sem·mon·ka
speed (velocity) ⓝ スピード spī·do
speed limit 制限速度 sē·gen·so·ku·do
spicy スパイシー spai·shī
spider クモ ku·mo
spinach ホウレンソウ hō·ren·sō
spoiled 悪くなった wa·ru·ku nat·ta
spoke スポーク spō·ku
spoon スプーン spūn
sport スポーツ spō·tsu
sports store/shop スポーツ用品店
spō·tsu·yō·hin·ten
sportsperson スポーツマン
spō·tsu·man
sprain 捻挫 nen·za
spring (coil) スプリング sprin·gu
spring (season) 春 ha·ru
spring onion ねぎ ne·gi
square (town) 広場 hi·ro·ba
squid イカ i·ka
stadium スタジアム sta·ji·a·mu
stairway 階段 kai·dan
stale 新鮮じゃない shin·sen ja nai
stamp ⓝ 切手 kit·te

stand-by ticket スタンドバイチケット stan·do·bai·chi·ket·to

star 星 ho·shi

(three-/four-)star (3つ/4つ)星 (mi·tsu/yo·tsu)·bo·shi

start ⑩ スタート stā·to

start ⑨ 始めます ha·ji·me·mas

station 駅 e·ki

stationer's (shop) 文房具(店) bum·bō·gu(·ten)

statue 像 zō

stay (at a hotel) ⑨ 泊まります to·ma·ri·mas

stay (in one place) ⑨ 滞在します tai·zai shi·mas

steak (beef) ステーキ stē·ki

steal 盗みます nu·su·mi·mas

steamed 蒸して mu·shi·te

steep 急な kyū na

step ⑩ 段 dan

stereo ステレオ ste·re·o

still water 静かな水 shi·zu·ka na mi·zu

stock (food) 食料 sho·ku·ryō

stockings ストッキング stok·kin·gu

stolen 盗まれた nu·su·ma·re·ta

stomach 胃 i

stomachache 腹痛 fu·ku·tsū

stone 石 i·shi

toned (drugged) ラリった ra·rit·ta

stop (bus, tram, etc) ⑩ 停留所 ē·ryū·jo

top (cease) ⑨ 止まります to·ma·ri·mas

stop (prevent) ⑨ 止めさせます ya·me·sa·se·mas

storm 嵐 a·ra·shi

story 話 ha·na·shi

stove ストーブ stō·bu

straight まっすぐな mas·su·gu na

strange 変な hen na

stranger よそ者 yo·so·mo·no

strawberry イチゴ i·chi·go

stream 流れ na·ga·re

street 道 mi·chi

street market 青空市場 a·o·zo·ra·i·chi·ba

strike ⑩ ストライキ sto·rai·ki

string ひも hi·mo

stroke (health) ⑩ 発作 hos·sa

stroller ベビーカー be·bī·kâ

strong 強い tsu·yoy

stubborn 頑固な gan·ko na

student 生徒 sē·to

studio スタジオ sta·ji·o

stupid ばかな ba·ka na

style スタイル stai·ru

subtitles 字幕 ji·ma·ku

suburb 郊外 kō·gai

subway (underpass) 地下道 chi·ka·dō

subway (train) 地下鉄 chi·ka·te·tsu

sugar 砂糖 sa·tō

suitcase スーツケース sūts·kēs

sultana レーズン rē·zun

summer 夏 na·tsu

sun 太陽 tai·yō

sunblock 日焼け止め hi·ya·ke·do·me

sunburn 日焼け hi·ya·ke

sunglasses サングラス san·gu·ras

sunny 晴れた ha·re·ta

sunrise 日の出 hi·no·de

sunscreen 日焼け止め hi·ya·ke·do·me

sunset 日の入り hi·no·i·ri

sunstroke 日射病 nis·sha·byō

supermarket スーパー sū·pâ

superstition 迷信 mē·shin

supporter (politics) 支持者 shi·ji·sha

supporter (sport) ファン fan

surf ⑨ サーフィンをします sā·fin o shi·mas

surface mail (land) 普通便 fu·tsū·bin

surface mail (sea) 船便 fu·na·bin

surfboard サーフボード sā·fu·bō·do

surfing ⑩ サーフィン sā·fin

surname 名字 myō·ji

surprise ⑩ 驚き o·do·ro·ki

sushi bar すし屋 su·shi·ya

sweater セーター sē·tâ

Sweden スウェーデン swē·den

sweet ⓐ 甘い a·mai

sweets お菓子 o·ka·shi

swelling 腫れ ha·re

swim ⑨ 泳ぎます o·yo·gi·mas

T

swimming (sport) ⓝ 水泳 su·i·ē
swimming pool プール pū·ru
swimsuit 水着 mi·zu·gi
Switzerland スイス su·i·su
sword 刀 ka·ta·na
synagogue シナゴーグ shi·na·gō·gu
synthetic 合成の gō·sē no
syringe 注射器 chū·sha·ki

T

table テーブル tē·bu·ru
table (low) ちゃぶ台 cha·bu·dai
table tennis 卓球 tak·kyū
tablecloth テーブルクロス
tē·bu·ru·ku·ros
tail 尻尾 ship·po
tailor テーラー tē·rā
take 取ります to·ri·mas
take a photo 写真を撮ります sha·shin
o to·ri·mas
talk 話します ha·na·shi·mas
tall 高い ta·kai
tampon タンポン tam·pon
tanning lotion 日焼けローション
hi·ya·ke·rō·shon
tap 蛇口 ja·gu·chi
tape (music, video) ⓝ テープ tē·pu
tap water 水道水 su·i·dō·su·i
tasty おいしい oy·shī
tattoo 刺青 i·re·zu·mi
tattooing ⓝ 刺青 i·re·zu·mi
tax 税金 zē·kin
taxi タクシー tak·shī
taxi stand タクシー乗り場
tak·shī·no·ri·ba
tea (Japanese) お茶 o·cha
tea (Western) 紅茶 kō·cha
tea ceremony 茶道 sa·dō
tea cup 湯飲み茶碗 yu·no·mi·ja·wan
tea garden 茶畑 cha·ba·ta·ke
teacher 教師 kyō·shi
team チーム chī·mu
teapot ティーポット・急須
tī·pot·to · kyū·su
teaspoon ティースプーン tī·spūn
technique 技術 gi·ju·tsu

teeth 歯 ha
telegram 電報 dem·pô
telephone ⓝ 電話 den·wa
telephone ⓥ 電話します den·wa
shi·mas
telephone box 電話ボックス
den·wa·bok·kus
telescope 望遠鏡 bō·en·kyō
television テレビ te·re·bi
tell 言います ī·mas
temperature (fever) 体温 tai·on
temperature (weather) 気温 ki·on
temple 寺 te·ra
tennis テニス te·nis
tennis court テニスコート te·nis
kō·to
tent テント ten·to
tent peg ペグ pe·gu
terrible ひどい hi·doy
test ⓝ テスト tes·to
thank 感謝します kan·sha shi·mas
that (one) あれ a·re
theatre 劇場 ge·ki·jō
their 彼らの ka·re·ra no
there そこに so·ko ni
thermometer 体温計 tai·on·kē
they 彼らは ka·re·ra wa
thick 厚い a·tsu·i
thief どろぼう do·ro·bō
thin 薄い u·su·i
think 思います o·moy·mas
third 3番の sam·ban no
(to be) thirsty ⓐ のどが渇い no·do
ga ka·wai·ta
this (one) これ ko·re
this month 今月 kon·ge·tsu
this week 今週 kon·shū
this year 今年 ko·to·shi
thread 糸 i·to
throat のど no·do
thrush (health) 口腔カンジダ症
kō·kū·kan·ji·da·shō
thunderstorm 嵐 a·ra·shi
ticket 切符 kip·pu
ticket collector 切符回収
kip·pu·kai·shū·ga·ka·ri

ticket machine 切符販売 kip·pu·ham·bai·ki

ticket office 切符売り kip·pu·u·ri·ba

tide 潮 shi·o

tight きつい ki·tsu·i

time 時間 ji·kan

time difference 時差 ji·sa

timetable 時刻表 ji·ko·ku·hyō

tin (can) 缶 kan

tin opener 缶切 kan·ki·ri

tiny とても小さい to·te·mo chī·sai

tip (gratuity) ⓝ チップ chip·pu

tire タイヤ tai·ya

tired 疲れた tsu·ka·re·ta

tissues ティッシュ tis·shu

to へ e

toast ⓝ トースト tōs·to

toaster トースター tōs·tā

tobacco タバコ tabako

tobacconist タバコ屋 ta·ba·ko·ya

tobogganing ⓝ そり so·ri

today 今日 kyō

toe つま先 tsu·ma·sa·ki

tofu 豆腐 tō·fu

together いっしょに is·sho ni

toilet トイレ toy·re

toilet paper トイレットペーパー toy·ret·to·pē·pā

token トークン tō·kun

toll ⓝ 通行料 tsū·kō·ryō

tomato トマト to·ma·to

tomato sauce トマトソース to·ma·to·sō·su

tomorrow 明日 a·shi·ta

tomorrow afternoon 明日の午後 a·shi·ta no go·go

tomorrow evening 明日の夜 a·shi·ta no yo·ru

tomorrow morning 明日の朝 a·shi·ta no a·sa

tonight 今夜 kon·ya

too (expensive etc) すぎる su·gi·ru

too many/much 多すぎます ō·su·gi·mas

tooth 歯 ha

toothache 歯痛 hai·ta

toothbrush 歯ブラシ ha·bu·ra·shi

toothpaste 練り歯磨き ne·ri·ha·mi·ga·ki

toothpick 楊枝 yō·ji

torch (flashlight) 懐中電灯 kai·chū·den·tō

touch ⓥ 触ります sa·wa·ri·mas

tour ⓝ ツアー tsu·ā

tourist 旅行者 ryo·kō·sha

tourist office 観光案内所 kan·kō·an·nai·jo

towel タオル tow·ru

tower 搭 tō

toxic waste 有害廃棄物 yū·gai·hai·ki·bu·tsu

toy shop おもちゃ屋 o·mo·cha·ya

track (path) ⓝ 通路 tsū·ro

track (sport) ⓝ トラック競技 to·rak·ku·kyō·gi

trade 貿易 bō·e·ki

tradesperson 貿易商 bō·e·ki·shō

traffic 交通 kō·tsū

traffic jam 渋滞 jū·tai

traffic light 信号 shin·gō

trail ⓝ 足跡 a·shi·a·to

train 電車 den·sha

train station 駅 e·ki

tram 市電 shi·den

transfer ⓝ 乗り換え no·ri·ka·e

transit lounge 待合室 ma·chi·ai·shi·tsu

translate 翻訳します hon·ya·ku shi·mas

transport ⓝ 輸送 yu·sō

travel ⓥ 旅行します ryo·kō shi·mas

travel agency 旅行代理店 ryo·kō·dai·ri·ten

travel sickness 乗り物酔い no·ri·mo·no·yoy

travellers cheque トラベラーズチェック to·ra·be·rāz·chek·ku

tree 木 ki

trip (journey) 旅 ta·bi

trolley トロリー to·ro·rī

trousers ズボン zu·bon

truck トラック to·rak·ku

U

true 本当の hon·tô no
try (attempt) ⓥ 試します ta·me·shi·mas
T-shirt Tシャツ tî·sha·tsu
tube (tyre) チューブ chû·bu
tumour 腫瘍 shu·yô
tuna マグロ ma·gu·ro
tune チューン chûn
turkey 七面鳥 shi·chi·men·chô
turn ⓥ 曲がります ma·ga·ri·mas
TV テレビ te·re·bi
tweezers 毛抜き ke·nu·ki
twice 2倍に ni·bai·ni
twin beds ツインベッド tsu·in·bed·do
twins 双子 fu·ta·go
two 2 ni
type ⓝ タイプ tai·pu
typical 典型的な ten·kê·te·ki na
typhoon 台風 tai·fû
tyre タイヤ tai·ya

U

ugly みにくい mi·ni·ku·i
ultrasound 超音波 chôm·pa
umbrella かさ ka·sa
uncomfortable 不安な fu·an na
understand 理解します ri·kai shi·mas
underwear 下着 shi·ta·gi
unemployed 失業した shi·tsu·gyô shi·ta
unfair 不公平な fu·kô·hê na
uniform ⓝ 制服 sê·fu·ku
universe 宇宙 u·chû
university 大学 dai·ga·ku
unleaded 無鉛の mu·en no
unsafe 安全じゃない an·zen ja nai
until (time) まで ma·de
unusual 珍しい me·zu·ra·shî
up 上に u·e ni
uphill 上り坂の no·bo·ri·za·ka no
urgent 緊急の kin·kyû no
urinary infection 尿道炎 nyô·dô·en
USA アメリカ a·me·ri·ka
useful 便利な ben·ri na

V

vacancy 空室の kû·shi·tsu no
no vacancy 満室 man·shi·tsu
vacant 空いている ai·te·i·ru
vacation 休暇 kyû·ka
vaccination 予防注射 yo·bô·chû·sha
vagina ヴァギナ va·gi·na
validate 有効にします yû·kô ni shi·mas
valley 谷 ta·ni
valuable ⓐ 高価な kô·ka na
valuables ⓝ 貴重品 ki·chô·hin
value (price) ⓝ 価値 ka·chi
van バン ban
veal 子牛 ko·u·shi
vegan 厳格な菜食主義者 gen·ka·ku na sai·sho·ku·shu·gi·sha
vegetable(s) 野菜 ya·sai
vegetables (fried) 野菜炒め ya·sai·i·ta·me
vegetarian ベジタリアン be·ji·ta·ri·an
vein 静脈 jô·mya·ku
vending machine 自動販売機 ji·dô·ham·bai·ki
venereal disease 性病 sê·byô
venue 現場 gem·ba
very とても to·te·mo
video camera ビデオカメラ bi·de·o·ka·me·ra
view ⓝ 眺め na·ga·me
village 村 mu·ra
vinegar 酢 su
vineyard ブドウ畑 bu·dô·ba·ta·ke
virus ウィルス wi·ru·su
visa ビザ bi·za
visit ⓥ 訪問します hô·mon shi·mas
vitamins ビタミン bi·ta·min
vodka ウォッカ wok·ka
voice ⓝ 声 ko·e
volcano 火山 ka·zan
volleyball バレーボール ba·rê·bô·ru
volume 量 ryô
vote ⓥ 投票します tô·hyô shi·mas

W

wage 賃金 chin·gin

wait (for) ⓥ 待ちます ma·chi·mas

waiter ウェイター wē·tā

waiting room 待合室 ma·chi·ai·shi·tsu

wake (someone) up 起こします o·ko·shi·mas

Wales ウェールズ wē·ru·zu

walk 歩きます a·ru·ki·mas

wallet 財布 sai·fu

wall 壁 ka·be

want ⓥ 欲しいです ho·shī des

war 戦争 sen·sō

wardrobe たんす tan·su

warm あたたかい a·ta·ta·kai

warn 警告します kē·ko·ku shi·mas

wash (oneself/something) 洗います a·rai·mas

wash cloth (flannel) 洗濯します sen·ta·ku shi·mas

washing machine 洗濯機 sen·tak·ki

watch ⓝ 腕時計 u·de·do·kē

watch ⓥ 見ます mi·mas

water 水 mi·zu

water bottle 水筒 su·i·tō

water bottle (hot) ポット pot·to

waterfall 滝 ta·ki

watermelon スイカ su·i·ka

waterproof 防水 bō·su·i

water-skiing ⓥ 水上スキー su·i·jō·skī

wave ⓝ 波 na·mi

way 道 mi·chi

we 私たちは wa·ta·shi·ta·chi wa

weak 弱い yo·wai

wealthy 裕福な yū·fu·ku na

wear 着ます ki·mas

weather 天気 ten·ki

wedding 結婚式 kek·kon·shi·ki

week 週 shū

weekend 週末 shū·ma·tsu

weekly 1週間 is·shū·kan

weight 重さ o·mo·sa

welfare 福祉 fu·ku·shi

well よく yo·ku

west 西 ni·shi

wet ⓐ 濡れている nu·re·te i·ru

whale くじら ku·ji·ra

what なに na·ni

wheel 車輪 sha·rin

wheelchair 車椅子 ku·ru·ma·i·su

when いつ i·tsu

where どこ do·ko

which どちら do·chi·ra

whisky ウィスキー wis·kī

white 白い shi·roy

white (coffee) ホワイト ho·wai·to

white wine 白ワイン shi·ro·wain

who だれ da·re

wholemeal bread ホールミールの パン hō·ru·mī·ru no pan

why なぜ na·ze

wide 広く hi·ro·ku

wife 妻 tsu·ma

wild 野生 ya·sē

wild rice ワイルドライス wai·ru·do·rai·su

win ⓥ 勝ちます ka·chi·mas

wind 風 ka·ze

wineglass ワイングラス wain·gu·ra·su

window 窓 ma·do

windscreen フロントガラス fu·ron·to·ga·ra·su

windsurfing ⓝ ウィンドサーフィン win·do·sā·fin

wine ワイン wain

wing 翼 tsu·ba·sa

winner 受賞者 ju·shō·sha

winter 冬 fu·yu

with いっしょに is·sho ni

within (an hour) （1時間）内に (i·chi·ji·kan) nai ni

without なしで na·shi de

wok 中華鍋 chū·ka·na·be

woman 女性 jo·sē

wonderful 素晴らしい su·ba·ra·shī

wood 木 ki

wood-block prints 浮世絵 u·ki·yo·e

wool ウール ū·ru

word 言葉 ko·to·ba

work ⓝ 仕事 shi·go·to

work ⓥ 働きます ha·ta·ra·ki·mas

Y

work experience 職歴 sho·ku·re·ki
work permit 就労許可 shū·rō·kyo·ka
workout ⓝ 練習 ren·shū
world 世界 se·kai
World Cup ワールドカップ wā·ru·do·kap·pu
worms イモムシ i·mo·mu·shi
worried 心配な shim·pai na
wrist 手首 te·ku·bi
write 書きます ka·ki·mas
writer 作家 sak·ka
wrong 間違った ma·chi·gat·ta

Y

year 年 nen
yellow 黄色い kī·roy
yes はい hai
yesterday きのう ki·nō

yoga ヨガ yo·ga
yogurt ヨーグルト yō·gu·ru·to
you sg あなた a·na·ta
you pl あなたたち a·na·ta·ta·chi
young 若い wa·kai
your あなたの a·na·ta no
youth hostel ユースホステル yū·su·ho·su·te·ru

Z

zip(per) ジッパー jip·pā
zodiac 12宮 jū·ni·gū
zoo 動物園 dō·bu·tsu·en
zucchini ズッキーニ zuk·kī·ni

Dictionary

JAPANESE *to* ENGLISH

日本語–英語

The entries in this Japanese–English dictionary are ordered according to the gojūon (or aiueo) system, which is widely used in Japan. The order is: **a**-i-u-e-o-**ka**-ga-ki-gi-kya-gya-kyu-gyu-kyo-gyo-ku-gu-ke-ge-ko-go-**sa**-za-shi-ji-sha-ja-shu-ju-sho-jo-su-zu-se-ze-so-zo-**ta**-da-chi-(ji)-cha-chu-cho-tsu-(zu)-te-de-to-do-**na**-ni-nya-nyu-nyo-nu-ne-no-**ha**-ba-pa-hi-bi-pi-hya-bya-pya-hyu-byu-pyu-hyo-byo-pyo-fu-bu-pu-he-be-pe-ho-bo-po-**ma**-mi-mya-myu-myo-mu-me-mo-**ya**-yu-yo-ra-ri-rya-ryu-ryo-ru-re-ro-**wa**-n

Verbs in the dictionary are given in their ·mas (ます) form (for more information on this, see **grammar**). The symbols ⓝ, ⓐ and ⓥ (indicating noun, adjective and verb) have been added for clarity where an English term could be either.

あ A

愛 ai love ⓝ
愛します ai shi·mas love ⓥ
アイスクリーム ais·ku·rī·mu ice cream
空いている ai·te i·ru vacant
アイルランド ai·ru·ran·do Ireland
アイロン ai·ron iron (for clothes) ⓝ
青い a·oy blue
青空市場 a·o·zo·ra·i·chi·ba street market
赤い a·kai red
赤ちゃん a·ka·chan baby
明るい a·ka·ru·i light (of colour) ⓐ
赤ワイン a·ka·wain red wine
秋 a·ki autumn • fall
揚げます a·ge·mas fry
朝 a·sa morning

朝ごはん a·sa·go·han breakfast
あさって a·sat·te (the) day after tomorrow
足 a·shi foot
脚 a·shi leg (body part)
足首 a·shi·ku·bi ankle
明日 a·shi·ta tomorrow
明日の朝 a·shi·ta no a·sa tomorrow morning
明日の午後 a·shi·ta no go·go tomorrow afternoon
明日の夜 a·shi·ta no yo·ru tomorrow evening
アスピリン as·pi·rin aspirin
あたたかい a·ta·ta·kai warm
頭 a·ta·ma head ⓝ
新しい a·ta·ra·shī new
熱い a·tsu·i hot
熱くなった a·tsu·ku nat·ta heated

あ

あと a·to after
あとで a·to de later
あなた a·na·ta you sg
あなたたち a·na·ta·ta·chi you pl
危ない a·bu·nai dangerous
油 a·bu·ra oil (food)
甘い a·mai sweet ⓐ
雨 a·me rain
アメリカ a·me·ri·ka USA
歩きます a·ru·ki·mas walk
アルコール a·ru·kō·ru alcohol
あれ a·re that (one)
アレルギー a·re·ru·gī allergy
アントレー an·to·rē entrée
案内所 an·nai·jo information office
胃 i stomach
いい ī good
いいえ ī·e no
Eメール ī·mē·ru email ⓝ
医学 i·ga·ku medicine (study, profession)
行きます i·ki·mas go ⓥ
イギリス i·gi·ri·su England
遺失物取扱所 i·shi·tsu·bu·tsu·to·ri·a·tsu·kai·jo lost property office
医者 i·sha doctor
椅子 i·su chair
忙しい i·so·ga·shī busy
痛み i·ta·mi pain
いたんだ i·tan·da off (spoiled)
1 i·chi one
市場 i·chi·ba market
いちばん大きい i·chi·ban ō·kī biggest
いちばん小さい i·chi·ban chī·sai smallest
いちばん近くの i·chi·ban chi·ka·ku no nearest
胃腸炎 i·chō·en gastroenteritis
いつ i·tsu when
いっしょに is·sho ni together
いっぱいの ip·pai no full
田舎 i·na·ka countryside
犬 i·nu dog
今 i·ma now
妹 i·mō·to younger sister
衣料店 i·ryō·ten clothing store

衣類 i·ru·i clothing
刺青 i·re·zu·mi tattoo • tattooing
色 i·ro colour
インターネット in·tā·net·to internet
インターネットカフェ in·tā·net·to·ka·fe internet cafe
インフルエンザ in·fu·ru·en·za flu • influenza
ウール ū·ru wool
ウェイター wē·tā waiter
ウェールズ wē·ru·zu Wales
上に u·e ni on • up
うしろ u·shi·ro behind
後ろの u·shi·ro no rear (seat etc) ⓐ
美しい u·tsu·ku·shī beautiful
腕 u·de arm
腕時計 u·de·do·kē watch ⓝ
海 u·mi sea
うるさい u·ru·sai loud • noisy
運転します un·ten shi·mas drive
運転手 un·ten·shu driver
運転免許証 un·ten·men·kyo·shō drivers licence
絵 e painting (a work)
エアコン付きの air·kon·tsu·ki no air-conditioned
映画 ē·ga film (cinema) • movie
映画館 ē·ga·kan cinema
英語 ē·go English
ATM ē·tī·e·mu automated teller machine (ATM)
駅 e·ki (train) station
エコノミークラス e·ko·no·mī·ku·ras economy class
エスカレータ es·ka·rē·ta escalator
エレベータ e·re·bē·ta elevator • lift
エンジン en·jin engine
エンターテイメントガイド en·tā·tē·men·to·gai·do entertainment guide
エンピツ em·pi·tsu pencil
おいしい oy·shī tasty
往復切符 ō·fu·ku·kip·pu return ticket
OL ō·e·ru female office worker
大きい ō·kī big
オーストラリア ō·sto·ra·rya Australia

オートバイ ō·to·bai motorcycle
オートマチック ō·to·ma·chik·ku automatic ⓐ
大晦日 ō·mi·so·ka New Year's Eve
お母さん o·kā·san mother
おかしい o·ka·shī funny
お金 o·ka·ne money
贈物 o·ku·ri·mo·no gift
遅れ o·ku·re delay
起こします o·ko·shi·mas wake (someone) up
おじいさん o·jī·san grandfather
おしゃぶり o·sha·bu·ri dummy • pacifier
遅い o·soy late
お茶 o·cha tea (Japanese)
夫 ot·to husband
お父さん o·tō·san father
弟 o·tō·to younger brother
男の子 o·to·ko no ko boy
おととい o·to·toy (the) day before yesterday
踊ります o·do·ri·mas dance
お腹がすいた o·na·ka ga su·i·ta (to be) hungry
お兄さん o·nī·san older brother
お姉さん o·nē·san older sister
おばあさん o·bā·san grandmother
おばさん o·ba·san aunt
お話し中 o·ha·na·shi·chū engaged (phone)
お風呂 o·fu·ro bath ⓝ
お土産 o·mi·ya·ge souvenir
お土産屋 o·mi·ya·ge·ya souvenir shop
オムツ o·mu·tsu diaper • nappy
おめでとう o·me·de·tō congratulations
重い o·moy heavy
泳ぎます o·yo·gi·mas swim
オランダ o·ran·da Netherlands
降ります o·ri·mas get off (a train, etc)
オレンジ o·ren·ji orange (colour) • orange (fruit)
おわり o·wa·ri end ⓝ
お椀 o·wan miso-soup bowl • soup bowl

音楽 on·ga·ku music
温泉 on·sen mineral hot-spring spa
女の子 on·na no ko girl

か **KA**

ガールフレンド gā·ru·fu·ren·do girlfriend
階 kai floor (storey)
絵画 kai·ga painting (the art)
海外 kai·gai abroad • overseas
外国の gai·ko·ku no foreign
会社 kai·sha company (firm)
快速 kai·so·ku rapid train
階段 kai·dan stairway
懐中電灯 kai·chū·den·tō torch (flashlight)
開店時間 kai·ten·ji·kan opening hours
ガイド gai·do guide (person)
ガイド付きツアー gai·do·tsu·ki·tsu·ā guided tour
ガイドブック gai·do·buk·ku guidebook
買います kai·mas buy
買い物をします kai·mo·no o shi·mas shop ⓥ
顔 ka·o face
画家 ga·ka painter
科学 ka·ga·ku science
鏡 ka·ga·mi mirror
鍵 ka·gi key
書留 ka·ki·to·me registered mail
書きます ka·ki·mas write
鍵をかけた ka·gi o ka·ke·ta locked
鍵をかけます ka·gi o ka·ke·mas lock ⓥ
家具 ka·gu furniture
カクテル ka·ku·te·ru cocktail
確認する ka·ku·nin su·ru confirm
かさ ka·sa umbrella
貸します ka·shi·mas rent ⓥ
ガス ga·su gas (for cooking)
カセット ka·set·to cassette
家族 ka·zo·ku family
ガソリン ga·so·rin gas • petrol
ガソリンスタンド ga·so·rin·stan·do petrol station • service station
肩 ka·ta shoulder

か

かたい ka·tai hard (not soft)
片道切符 ka·ta·mi·chi·ki·pu one-way ticket
月 ga·tsu month
カップ kap·pu cup
カナダ ka·na·da Canada
彼女の ka·no·jo no her (ownership)
彼女は ka·no·jo wa she
彼女を ka·no·jo o her (as object of sentence)
カバーチャージ ka·bā·chā·ji cover charge
かばん ka·ban bag
カフェ ka·fe café
カプセルホテル ka·pu·se·ru·ho·te·ru capsule hotel
花粉症 ka·fun·shō hay fever
紙 ka·mi paper
剃刀 ka·mi·so·ri razor
剃刀の刃 ka·mi·so·ri no ha razor blade
カメラ ka·me·ra camera
かゆみ ka·yu·mi itch ⓝ
から ka·ra from
空の ka·ra no empty
軽い ka·ru·i light (not heavy) ⓐ
彼の ka·re no his
彼は ka·re wa he
彼を kare o him
皮 ka·wa leather ⓝ
川 ka·wa river
乾いた ka·wai·ta dry ⓐ
乾かします ka·wa·ka·shi·mas dry (clothes) ⓥ
為替 ka·wa·se currency exchange
為替レート ka·wa·se·rē·to exchange rate
缶 kan can • tin
缶切 kan·ki·ri can opener • tin opener
換金します kan·kin shi·mas change (money) ⓥ
間欠泉 kan·kets·sen geyser
観光案内所 kan·kō·an·nai·jo tourist office
看護婦 kan·go·fu nurse
感謝している kan·sha shi·te i·ru grateful

勘定 kan·jō bill (restaurant etc) ⓝ
感触 kan·sho·ku feeling (physical)
感染 kan·sen infection
幹線道路 kan·sen·dō·ro highway
元旦 gan·tan New Year's Day
黄色い kī·roy yellow
気温 ki·on temperature (weather)
聴きます ki·ki·mas listen (to)
既婚 ki·kon married
技術者 gi·ju·tsu·sha engineer
季節 ki·se·tsu season
北 ki·ta north
汚い ki·ta·nai dirty
喫煙 ki·tsu·en smoking ⓐ
切って kit·te stamp ⓝ
切符 kip·pu ticket
切符売り kip·pu·u·ri·ba ticket office
切符販売機 kip·pu·ham·bai·ki ticket machine
絹 ki·nu silk ⓝ
きのう ki·nō yesterday
キャンセル kyan·se·ru cancel ⓥ
キャンプ場 kyam·pu·jō camping ground
休暇 kyū·ka holidays • vacation
救急 kyū·kyū emergency
救急車 kyū·kyū·sha ambulance
救急箱 kyū·kyū·ba·ko first-aid kit
宮殿 kyū·den palace
救命胴衣 kyū·mē·dōy life jacket
今日 kyō today
境界 kyō·kai border
教会 kyō·kai church
教師 kyō·shi teacher
兄弟 kyō·dai brother
キヨスク ki·yos·ku kiosk
義理のお母さん gi·ri no o·kā·san mother-in-law
義理のお父さん gi·ri no o·tō·san father-in-law
切ります ki·ri·mas cut ⓥ
きれいな ki·rē na clean ⓐ
キロ（グラム）ki·ro(·gu·ra·mu) kilo(gram)
キロメートル ki·ro·mē·to·ru kilometre
金 kin gold ⓝ

銀 gin silver ⓝ

禁煙の kin·en no nonsmoking

緊急の kin·kyū no urgent

金庫 kin·ko safe ⓝ

銀行 gin·kō bank (money) ⓝ

銀行口座 gin·kō·kō·za bank account

航空 kō·kū airline

空港 kū·kō airport

空港税 kū·kō·zē airport tax

航空便 kō·kū·bin airmail

空室 kū·shi·tsu vacancy

くし ku·shi comb

苦情 ku·jō complaint

薬 ku·su·ri drug (medicine) • medication

果物 ku·da·mo·no fruit

口 ku·chi mouth

口紅 ku·chi·be·ni lipstick

靴 ku·tsu shoe

靴下 ku·tsu·shi·ta socks

靴屋 ku·tsu·ya shoe shop

首 ku·bi neck

暗い ku·rai dark

クラシックの ku·ra·shik·ku no classical

グラス gu·ra·su glass (for drinking)

グラム gu·ra·mu gram

クリーニング ku·rī·nin·gu cleaning ⓝ

クリーム ku·rī·mu cream

クリスマス ku·ri·su·mas Christmas

車椅子 ku·ru·ma·i·su wheelchair

クレジットカード ku·re·jit·to·kā·do credit card

黒い ku·roy black

クローク ku·rō·ku cloakroom

警官 kē·kan police officer

警察 kē·sa·tsu police

警察署 kē·sa·tsu·sho police station

計算機 kē·san·ki calculator

芸術家 gē·ju·tsu·ka artist

軽食 kē·sho·ku snack

携帯電話 kē·tai·den·wa mobile phone

ゲイの gē no gay ⓐ

けが ke·ga injury ⓝ

劇 ge·ki play (theatre) ⓝ

劇場 ge·ki·jō theatre

下剤 ge·zai laxative ⓝ

下宿屋 ge·shu·ku·ya boarding house

ゲストハウス ges·to·how·su guesthouse

血液型 ke·tsu·e·ki·ga·ta blood group

欠点のある ket·ten no a·ru faulty

毛抜き ke·nu·ki tweezers

下痢 ge·ri diarrhoea

現金 gen·kin cash ⓝ

現金化します gen·kin·ka shi·mas cash (a cheque) ⓥ

言語 gen·go language

建築 ken·chi·ku architecture

建築家 ken·chi·ku·ka architect

コイン ko·in coins

コインランドリー ko·in·ran·do·rī launderette

更衣室 kōy·shi·tsu changing room (for sport)

公園 kō·en park ⓝ

工学会 kō·ga·ku engineering

高価な kō·ka na valuable ⓝ

豪華な gō·ka na luxury ⓐ

交換 kō·kan exchange ⓝ

交換します kō·kan shi·mas exchange ⓥ

航空便 kō·kū·bin flight

工芸品 kō·gē·hin crafts

公衆電話 kō·shū·den·wa public telephone

公衆トイレ kō·shū·toy·re public toilet

香水 kō·su·i perfume

抗生剤 kō·sē·zai antibiotics

高速道路 kō·so·ku·dō·ro motorway (tollway)

紅茶 kō·cha tea (Western)

交番 kō·ban police box

コークスクリュー kō·ku·sku·ryū corkscrew

凍った kōt·ta frozen

コート kō·to coat • court (tennis)

コーヒー kō·hī coffee

氷 kō·ri ice

小切 ko·git·te check (banking) ⓝ

顧客 ko·kya·ku client

午後 go·go afternoon

心地よい ko·ko·chi·yoy comfortable

ここで ko·ko de here

小皿 ko·za·ra plate (small)
故障した ko·shō·shi·ta broken down
故障中 ko·shō·chū out of order
個人的な ko·jin·te·ki na private
小銭 ko·ze·ni change (coins) ⓝ
コック kok·ku cook ⓝ
小包 ko·zu·tsu·mi packet (general) • parcel
子供 ko·do·mo child • children
ごはん go·han rice (cooked)
小道 ko·mi·chi path
ごみ箱 go·mi·ba·ko garbage can
米 ko·me rice (uncooked)
子守り ko·mo·ri childminding ⓝ
ゴルフ go·ru·fu golf
ゴルフコース go·ru·fu·kō·su golf course
これ ko·re this (one)
コレクトコール ko·re·ku·to·kō·ru collect call
壊れた ko·wa·re·ta broken
壊れやすい ko·wa·re·ya·su·i fragile
コンサート kon·sā·to concert
コンタクトレンズ kon·ta·ku·to·ren·zu contact lenses
コンドーム kon·dō·mu condom
コンパニオン kom·pa·ni·on companion
コンビニ kom·bi·ni convenience store
コンピュータ kom·pyū·ta computer
コンファーム kon·fā·mu confirm (a booking)
コンファレンス kon·fa·ren·su conference (big)
今夜 kon·ya tonight
婚約者 kon·ya·ku·sha fiancé(e)

さ SA

サーカス sā·kas circus
サービス sā·bis service
サービス料 sā·bis·ryō service charge
最高の sai·kō no best
最後の sai·go no last (final)
祭日 sai·ji·tsu public holiday
(厳格な)菜食主義者 (gen·ka·ku na) sai·sho·ku·shu·gi·sha vegan
サイズ sai·zu size (general)

財布 sai·fu purse • wallet
魚 sa·ka·na fish
魚屋 sa·ka·na·ya fish shop
酒屋 sa·ka·ya liquor store
酒 sa·ke alcoholic drink • sake
サッカー sak·kā football (soccer)
茶道 sa·dō tea ceremony
寒い sa·mu·i cold (atmosphere)
皿 sa·ra dish • plate (big)
サラリーマン sa·ra·rī·man business man
さん ·san Mr • Mrs • Ms • Miss
サングラス san·gu·ras sunglasses
市 shi city
試合 shi·ai game (sport) • match
幸せな shi·a·wa·se na happy
シーツ shī·tsu bed linen • sheet (bed)
シートベルト shī·to·be·ru·to seatbelt
ジーンズ jīn·zu jeans
シェアします she·a shi·mas share (a dorm etc) ⓥ
シェービングクリーム she·bin·gu·ku·rī·mu shaving cream
シェフ she·fu chef
時間 ji·kan hour
時間どおり ji·kan·dō·ri on time
事故 ji·ko accident
時刻表 ji·ko·ku·hyō timetable
仕事 shi·go·to job
時差 ji·sa time difference
時差ぼけ ji·sa·bo·ke jet lag
辞書 ji·sho dictionary
静かな shi·zu·ka na quiet
下着 shi·ta·gi underwear
下へ shi·ta e down
試着室 shi·cha·ku·shi·tsu changing room (in shop)
失業した shi·tsu·gyō shi·ta unemployed
ジッパー jip·pā zip • zipper
自転車 ji·ten·sha bicycle
自動車 ji·dō·sha car
自動車所有権 ji·dō·sha·sho·yū·ken car owner's title
自動車登録 ji·dō·sha·tō·ro·ku car registration

自動販売機 ji·dō·ham·bai·ki vending machine

市の中心 shi no chū·shin city centre

支払い shi·ha·rai payment

紙幣 shi·hē banknote

島 shi·ma island

姉妹 shi·mai sister

字幕 ji·ma·ku subtitles

閉まった shi·mat·ta shut

ジム ji·mu gym (place)

事務処理 ji·mu·sho·ri paperwork

閉めます shi·me·mas close ⓥ

地元 ji·mo·to local

ジャーナリスト jā·na·ris·to journalist

蛇口 ja·gu·chi faucet • tap

ジャケット ja·ket·to jacket

写真 sha·shin photo • photography

写真家 sha·shin·ka photographer

シャツ sha·tsu shirt

シャワー sha·wā shower

シャンペン sham·pen champagne

週 shū week

習慣 shū·kan custom

住所 jū·sho address

充分な jū·bun na enough

週末 shū·ma·tsu weekend

修理します shū·ri shi·mas repair ⓥ

手芸品 shu·gē·hin handicrafts

出張 shut·chō business trip

出発 shup·pa·tsu departure

潤滑油 jun·ka·tsu·yu lubricant

障害をもつ shō·gai o mo·tsu disabled ⓐ

消化不良 shō·ka·fu·ryō indigestion

乗客 jō·kya·ku passenger

正午 shō·go midday • noon

錠剤 jō·zai pill

消臭剤 shō·shū·zai deodorant

消毒剤 shō·do·ku·zai antiseptic ⓝ

乗馬 jō·ba horse riding

情報 jō·hō information

ショー shō show ⓝ

食事 sho·ku·ji meal

食前酒 sho·ku·zen·shu apéritif

食中毒 sho·ku·chū·do·ku food poisoning

食堂車 sho·ku·dō·sha dining car

食料 sho·ku·ryō food supplies

食料品 sho·ku·ryō·hin grocery

女性 jo·sē female • woman

ショッピングセンター shop·pin·gu·sen·tā shopping centre

処方箋 sho·hō·sen prescription

書類 sho·ru·i papers (documents)

城 shi·ro castle

白い shi·roy white

白黒 （フィルム） shi·ro·ku·ro (fi·ru·mu) B&W (film)

白ワイン shi·ro·wain white wine

新幹線 shin·kan·sen bullet train

シングルルーム shin·gu·ru·rū·mu single room

寝室 shin·shi·tsu bedroom

親切 shin·se·tsu na kind (nice)

新鮮 shin·sen na fresh

心臓 shin·zō heart

心臓病 shin·zō·byō heart condition

寝台車 shin·dai·sha sleeping car

新聞 shim·bun newspaper

水筒 su·i·tō water bottle

炊飯器 su·i·han·ki rice cooker

水疱 su·i·hō blister

数字 sū·ji number

スーツケース sūts·kēs suitcase

スーパー sū·pā supermarket

スカート skā·to skirt

スカーフ skā·fu scarf

スキー skī skiing ⓝ

好きです su·ki des like ⓥ

すぎる su·gi·ru too (expensive etc)

少ない su·ku·nai less

すぐに su·gu ni soon

スコットランド skot·to·ran·do Scotland

涼しい su·zu·shī cool (temperature)

勧めます su·su·me·mas recommend ⓥ

スタンドバイチケット stan·do·bai·chi·ket·to stand-by ticket

頭痛 zu·tsū headache

ストッキング stok·kin·gu stockings

ストライキ sto·rai·ki strike ⓝ

素晴らしい su·ba·ra·shī great (fantastic)

スプーン spūn spoon

スポーツ用品店 spō·tsu·yō·hin·ten sports shop • sports store

ズボン zu·bon pants • trousers

スライス su·rai·su slice ⓝ

スライド su·rai·do slide (film) ⓝ

税関 zē·kan customs

税金 zē·kin tax

制限速度 sē·gen·so·ku·do speed limit

生徒 sē·to student

生理用ナプキン sē·ri·yō·na·pu·kin panty liners • sanitary napkins

セーター sē·tā jumper • sweater

セーフセックス sē·fu·sek·kus safe sex

セカンドクラス se·kan·do·ku·ras second class ⓝ

席 se·ki seat (place)

せきが出ます se·ki ga de·mas cough ⓥ

せき止め se·ki·do·me cough medicine ⓝ

石油 se·ki·yu oil (petrol)

セックス sek·kus sex

石鹸 sek·ken soap

接続 se·tsu·zo·ku connection (transport)

背中 se·na·ka back (body part)

セルフサービスの se·ru·fu·sā·bis no self service

栓 sen plug (bath)

前菜 zen·sai appetiser

洗濯場 sen·ta·ku·ba laundry (place)

洗濯物 sen·ta·ku·mo·no laundry (clothes)

洗濯機 sen·tak·ki washing machine

センチ sen·chi centimetre

銭湯 sen·tō bath house • public baths

栓抜き sen·nu·ki bottle opener

全部 zem·bu all • everything

掃除をします sō·ji o shi·mas clean ⓥ

速達 so·ku·ta·tsu express (mail) ⓝ

そこに so·ko ni there

そして so·shi·te and

外側の so·to·ga·wa no outside

剃ります so·ri·mas shave ⓥ

それぞれ so·re·zo·re each

た TA

ダイアルトーン dai·a·ru·tōn dial tone

大学 dai·ga·ku university

退屈な tai·ku·tsu na boring

大使館 tai·shi·kan embassy

大聖堂 dai·sē·dō cathedral

大切な tai·se·tsu na important

台所 dai·do·ko·ro kitchen

たいへんな tai·hen na hard (not easy)

タイヤ tai·ya tire • tyre

太陽 tai·yō sun

タオル tow·ru towel

高い ta·kai expensive • high

タクシー tak·shī taxi

タクシー乗り場 tak·shī·no·ri·ba taxi stand

たすけ tas·ke help ⓝ

たすけます tas·ke·mas help ⓥ

脱脂綿 das·shi·men cotton balls

建物 ta·te·mo·no building

タバコ ta·ba·ko cigarette

タバコを吸います ta·ba·ko o su·i·mas smoke ⓥ

旅 ta·bi journey

ダブルベッド da·bu·ru·bed·do double bed

ダブルルーム da·bu·ru·rū·mu double room

食べます ta·be·mas eat

食べ物 ta·be·mo·no food

だれ da·re who

誕生日 tan·jō·bi birthday • date of birth

ダンス dan·su dancing ⓝ

タンポン tam·pon tampon

血 chi blood

小さい chī·sai small

チーズ chī·zu cheese

チーム chī·mu team

チェックイン chek·ku·in check-in (desk) ⓝ

違う chi·ga·u different

近く chi·ka·ku close • near • nearby

地下鉄の駅 chi·ka·te·tsu no eki subway/metro station

地下道 chi·ka·dō subway (underpass)

地図 chi·zu map

チップ chip·pu tip (gratuity) Ⓝ

チャイルドシート chai·ru·do·shī·to child seat

茶色い chai·roy brown Ⓐ

茶畑 cha·ba·ta·ke tea garden

茶碗 cha·wan rice bowl

中央 chū·ō centre

中止 chū·shi intermission

注射 chū·sha injection

駐車します chū·sha shi·mas park (a car) Ⓥ

駐車場 chū·sha·jō car park

注射針 chū·sha·ba·ri needle (syringe)

昼食 chū·sho·ku lunch

超過 chō·ka excess (baggage)

彫刻 chō·ko·ku sculpture

朝食 chō·sho·ku breakfast

ちょうど chō·do exactly

直接に cho·ku·se·tsu ni direct

直通 cho·ku·tsū direct-dial

チョコレート cho·ko·rē·to chocolate

賃貸します chin·tai shi·mas hire

鎮痛剤 chin·tsū·zai painkiller

ツアー tsu·ā tour

ツインベッド tsu·in·bed·do twin beds

通信社 tsū·shin·sha newsagency

通訳 tsū·ya·ku interpreter

通路 tsū·ro aisle (on plane)

疲れた tsu·ka·re·ta tired

つぎ tsu·gi next

包み tsu·tsu·mi package

妻 tsu·ma wife

つまります tsu·ma·ri·mas blocked

爪切 tsu·me·ki·ri nail clippers

冷たい tsu·me·tai cold (to the touch) Ⓐ

釣り tsu·ri fishing Ⓝ

手 te hand

で de at

Tシャツ tī·sha·tsu T-shirt

ティースプーン tī·spūn teaspoon

ティーポット tī·pot·to teapot

ティッシュ tis·shu tissues

テーラー tē·rā tailor

手形 te·ga·ta check (bill)

出かけます de·ka·ke·mas go out

手紙 te·ga·mi letter (mail)

出口 de·gu·chi exit Ⓝ

デザート de·zā·to dessert

手数料 te·sū·ryō commission

手作りの te·zu·ku·ri no handmade

テニス te·nis tennis

テニスコート te·nis kō·to tennis court

手荷物 te·ni·mo·tsu baggage • luggage

手荷物預かり所 te·ni·mo·tsu·a·zu·ka·ri·sho left luggage (office)

手荷物許容量 te·ni·mo·tsu·kyo·yō·ryō baggage allowance

デパート de·pā·to department store

手袋 te·bu·ku·ro gloves

寺 te·ra temple

デリカテッセン de·ri·ka·tes·sen delicatessen

テレビ te·re·bi television

テレフォンカード te·re·fon·kā·do phone card

電化製品店 den·ka·sē·hin electrical store

電気 den·ki electricity • light

電気技師 den·ki·gi·shi electrician

伝言 den·gon message

電車 den·sha train

電子レンジ den·shi·ren·ji microwave (oven)

電池 den·chi battery (general)

電報 dem·pō telegram

展覧会 ten·ran·kai exhibition

電流 den·ryū current (electricity)

電話 den·wa telephone • phone call Ⓝ

電話します den·wa shi·mas telephone Ⓥ

電話帳 den·wa·chō phone book

電話番号 den·wa·ban·gō phone number

な

電話ボックス den·wa·bok·kus phone box
ドイツ doy·tsu Germany
トイレ toy·re toilet
トイレットペーパー toy·ret·to·pē·pā toilet paper
搭乗券 tō·jō·ken boarding pass
到着 tō·cha·ku arrivals
糖尿病 tō·nyō·byō diabetes
動物園 dō·bu·tsu·en zoo
同僚 dō·ryō colleague
遠い tōy far
トースター tōs·tā toaster
トースト tōs·to toast
独身 do·ku·shin single (person)
毒の do·ku no poisonous
どこ do·ko where
図書館 to·sho·kan library
どちら do·chi·ra which
飛びます to·bi·mas fly Ⓥ
友達 to·mo·da·chi friend
トラベラーズチェック to·ra·be·rāz·chek·ku travellers cheque
鶏肉 to·ri·ni·ku chicken (meat)
努力します do·ryo·ku shi·mas try Ⓥ
ドル do·ru dollar
ドレス do·res dress
トロリー to·ro·rī trolley

な NA

ナイトクラブ nai·to·ku·ra·bu nightclub
ナイフ nai·fu knife
ナイフとフォーク nai·fu to fō·ku cutlery (lit: knife and fork)
なか na·ka in
長い na·gai long
眺め na·ga·me view
なくした na·ku·shi·ta lost (item)
なしで na·shi de without
なぜ na·ze why
夏 na·tsu summer
なに na·ni what
何もない na·ni·mo nai nothing
ナプキン na·pu·kin napkin

名前 na·ma·e name Ⓝ
南京錠 nan·kin·jō padlock
2 ni two
におい ni·oy smell Ⓝ
肉 ni·ku meat
肉屋 ni·ku·ya butcher's shop
西 ni·shi west
2週間 ni·shū·kan fortnight
日記 nik·ki diary
日中 nit·chū day
ニュージーランド nyū·jī·ran·do New Zealand
入場券 nyū·jō·ken entry
入場料 nyū·jō·ryō admission (price)
ニュース nyū·su news
庭 ni·wa garden
妊娠している nin·shin shi·te i·ru pregnant
盗まれた nu·su·ma·re·ta stolen
値段 ne·dan price
熱 ne·tsu heat • fever
寝袋 ne·bu·ku·ro sleeping bag
眠ります ne·mu·ri·mas sleep Ⓥ
練り歯磨き ne·ri·ha·mi·ga·ki toothpaste
年 nen year
年金者 nen·kin·sha pensioner
捻挫 nen·za sprain
脳しんとう nō·shin·tō concussion
ノート nō·to notebook (paper)
乗って not·te aboard
のど no·do throat
のどが渇いた no·do ga ka·wai·ta (to be) thirsty
飲みます no·mi·mas drink Ⓥ
飲み物 no·mi·mo·no drink Ⓝ
乗り換え no·ri·ka·e transfer Ⓝ
乗ります no·ri·mas board (a plane, ship etc)
乗り物酔い no·ri·mo·no·yoy travel sickness

は HA

バー bā bar
パーティー pā·tī party (night out)
パートナー pā·to·nā partner (intimate)

はい hai yes
灰色の hai-iro no grey
廃墟 hai-kyo ruins
ハイキング hai-kin-gu hiking ⓝ
灰皿 hai-za-ra ashtray
歯医者 ha-i-sha dentist
売春 bai-shun prostitute
歯痛 ha-i-ta toothache
配達します hai-ta-tsu shi-mas deliver
俳優 hai-yū actor
入ります hai-ri-mas enter
はがき ha-ga-ki postcard
吐き気 ha-ki-ke nausea
博物館 ha-ku-bu-tsu-kan museum
箱 ha-ko box
ハサミ ha-sa-mi scissors
橋 ha-shi bridge
箸 ha-shi (pair of) chopsticks
はしけ ha-shi-ke lighter
(市)バス (shi-)bas bus (city)
(長距離)バス (chō-kyo-ri-)bas bus (intercity)
バスターミナル bas-tā-mi-na-ru bus station
バス停 bas-tē bus stop
パスポート pas-pō-to passport
パスポート番号 pas-pō-to-ban-gō passport number
罰金 bak-kin fine (penalty)
バックパック bak-ku-pak-ku backpack
バッゲージクレーム bag-gē-ji-ku-rē-mu baggage claim
鼻 ha-na nose
話します ha-na-shi-mas speak
花屋 ha-na-ya florist
ハネムーン ha-ne-mūn honeymoon
パブ pa-bu pub (bar)
歯ブラシ ha-bu-ra-shi toothbrush
葉巻 ha-ma-ki cigar
速い ha-yai fast
早く ha-ya-ku early
払い戻し ha-rai-mo-do-shi refund ⓝ
針 ha-ri needle (sewing)
春 ha-ru spring (season)
晩 ban evening
パン pan bread

ハンカチ han-ka-chi handkerchief
晩ごはん ban-go-han dinner
半ズボン han-zu-bon shorts
バンド ban-do band (music)
バンドエイド ban-do-ēdo Band-Aids
ハンドバッグ han-do-bag-gu handbag
パンフレット pan-fu-ret-to brochure
半分 ham-bun half
パン屋 pan-ya bakery
ヒーター hī-tā heater
ビーチ bī-chi beach
ビール bī-ru beer
日陰 hi-ka-ge shade
東 hi-ga-shi east
低い hi-ku-i short (height)
ピクニック pi-ku-nik-ku picnic
飛行機 hi-kō-ki aeroplane • airplane
ひざ hi-za knee
ビザ bi-za visa
ビジネス bi-ji-nes business
ビジネスクラス bi-ji-nes-ku-ras business class
美術 bi-ju-tsu art
美術館 bi-ju-tsu-kan art gallery
左 hi-da-ri left (direction)
日付 hi-zu-ke date (day)
ヒッチハイク hit-chi-hai-ku hitchhike
ビデオカメラ bi-de-o-ka-me-ra video camera
人 hi-to person • human being
ひどい hi-doy awful
一晩 hi-to-ban overnight
ひとりで hi-to-ri de alone
日の入り hi-no-i-ri sunset
日の出 hi-no-de sunrise
日焼け hi-ya-ke sunburn
日焼け止め hi-ya-ke-do-me sunblock
日焼けローション hi-ya-ke-rō-shon tanning lotion
ビュッフェ byuf-fe buffet
病院 byō-in hospital
費用がかかります hi-yō ga ka-ka-ri-mas cost ⓥ
病気の byō-ki no ill • sick
美容師 bi-yō-shi hairdresser
昼ごはん hi-ru-go-han lunch

広場 hi·ro·ba square (town) ⓝ
ビン bin bottle
ピンクの pin·ku no pink
ピンボール pin·bō·ru pinball
ファーストクラス fā·sto·ku·ras first class ⓝ
ファックス fak·kus fax • fax machine
不安な fu·an na uncomfortable
フィルム fi·ru·mu film (for camera)
フィルムの感度 fi·ru·mu no kan·do film speed
封筒 fū·tō envelope
プール pū·ru swimming pool
フェリー fe·rī ferry ⓝ
フォーク fō·ku fork
不可能な fu·ka·nō na impossible
腹痛 fu·ku·tsū stomachache
含んで fu·kun·de included
普通便 fu·tsū·bin surface mail (land)
不動産屋 fu·dō·san·ya estate agency
太った fu·tot·ta fat ⓐ
ふとん fu·ton futon
船便 fu·na·bin surface mail (sea)
船 fu·ne boat
冬 fu·yu winter
フライパン fu·rai·pan frying pan
プラグ pu·ra·gu plug (electricity)
ブラシ bu·ra·shi brush ⓝ
ブラジャー bu·ra·jā bra
プラットフォーム pu·rat·to·fō·mu platform
ブリーフケース bu·rī·fu·kēs briefcase
フリーマーケット fu·rī·mā·ket·to fleamarket
プリンタ pu·rin·ta printer (computer)
古い fu·ru·i old
ブレーキ bu·rē·ki brakes
フレーズブック fu·rē·zu·buk·ku phrasebook
プレゼント pu·re·zen·to present (gift) ⓝ
風呂場 fu·ro·ba bathroom
分 fun minute
文房具 (店) bum·bō·gu(·ten) sta·tioner's (shop)
へ e to

ヘアカット hair·kat·to haircut
閉店した hē·ten·shi·ta closed
ベジタリアン be·ji·ta·ri·an vegetarian ⓝ
ベッド bed·do bed
ヘッドライト hed·do·rai·to headlights
ペニシリン pe·ni·shi·rin penicillin
ペニス pe·nis penis
ベビーカー be·bī·kā stroller
ベビーシッター be·bī·shit·tā baby-sitter
部屋 he·ya room
ペン pen pen (ballpoint)
変化 hen·ka change ⓝ
弁護士 ben·go·shi lawyer
ペンナイフ pen·nai·fu penknife
法学部 hō·ga·ku law (study, professsion)
方向 hō·kō direction
帽子 bō·shi hat
宝石 hō·se·ki jewellery
包帯 hō·tai bandage
ボーイフレンド bōy·fu·ren·do boyfriend
ボール bō·ru bowl
ほかの ho·ka no other
保険 ho·ken insurance
保証された ho·shō sa·re·ta guaranteed
墓地 bo·chi cemetery
ポット pot·to water bottle (hot)
ホテル ho·te·ru hotel
歩道 ho·dō footpath
ホモ ho·mo homosexual ⓝ
本 hon book ⓝ
ポンド pon·do pound (money, weight)
本屋 hon·ya bookshop
翻訳します hon·ya·ku shi·mas translate

ま MA

毎 mai every
毎 mai per (day etc)
毎日 mai·ni·chi daily
前 ma·e before
前の ma·e no last (previous)

枕 ma·ku·ra pillow
枕カバー ma·ku·ra·ka·bā pillowcase
孫 ma·go grandchild
また ma·ta again
待合室 ma·chi·ai·shi·tsu transit lounge • waiting room
待ちます ma·chi·mas wait (for) ⓥ
マッサージ mas·sā·ji massage
マッチ mat·chi matches (for lighting)
マットレス mat·to·res mattress
まで ma·de until (time)
窓 ma·do window
マネージャー ma·nē·jā manager (restaurant, hotel)
麻薬 ma·ya·ku drug (narcotic)
真夜中 ma·yo·na·ka midnight
マリファナ ma·ri·fa·na dope (drugs)
漫画 man·ga comics
満室 man·shi·tsu no vacancy
マンション man·shon apartment
ミーティング mī·tin·gu conference (small)
右 mi·gi right (direction) ⓐ
短い mi·ji·kai short (length)
水 mi·zu water
湖 mi·zū·mi lake
水着 mi·zu·gi swimsuit
店 mi·se shop ⓝ
見せます mi·se·mas show ⓥ
味噌汁 mi·so·shi·ru miso-soup
道 mi·chi street • road
緑の mi·do·ri no green
南 mi·na·mi south
ミネラルウォーター mi·ne·ra·ru·wō·tā mineral water
身分証明 mi·bun·shō·mē identification
身分証明書 mi·bun·shō·mē·sho identification card (ID)
耳 mi·mi ear
ミリ（メートル）mi·ri(·mē·to·ru) millimetre
ミルク mi·ru·ku milk
みんな min·na everyone
息子 mu·su·ko son
娘 mu·su·me daughter

胸 mu·ne chest (body part)
無料の mu·ryō no free (gratis) • complimentary (free)
目 me eye
名刺 mē·shi business card
メインコース mēn·kō·su main course
メーキャップ mē·kyap·pu make-up
メートル mē·to·ru metre
眼鏡 me·ga·ne glasses (spectacles)
目覚し時計 me·za·ma·shi·do·kē alarm clock
珍しい me·zu·ra·shī rare (uncommon)
メニュー me·nyū menu
綿 men cotton
もう一つの mō·hi·to·tsu no another
毛布 mō·fu blanket
モーテル mō·te·ru motel
目的地 mo·ku·te·ki·chi destination
モダンな mo·dan na modern
持っています mot·te i·mas have
もっと mot·to more
モデム mo·de·mu modem
もどります mo·do·ri·mas return (come back) ⓥ
森 mo·ri forest

や YA

薬剤師 ya·ku·zai·shi chemist (person)
野菜 ya·sai vegetable
安い ya·su·i cheap
薬局 yak·kyo·ku chemist (shop) • pharmacy
山 ya·ma mountain
有効にします yū·kō ni shi·mas validate
夕食 yū·sho·ku dinner
ユースホステル yū·su·ho·su·te·ru youth hostel
郵送 yū·sō mail (letters)
郵便 yū·bin mail (postal system)
郵便局 yū·bin·kyo·ku post office
郵便番号 yū·bin·ban·gō postcode
郵便ポスト yū·bin·pos·to mailbox
ユーロ yū·ro euro
雪 yu·ki snow
ゆっくり yuk·ku·ri slowly

湯飲み茶碗 yu·no·mi·ja·wan tea cup
yu·bi finger
指 yu·bi·wa ring (on finger) ⓝ
夜明け yo·a·ke dawn
夜遊び yo·a·so·bi night out
ヨーロッパ yō·rop·pa Europe
預金 yo·kin credit • deposit (bank)
横 yo·ko beside
予算 yo·san budget
酔った yot·ta drunk ⓐ
呼びます yo·bi·mas call ⓥ
予防注射 yo·bō·chū·sha vaccination
予約 yo·ya·ku appointment • reservation (booking)
予約します yo·ya·ku shi·mas book (make a booking) ⓥ
より大きい yo·ri ō·kī bigger
より小さい yo·ri chī·sai smaller
より良い yo·ri yoy better
夜 yo·ru night

ら RA

来(月) rai(·ge·tsu) next (month)
ライター rai·tā cigarette lighter
ラジオ ra·ji·o radio
ラップトップ rap·pu·top·pu laptop
離婚した ri·kon shi·ta divorced
離乳食 ri·nyū·sho·ku baby food
リネン ri·nen linen (sheets etc)
リフト ri·fu·to chairlift (skiing)
リモコン ri·mo·kon remote control
料金 ryō·kin fare • toll
領事館 ryō·ji·kan consulate
両親 ryō·shin parents
両方 ryō·hō both

料理します ryō·ri shi·mas cook ⓥ
旅館 ryo·kan traditional Japanese inn
旅行代理店 ryo·kō·dai·ri·ten travel agency
旅行日程 ryo·kō·nit·tē itinerary
リンネル rin·ne·ru linen (material)
ルームナンバー rū·mu·nam·bā room number
冷蔵庫 rē·zō·ko fridge • refrigerator
レインコート re·in·kō·to raincoat
レコード店 re·kō·do·ten music shop
レジ re·ji cashier • cash register
レシート re·shī·to receipt
レズ re·zu lesbian ⓝ
レストラン res·to·ran restaurant
レンズ ren·zu lens
レンタカー ren·ta·kā car hire
ローカル線 rō·ka·ru·sen local train (country)
ロッカー rok·kā luggage lockers
ロック rok·ku rock (music) ⓝ
露天風呂 ro·tem·bu·ro open-air baths
ロマンチックな ro·man·chik·ku na romantic
ワイン wain wine

わ WA

分け合います wa·ke·ai·mas share (with)
私たちの wa·ta·shi·ta·chi no our
私の wa·ta·shi no my
私は wa·ta·shi wa I
私を wa·ta·shi o me
割引 wa·ri·bi·ki discount
悪い wa·ru·i bad

Index

For topics that are covered in several sections of this book, we've indicated the most relevant page number in bold.

A

abbreviations 3
accommodation........................... 68
activities (social).......................... 132
addresses 64, **67**
addressing people 115
adjectives (grammar)............... **16**, 21
adverbs (grammar)........................ 16
age 117
airports 52
allergies 167, 194
alphabet .... see *writing Japanese*
amounts **36**, 39, 190
apologies **113**, 143
appointments.................... 100, 135
art...104
articles (grammar) 17
asking someone out 135, 138
automated teller machines............. 96

B

babies (travelling with) 109
baggage 51
banking 96
bar (drinking) 186
bargaining.................................... 82
baseball 149
basic language 112
beach 155
beliefs 142
be (verb) 17
bicycle... 60
bills (accommodation) **69**, 76, 95

bills (restaurant) 95, 175, **181**
boat.................................... 46, **54**
body parts (diagram) 168
booking (accommodation) 69
booking (restaurant) 173, **174**
books 84
border crossing............................. 62
bowing 113
breakfast.................................... 172
bullet train 46, 53
bus 46, 52
business 98
buying food................................ 189
buying stuff **80**, 83, 95
buying tickets 48

C

calendar...................................... 42
calls (phone) 90
camping.............................. 68, **76**
cancelling tickets 50
car 56
car parts (diagram)........................ 57
CDs (shopping) 85
cell phone 92
changing money 96
chatting 115
checking in (accommodation)........ 69
checking out (accommodation) 75
chemist.............................. 162, **170**
children **109**, 120
cinema 124
classifiers (grammar).......................37

clothes 84
coach (bus) 52
commission (banking) 95
communication problems 34
compass points 66
complaints (accommodation) 74
compliments (accommodation) 76
compliments (food) 179
compliments (language) 128
computers **92**, 100
concerts 133, 134
conditions (medical) 164
confirming tickets 50
consonant sounds 11
contact details 99, 120
conversation 115
cooking 178, **191**
counters (grammar) 37
countries of origin 117
credit cards 95
cultural differences 142
cultural tips 79, 84, 99, 100, 113, 116, 128, 131, 141, 184, 187
customs (border crossing) 63
customs (cultural) 143
cycling 60

D

dates (time) 43
days of the week 42
debit cards 95
declarations (customs) 63
delays (transport) 47, 51
demonstratives (grammar) 19
dentist 169
dialects 6
dictionary English–Japanese 219
dictionary Japanese–English 253
diets (special) 193
differences (cultural & religious) ... 143
digital photography 86
dining tips 184
dinner 172
directions 64
disabled travellers 107
discounts 82, 104

dishes (menu decoder) 196
diving 156
doctor 162
drinks 181, 184, 186
drugs (illegal) 137
drugs (medical) 163, 165, 166, **170**
duty-free 52, 63
DVDs (shopping) 85

E

eating out **172**, 175
eateries 183
elevator 72, 108
email 94, 99
emergencies 158
entertainment 124, 132
environment 130
etiquette (business) 99, 100
etiquette (eating & drinking) ... 184, 187
etiquette
  (general) 79, 113, 115, 116, 128, 131
etiquette (photography) 103
exchange (money) 96, 97

F

facilities (camping) 76
facilities (for children) 109
facilities
  (for older & disabled people) 107
facilities (sport) 148
families with children 109
family (kinship terms) 119
farewells 120
fax 100
feelings 126
ferry 54
film (cinema) 124
film (photography) 86
flights (plane) 52
food-related allergies 193
food (general) 171
food (buying) 189
food (menu decoder) 196
football (soccer) 152
formalities (grammar) 24

fractions (numbers) 39
future (grammar)............................. 31
future (time)................................... 44

G

gas (petrol).......................... 57, 58, 59
gay venues..................................... 132
gender (grammar)............................ 21
going out.. 132
golf... 148
goodbyes............................... **113**, 120
grammar... 16
greetings.. 113
guides (hiking)............................... 154
guides (sightseeing) 102

H

halal food....................................... 194
handshakes.................................... 113
have (verb) 20
health... 162
health (special diets)..................... 193
hiking... 153
hiragana (script) 13, 15
hire (sporting equipment)...... 149, 150
hiring (car & motorbike)................. 56
hiring (bicycle) 60
hobbies... 122
homestays.. 78
hotel.. **68**, 71
hugging.. 113

I

illnesses... 164
immigration...................................... 62
ingredients (menu decoder)........... 196
injuries.......................... 158, **165**, 169
interests... 122
internet.. 92
intersection (diagram).................... 66
intimacy... 140
introduction (to Japanese).............. 6
introductions (meeting
people).............................. 112, **114**
invitations........................... 101, **133**

J

Japanese food
(menu decoder) 196

K

kanji (script) 13
karaoke.. 136
katakana (script)...................... 14, 15
kinship terms 119
kissing.................................... 113, 140
kosher food 193

L

language difficulties........................ 34
laundry... 72
legal assistance............................. 161
lift (elevator)........................... 72, 108
locals (staying with)........................ 78
lockers (luggage) 51
loss of valuables............................ 161
love... 141
luggage.. 51
lunch.. 172

M

mail.................................... 60, 64, **102**
maps.................................... 60, 64, **102**
meal requests.............. 177, **178**, 195
medical (health)............................. 162
medication 163, 165, 166, **170**
meeting people.............................. 112
meeting up 135
menu (terminology) 181
menu decoder................................ 196
messages................................. **73**, 91
metro... 52
mobile phone 92
money.. 95
monorail 55
months 42
motorbike 56
museums (art)............................... 104
music 85
movies 124

N

names	**114**, 116, 141
nationalities	117
nature	130
negatives (grammar)	17, **20**
nonsmoking section	50, 176
nouns (grammar)	21
numbers	36

O

occupations	118
older travellers	107
opening times	103
opinions	127
ordering (drinks)	181, 184, **186**
ordering (food)	174, **177**, 195
ordering (taxi)	**55**, 75
organic produce	189, 195
outdoor pursuits	153
ownership (grammar)	20, 22, 23, **25**

P

parcels	81, **88**
particles (grammar)	22
parts of the body (diagram)	168
passport control	62
past (grammar)	31
past (time)	44
pastimes	122
payment (methods of)	95
petrol	57, 58, 59
pharmacy	162, **170**
phone	90
photography (etiquette)	103
photography (shopping)	86
pick-up lines	138
PINs	97
plane	46, **52**
play (theatre)	**124**, 133
playing sport	148
pleasantries	115
plurals (grammar)	21, **24**
police	158, **160**
polite forms (grammar)	24
politics	128
possession (grammar)	20, 22, 23, **25**

post office	88
preparation (food)	178, 195
prepositions (grammar)	26
prescriptions	170
present (time)	43
presents (giving & receiving)	79, **131**
problems (accommodation)	74
problems (banking)	97
problems (car & motorbike)	59
problems (emergencies)	158
problems (food-related)	195
problems (health)	162
problems (internet)	94
problems (language)	34
problems (legal)	160
problems (phone)	91
problems (restaurant)	180
problems (with the bill)	96, **181**
professions	118
pronouns (grammar)	27
pronunciation	10
public transport	46

Q

quantities (food)	190
quarantine (customs)	63
queries (accommodation)	72
questions (grammar)	28

R

rates (accommodation)	**69**, 7?
rates (communications)	90, 92, 94
rates (sports facilities)	148, 149
reading (books)	84
reading Japanese	1?
receipts (payment)	**82**, 96
recommendations (accommodation)	69
recommendations (food)	173, **175**, 176
recycling	130
refunds	82
regional variations (language)	?
rejections	135, **13?**
religion	14?
renting (accommodation)	7?
repairs (general)	8?

repairs (car & motorbike)................59
requests (accommodation)..............72
reservations .... see booking
restaurant........................172, 175
returns (purchases).........................82
road signs 58
romance 138
room (diagram).................................72
rooms.............................**70**, 71, 78
routes (hiking)...............................153
routes (transport).....................50, 53

S

safe (for valuables) 72
safety 156, 158, **159**
school 118, 120
scooter...56
script (table)....................................15
seasons 42
seating 47, 48, **50**,
   100, 108, 124, 174, 176
self-catering.................................189
senior travellers...........................107
sex..140
shopping (general).........................80
shopping (food)............................189
sightseeing....................................102
signs (accommodation)..................70
signs (customs & immigration).....63
signs (emergencies).....................159
signs (shops)...................................81
signs (road)......................................58
SIM cards...92
skiing 150
small talk.......................................115
soccer 152
social issues..................................128
socialising 132
souvenirs 84
special diets..................................193
specialities............174, 177, 189, 196
sport..145
stations (train)................................52
stops (bus & train)...................52, 53
street scene (diagram)...................66
studies 118
subtitles (cinema).........................124

subway 55
sumo..146
swimming 156
symptoms (medical).....................164

T

table (diagram)..............................180
table etiquette...............**184**, 187
taxi 55
telephone...90
telling the time................................40
tennis 145, 148
thanking people...........................112
theatre 124
tickets (transport)..............**48**, 49
time..40
titles (for people)...................100, 115
toilets.................50, 107, 155, **159**, 187
tooth problems.............................169
tours (sightseeing).......................105
train.............................46, 49, **52**
tram...55
transit (border crossing)...............62
transport..46
travellers cheques..........................96
trekking..153

V

valuables......................76, 160, 161
vaccinations..................................163
vegan food....................................194
vegetarian food............................194
verbs (grammar)..............................30
vowel sounds...................................10

W

walking (hiking).............................153
water (drinkable) 77, 155, **181**
weather...156
withdrawing money........................96
women's health.............................167
word order (grammar) 32
word stress 12
work .... see business
writing Japanese.....................13, 15

10 Ways to Start a Sentence

What time's (the next bus)?	(次のバスは)何時ですか?	(tsu·gi no bas wa) nan·ji des ka
Where's (the station)?	(駅)はどこですか?	(e·ki) wa do·ko des ka
How much is (a room)?	(ルーム)はいくらですか?	(rū·mu) wa i·ku·ra des ka
Do you have (a map)?	(地図)がありますか?	(chi·zu) ga a·ri·mas ka
Is there (a toilet)?	(トイレ)がありますか?	(toy·re) ga a·ri·mas ka
I'd like (the menu).	(メニュー)をお願いします。	(me·nyū) o o·ne·gai shi·mas
Can I (sit here)?	(ここに座って)もいいですか?	(ko·ko ni su·wat·te) mo ī des ka
I need (a can opener).	(缶切り)が必要です。	(kan·ki·ri) ga hi·tsu·yō des
Do I need (a visa)?	(ビザ)が必要ですか?	(bi·za) ga hi·tsu·yō des ka
I have (a reservation).	(予約)があります。	(yo·ya·ku) ga a·ri·mas